International's Series in
ECONOMICS

International Economics

International Economics

David Young
University of Dundee
Scotland

Intext Educational Publishers
Scranton   Toronto   London

382
Y69i
1970

ISBN 0–7002–2316–9

Contents

International Economics

CHAPTER 1

The Study of International Trade

To MY mind, there can be two main reasons for studying International Economics – firstly international trade is of significant importance to a large number of countries and it is desirable therefore that some understanding is achieved of the reasons why trade takes place, what its effects on the participating countries are, what its effects on non-participating countries are, and so on. If governments are to formulate adequate economic policies, then they would have to take into account the effects such policies would have on trade and related variables both at the domestic and international levels. In order to do this successfully, some knowledge of the underlying economic relationships between the relevant variables is required.

A second reason for studying the theory of international trade (taken in its widest sense) is that it should enable the student to understand how it is that well-trained knowledgeable people can hold opposing views on what appear to be basically simple problems. For instance, how is it that so many plans have been put forward to solve the problem of international liquidity, a problem, furthermore, which others claim does not exist? It is hoped that part of the answer to such a problem will be found within the covers of this book, the main aim of which is to provide the undergraduate student with a grounding in the theory of international trade, and show how, on the basis of differing analyses and explanations, various conclusions can be drawn relating to a particular problem. This awareness that there is no unique method of analyzing a problem, that there is no one answer which is *the* answer should, it is hoped, contribute to a better understanding of the role of economic theory in policy formation. It is with this aim in mind that the author has selected 10 basic fields of analysis which have received fairly intensive study in recent years and which bear directly on a fair number of current international economic problems.

Before giving a brief outline of each of the chapters of this book, it might be worthwhile to examine the importance of international trade in order to find out just how important it is. The first thing which strikes one when analyzing trade statistics is that international trade is not of equal importance to all countries. To show this, let us examine the ratio of imports and exports to the national income of selected countries in 1967.

TABLE 1

IMPORTS AND EXPORTS AS A PERCENTAGE OF
NATIONAL INCOME, SELECTED COUNTRIES, 1966

Country	Imports	Exports
Belgium	50	47
Netherlands	40	47
Norway	41	27
Denmark	29	28
Canada	25	27
United Kingdom	20	18
West Germany	20	17
France	16	14
Japan	12	12
United States	4	5

As can be seen, of the countries selected Belgium has the highest ratio of imports to national income and the highest-equal ratio of exports to national income. At the other extreme, the United States has the lowest ratios. However, if we compare the dependence of countries on international trade with the absolute volumes of trade carried out by each country, the picture looks somewhat different.

TABLE 2

IMPORTS AND EXPORTS OF SELECTED COUNTRIES, 1966 ($M.)

Country	Imports c.i.f.	Exports f.o.b.
Belgium	7,182	6,832
Netherlands	8,016	6,751
Norway	2,404	1,564
Denmark	3,003	2,454
Canada	10,170	9,988
United Kingdom	16,651	14,676
West Germany	18,036	20,145
France	11,843	10,890
Japan	9,524	9,777
United States	27,747	30,434

Thus it can be seen that the U.S. trade volume dominates for the countries selected, whilst a country like Norway, which has a relatively high dependence on international trade, has a relatively small absolute volume of trade. It should not be assumed therefore that because a country has a relatively low dependence[1] on international trade that it does not have a significant interest in trade and its expansion. Nor should it be assumed that because a country has a low ratio of imports to national income, it is not very dependent on international trade and could survive virtually unaffected by a cessation of its import flows. For example, the United States is lacking virtually entirely in a number of vital raw materials which are important for national defense (e.g. manganese, asbestos, mica, nickel, cobalt, mercury, etc.) and for other industries (industrial diamonds, bananas, tea, copra, etc.). One could also argue that the United States, by trading, can obtain imports of certain foodstuffs and consumer items which would cease to be available should imports cease (e.g. Rolls Royce cars). On the export side, also, the United States would lose a large proportion of certain markets if trade did not take place, and the loss of these markets could have serious adverse effects on the domestic economy through, for instance, economies of scale (e.g. wheat, cotton). It can be argued, therefore, that although the ratio of trade to national income is fairly low, the importance of trade to a country is in no way directly reflected by this ratio. What this means is that a higher level of real income of a country tends to be achieved when international trade is undertaken compared with the situation where the economy is closed.

This is a convenient point at which to describe briefly the contents of the chapters which follow.[2]

Chapter 2 examines the question "Why does trade take place?" tracing the theoretical developments from Adam Smith to Ricardo, with a detailed examination of the *Theory of Comparative Costs*. It will be shown how in line with comparative costs trade can benefit the countries which engage in it. However, the reason why such differences in comparative costs arise will not be studied here. This is done in Chapter 3, which examines the *Ohlin-Heckscher Theory of Trade* which relies on the concept of relative factor endowments. These factor endowments differ internationally, and it is argued that this explains the comparative costs and is therefore the underlying basis of all trade. Other bases for trading will also be looked at (differing factor qualities, returns to scale, etc.), and finally a survey of empirical analyses of comparative cost and factor endowment theory will be given. In Chapter 4, we shall look at the way in which international trade may affect the relative and absolute levels of factor prices. Using a very restrictive set of assumptions the *Factor-Price Equalization Theorem* will be derived and criticized. Chapter 5 will analyze how, using the Offer Curve technique, the demand side of international trade theory is developed and how demand and supply interact to determine the *Terms of Trade*. This opens the way for a study of the various Terms of Trade concepts and a discussion of the way in which various factors can affect a country's terms of trade (economic growth, demand shifts, capital transfers, etc.). Having seen how the terms of trade are determined, Chapter 6 examines the *Theory of Customs Unions* and how the formation of such a Union can alter the production consumption patterns of its members and the terms of trade. The concept of the Optimum Tariff is also dealt with here. Chapter 7, in a sense, represents a break with the pure theory of trade and moves on to the monetary aspects of trade as they find expression in the *foreign exchange market* and *balance of payments*. A detailed study is made of the various meanings which can be given to "the balance of payments," as well as an analysis of how the exchange rate is determined and whether or not the rate will be stable. Chapter 8 follows on by looking at the way in which imbalances can arise in the balance of payments and how these imbalances are dealt with under the Classical gold standard, flexible rates and under the current gold-exchange-standard. This, of course, involves a fairly detailed study of the *income and price-adjustment mechanisms*. The Chapter concludes with a synthesis of the income and price approaches to payments adjustment. Chapter 9 is a follow on to Chapter 8, examining the various possible ways of adjusting to payments' imbalances (inflation/deflation, flexible exchange rates, modified flexible rates, etc.). The major part of this chapter is taken up with the controversy over the *fixed* versus *flexible exchange rate systems*.

Chapter 10 divides itself into two parts: the first being an analysis of the theory of *international disequilibrium*, its causes and effects; the second being a study of *the U.S.' recent balance of payments experience* in the light of the preceding discussion. An attempt is made to discover the causes of its persistent balance of payments deficits and possible remedies. Finally, Chapter 11 is concerned with the *current international monetary system* and the problems which appear to be associated with it – particularly the so-called International Liquidity problem. The question of whether or not such a problem actually exists is examined, as well as a critique of current plans for international monetary reform.

It is hoped, therefore, that by the time the student has mastered the contents of this book, he will have a fairly thorough understanding of international trade theory as well as a knowledge of some of the current economic problems facing the world economy.

[1] As measured by Table 1.

[2] Note that a certain knowledge of mathematics is required to follow some of the detailed arguments of Chapters 4, 8 and 9, although the standard involved does not exceed high school mathematics. The student is also expected to be familiar with basic economic price theory involving the use of such concepts as "elasticities," "demand," "supply," etc.

CHAPTER 2

The Theoretical Basis of Trade (i)

THE AIM of this and the following chapter will be to make a detailed survey of the theories which have been put forward in order to explain why trade takes place between nations. This chapter deals with the so-called classical theories of trade propounded by Adam Smith and David Ricardo. The following chapter deals with the more modern theories of Ohlin-Heckscher, Kravis and Linder, and contains a brief survey of empirical analyses of these theories.

At first sight, the answer to the question "Why does trade take place between nations?" seems fairly obvious – trade takes place because, by trading, nations can benefit economically. In other words, nations can increase their economic welfare by taking part in international trade. If this were not the case, there would seem to be little point (economically speaking) in trading.

However, although this is all quite true, it is not enough to satisfy the analytical mind of the economist – he must go behind the obvious and ask the question – "How is it that nations can benefit by engaging in international trade?" Fundamentally, it is this question which concerned such economists as Ricardo and Ohlin and which will concern us for this and the following chapter. It should be noted that implied in this basic question are other questions such as: "Why does the United States specialize in the production of mass-produced consumer goods and export these to the rest of the world?" "Why does Brazil specialize in the production of coffee?" "Why do countries specialize in production at all?"

It is hoped that, having read this and the following chapter, the student will be able to provide answers to these questions.

(i) ADAM SMITH[1] – THE THEORY OF ABSOLUTE ADVANTAGES

In the writings of Smith are to be found the origins of the classical theory of international trade. Smith was a great defender of Free Trade on the grounds that this promoted the international division of labor by allowing nations to concentrate their production on the goods which could be made most cheaply, with all the consequent benefits of division of labor.

In Smith's opinion, it was far better for a nation to import goods which could be produced abroad more efficiently in terms of real resources than to manufacture them itself. As an example of this, he gave the case of Scotland which *could* (if it used, relative to other factors of production, a lot of capital) produce grapes for wine making. However, Italy could perform this function more efficiently than Scotland, and so it would benefit Scotland to import wine from Italy and pay for it with goods which required in their production less capital than grapes.

Smith's theory can best be summed up in his own words.[2]

"If a foreign country can supply us with a commodity cheaper than we ourselves can make it, better buy it off them with some part of the produce of our own industry employed in a way in which we have some advantage. Whether the advantages which one country has over another be natural or acquired, is in this respect of no consequence."

What is important to note here is that Smith's analysis was presented entirely in terms of *absolute advantages* – in other words, countries would export goods in the production of which they possessed an absolute advantage over the importing country. Italy had an absolute advantage over Scotland in wine production and so she would export this to Scotland. On the other hand, Scotland had an absolute advantage over Italy in the production of, say, ships and so she would export these in exchange.

Smith's emphasis, therefore, was placed on these *absolute* advantages.

What this means, in effect, is that production conditions differ between countries and also within countries. Thus, coal may be more efficiently mined, in terms of real resource usage, in Wales than in the North of Scotland. As a result it would benefit Britain to "export" coal from Wales to Scotland. Similarly, Scotland may have an advantage in beef raising and so she will "export" cattle to the rest of Britain. By means of such specialization within a country (and between countries as Smith has shown), the economic welfare of nations can be increased. This applies, of course, even although the two countries (or parts of the same country) can produce the same commodities. (In our example, Italy and Scotland could produce ships *and* wine.) However, what happens if one of our countries can produce *every* commodity more cheaply (in terms of real resource usage) than the other country? In this situation, one country will have an *absolute* advantage over the other country in the production of *every* commodity. On Smithian analysis, it would appear as if trade were impossible in such circumstances – why should the more efficient country (in every direction) bother trading with the less efficient? It was precisely this problem which Ricardo was able to solve through his analysis of *Comparative* (or relative) *Advantages* as opposed to absolute advantages.

(ii) DAVID RICARDO[3] – THE THEORY OF COMPARATIVE ADVANTAGES

At first sight, it would appear that where one country has an absolute advantage in the production of every commodity, trade would not take place. However, so long as differences exist in the *relative* efficiencies of production of the different goods in the two countries, trade can take place to the mutual advantage of both countries.

What this means is that the "rich" country must have an absolute advantage which is *relatively* greater than its other advantages; and the "poor" country will correspondingly have an absolute disadvantage which is relatively less than its other disadvantages.

It is this emphasis of Ricardo on *comparative* (or relative) advantages and disadvantages which marks his great advance over Smith.

To grasp this important distinction between absolute and comparative advantages, and therefore between Smith's and Ricardo's analyses of trade, consider the following situations in which we shall confine ourselves to a two-good, two-country model; the goods being food (F) and steel (S); the countries the United States and Australia.

Case (a). Absolute advantage in one country only.

Suppose the following table illustrates the production possibilities open to the two countries.

	United States	Australia
F	20	20
S	10	5

These outputs are alternatives for equal resource inputs which Ricardo regarded as labor-time units. Thus, if the United States uses one unit of factor input, it can produce either 20 units of food or 10 units of steel. Similarly, Australia with 1 unit of factor input can produce either 20 units of food of 5 units of steel.

In this example, the United States and Australia are equally efficient at producing food, but the United States is more efficient at producing steel. The United States, therefore, has an absolute advantage in steel production. Australia, on the other hand, has no absolute advantages, but has an absolute *dis*advantage in steel production.

In this example will trade take place? The answer would seem to be

"No!" The United States is just as efficient as Australia in food production and better in steel production, so what incentive is there for the United States to import anything from Australia?

However, trade will take place and both countries will gain from this trade. Suppose that the United States concentrates on steel production since it has an absolute advantage in this type of activity. Australia will concentrate on food production. Why? Because although it does not have an absolute advantage in food production, it has a *comparative* advantage in this type of activity – it is worse at producing steel, compared with the United States, than it is at producing food, compared with the United States.

The gain to be had from such specialization and trading, can be seen by noting that if neither country specializes, the maximum "world" output of food and steel possible (per unit of factor input for each country) is 20 F and $7\frac{1}{2}$ S – the United States producing 10 F and 5 S and Australia producing 10 F and $2\frac{1}{2}$ S.

However, with specialization taking place, the United States produces 10 S and Australia 20 F, thus increasing "world" ouput (per unit of factor input for each country) by $2\frac{1}{2}$ S units.

How this gain in "world" output is distributed between the two countries depends on demand factors, which will be discussed in a later chapter, but without doing this it is now possible to show how each country, individually, benefits from trade.

	United States	Australia		United States	Australia
F	20	20	F	10	10
	or	or		+	+
S	10	5	S	5	$2\frac{1}{2}$

By specializing in steel production, the United States is giving up 10 units of food production. Similarly, Australia, by specializing in food production is giving up $2\frac{1}{2}$ units of steel production. Therefore, unless the United States can obtain at least 10 units of food from Australia for every 5 units of steel it exports, it will not pay the United States to trade. Similarly, unless Australia can obtain at least $2\frac{1}{2}$ units of steel for every 10 units of food she exports to the United States, it will not pay Australia to trade. It can be seen, by inspection, therefore, that trade is possible and mutually advantageous, so long as the rate of exchange[4] between steel and food lies within the range specified by the above conditions (i.e., 10 F for at least $2\frac{1}{2}$ S but less than 5 S.)The exact rate of exchange will be determined by the relative strengths of demand in the United

States and Australia for food and steel respectively. This will be analyzed later, but it is obvious that if demand conditions are such that
the final F:S rate of exchange settles down near the 10 F for 5 S end of
the range, Australia will gain most by trading if it settles down closer
to the other end of the range, the United States will gain most.

The important point in all this is that trade will occur on the basis
of the *comparative* advantage which the United States possesses in steel
production.

Case (b).   Absolute advantages in both countries.
Suppose the following is the case.

	United States	Australia
F	20	25
S	10	5

Here, Australia has an absolute advantage in the production of food,
and the United States has an absolute advantage in the production of
steel. This, in essence, is Smith's case; trade will take place with the
United States specializing in steel production and Australia in food
production. Again, before trade, "world" output (per unit of factor
input for each country) had a maximum of 22 F$\frac{1}{2}$ and 7$\frac{1}{2}$ S. With specialization and trade, this increases to 25 F and 10 S – an absolute increase
in both goods. Again the distribution of the gain will depend on demand
factors; this time the range of exchange – rate possibilities stretching
between 10 F for at least 2 S but less than 5 S.

Trade is based in this example on absolute advantages; but it is also
true to say that it is based on comparative advantages which reinforce
these absolute advantages.

Case (c).   Absolute advantage of one country in both goods, but with
             a comparative advantage in one.
Suppose the production possibilities are as shown.

	United States	Australia
F	20	10
S	10	3

In this example, the United States has an absolute advantage in both food and steel production. However, it can be shown that trade will take place to the mutual advantage of both countries because the United States has a comparative (or relative) advantage in steel production. In other words, the United States is better at being better in steel production than it is at being better in food production – it is twice as efficient as Australia in food production, but three and one third times as efficient in steel production. The United States will concentrate on steel production, therefore, and Australia on food production.

Looked at from Australia's point of view, it is worse at everything, relative to the United States, but is "less worse" at producing food than it is at producing steel. It will therefore concentrate on food production.

The gains from this specialization can be shown in the usual way – before specialization "world" output (per unit of factor input for each country) was at a maximum of 15 F and $6\frac{1}{2}$ S. After specialization "world" output has increased[5] to 10 F and 10 S. Again, the distribution of the gain will depend on demand factors, the rate of exchange lying somewhere between 10 F for at least 3 S but less than 5 S.

Case (d).   Absolute advantage of one country in both goods, but with no comparative advantage in either.

Suppose the production possibilities are as shown.

	United States	Australia
F	20	10
S	10	5

Again, the United States has an absolute advantage over Australia in both food and steel production. However, in this situation, trade will not take place, because no comparative advantage exists. What this means is that the United States is as good at being better than Australia in food production as is at being better in steel production – twice as efficient in each case. For the sake of argument. however, suppose that the United States were to specialize in food production. Then, for every 10 units of food it exports to Australia, it would have to get in return at least 5 units of steel. But Australia would not be willing to export any more than 5 units of steel for 10 units of food. Similarly, should the United States specialize in steel production, for every 5 units of steel exported it would require at least 10 units of food in return, but again Australia would be unwilling to give up more than 10 units of food for 5 units of steel. Thus, neither the United States nor Australia gain anything by the United States specializing in either field of production. It can likewise be shown that no gains are to be had from Australia deciding to specialize. Trade, then, is not advantageous in such a situation where comparative advantages fail to arise.

It can also be observed by looking at the domestic price ratios between food and steel in each country that "world" output can't be increased by specialization – thus, before trade, "world" output (per unit of factor input for each country) has a maximum of 15 F and $7\frac{1}{2}$ S. If the United States specialized in food production and Australia in steel production "world" output would be 20 F and 5 S. Similarly, if the United States specialized in steel production and Australia in food production, "world" output would be 10 F and 10 S.

Can we say from this that "world" output before trade is less than that after trade? This was the sort of conclusion we reached in all the previous cases. After trade, "world" output had increased and there could be no doubt about it because the output of both goods[6] has increased.

However, in this case we have a choice, after trade of more food and less steel, or more steel and less food. How can we compare the pre- and post-trade positions? The answer is that we must look at the domestic price ratios for the two goods. In both the United States and Australia one units of steel is worth two units of food, or to be more correct, the production of one unit of steel requires the resources used to produce two units of food (so the real cost of steel in terms of food is "two"). Since the price ratio is the same in both countries, we can measure "world" output in either food units or steel units by converting our steel units into food units at the domestic price level, or by converting food units into steel units at the domestic price level.

Suppose we use food as our unit of measurement; thus, before trade, we had 15 F and $7\frac{1}{2}$ S as our "world" output/unit of input. This can be regarded as $[15+(7\frac{1}{2}\times2)]$ F units $\equiv$ 30 F units.

After trade, the two possibilities are 20 F + 5 S or 10 F + 10 S. Converting our steel units into food units we have either $[20+(5\times2)]$ F units or $[10+(10\times2)]$ F units, both of which are equal to 30 F units (i.e. the same as the pre-specialization position).[7] Thus "world" output cannot be increased in this situation by engaging in trade, the important reason for this being that no comparative advantage existed on either the United States' or Australia's part.

What we can say, therefore, is that the necessary and sufficient condition for trade to take place and be advantageous for the countries engaging in it is that a comparative advantage must occur in the production of one of the goods.

The Law of Comparative Advantages can be stated thus:

A country will concentrate its production on those things in which it has the greatest relative advantage over other countries and will get from abroad those things in the production of which it has the least relative advantage.

It was this principle which Ricardo propounded using his example of Portugal producing wine and England producing cloth – each country ends up specializing in the production of the goods in which it has the comparative advantage and imports the goods in which it has a comparative disadvantage.

Ricardo's analysis was conducted, however, in terms of a two-country, two-commodity situation with only one factor-input (labor time). This input was more efficient in one country than another with the result that wages would tend to be higher in the more efficient country. However, the disparity in wage levels between the two countries would not be ironed out by movements of labor from the less highly paid to the more highly paid country since, Ricardo argued, factors of production, though not completely immobile, were exceedingly immobile between countries as compared with movement within a country. It is this distinction between mobility of factors within a country and that between countries which is the basis of Ricardo's differentiation between international and inter-regional trade.

Whereas rates of return to productive factors will tend to equality as between the regions of a country, this would not occur (according to Ricardo) between nations simply because of factor immobilities. As we shall see later, this argument concerning the equalization of factor returns later came in for serious attack.

Criticisms of Ricardo

Despite the elegance and simplicity of Ricardo's model in demonstrating the welfare proposition that trade is beneficial to those who engage in it, his theory of comparative advantage has come in for serious criticism in various counts.

(i) The most serious attack on Ricardo is that he tied his theory of trade to labor costs and to labor costs alone. In essence, he relied on the labor theory of value which stated that the values of goods were determined by their labor content (i.e. the amount of labor time used in their production). However, obviously, goods are not produced by labor alone, but by a combination of all factors of production. If we compare the labor content of various goods, then this will not give us a true picture of their relative values. For example, the labor content of cars will probably be less than that of textiles, but this does not mean that cars are valued less, relative to textiles. We must take account of the fact that the capital content of cars will be higher than that for textiles. It is precisely these varying factor proportions in the production of different goods which makes it impossible to use the labor theory of value.

Ricardo realised that the structure of trade was determined by money costs and prices, but he assumed that these prices would be proportional to the labor time embodied in the goods and argued, therefore, that the pattern of trade would ultimately be governed by the relative amounts of labor expended in production.

However, both Mill[8] and Senior[9] later pointed out that prices could deviate from strict proportionality to labor time, and such deviations could affect the structure of trade. Mill also argued that the actual productivity of labor was important and not simply labor time expended. Such differences in productivity (which, of course, mean a difference in the quality of the labor, if we assume that land and capital are homogeneous between nations) would mean that wage levels would also differ between industries and between countries. Ricardo had regarded "labor" as being a homogeneous class of factor.

Cairnes[10] argued that factor prices would not, in general, be proportional to labor time, since wage levels could differ between industries simply because labor was not a homogeneous mass but was divided into a series of noncompeting groups. As a result, variations in the wage levels of these noncompeting groups could occur with consequent variations in the relative prices of the goods produced. Such differences in relative prices could, in turn, affect the pattern of international trade, the important point being that obstacles existed to prevent a wage increase or decrease in one industry from spreading to all industries and wage levels.

Thus, by taking account of money wages as being an important variable which could affect the pattern of trade and specialization and cause it to differ from that given by a concentration on labor time, another step forward was made in relating trade theory to the real world.

(ii) Ricardo's theory of comparative advantage was only a theory of the supply side of international trade – it took no account of demand. His theory could explain what goods a country would export and import but the actual rate of exchange (i.e. how much of exports had to be given up for a certain amount of imports) was left undetermined. In order to determine the rate of exchange between exports and imports or what is the same thing, the prices of internationally traded goods, demand had to be introduced into the analysis. This was the problem which Mill set himself and later Marshall[11] also. This problem will be discussed in detail in Chapter 5.

(iii) Ricardo took no account in his theory of the effects of transport costs. In the real world, transport costs must play an important part in determining the prices of internationally traded commodities. Therefore some account should be taken of their effect when considering the theory of trade.

Let us consider *Case* (*b*) again in order to see what modifications have to be made to our conclusion once we bring transport costs into the picture.

	United States	Australia
F	20	25
S	10	5

In this case, the final rate of exchange between food and steel will lie within the range 10 units of food for at least 2 units of steel but less than 5 units of steel. Suppose now that transport costs between the United States and Australia are such that Australia pays 1 unit of food in order to transport 10 units of food to the United States and the United States pays $\frac{1}{2}$ unit of steel to transport 5 units of steel to Australia.

It will now pay Australia to export 10 units of food to the United States so long as it can get at least 2 units of steel plus the equivalent of 1 unit of food to cover transport costs. To Australia, one unit of food is the same (in terms of real source usage) as $\frac{1}{5}$th unit of steel. Australia must get in return for 10 units of food, therefore, at least $2\frac{1}{5}$ units of steel.

The United States, on the other hand, was previously willing to export up to 5 units of steel in return for 10 units of food; but the transport costs for the United States are such that it will only be willing to give up to $4\frac{1}{2}$ units of steel in exchange for 10 units of food. The range within which the rate of exchange can now lie has narrowed from 10 units of food for at least 2 but less than 5 units of steel, to a range 10 units of food for at least $2\frac{1}{5}$ but less than $4\frac{1}{2}$ units of steel.

The more important transport costs become in relation to the real resources used in the actual production of the goods, the greater will be their effect on the possible range of final prices (rates of exchange); the higher transport costs become, the narrower becomes the range of exchange. Thus, it is possible to construct simple examples where the Law of Comparative Advantage would indicate that trade would occur, but transport costs are so high that the gains from trading are absorbed entirely by these transport charges.

So, once we take account of the fact that nations are separated by distance, it can be seen that the pattern of trade and specialization will be affected by the distances involved, and by the relative weight and bulkiness of the traded goods.

Empirical studies of the relation of transport costs to trade have been undertaken by Isard[12] and Beckerman[13] who both claim that the distance variable has a major influence on actual trade flows.

(iv) Ricardo dealt with only a two-country, two-commodity model. This objection is perfectly valid but is not damaging to Ricardo's conclusions. If we extend the analysis to cover more than two commodities (with two countries), it is no longer possible to apply the strong Ricardian theories that the pattern of trade will be determined solely by international differences in factor productivities. What we now have is a weaker proposition which states that it will always hold that each of a country's exports will have a higher factor-productivity ratio than each of its imports.

Thus, although it is possible to draw up a list of the goods produced in order of decreasing factor-productivity ratios, how can we determine which of these goods will be exported and which imported?

Jones[14] has demonstrated that, in order to discover the answer to this problem, we must bring demand into the analysis. He has also shown that the above so-called weak proposition will continue to hold when we extend the analysis to more than two countries – a country's exports will always have a higher factor-productivity ratio than its imports. It is possible, then, to extend Ricardo's simple analysis to cover a multi-commodity, multi-country model. In the multi-country analysis, so long as we can have free trade (i.e. no restrictions on exports or imports) then it is likely that the potential increase in world output (and therefore in world economic welfare) will be greater than would be the case if trade were confined to two-country situations (i.e. bilateral trade).

This is due to the fact that with multilateral trade, the possibility of indirect trading exists.

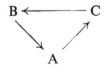

Thus, country A may find it profitable to trade indirectly with country C, which sells very little to country A. Country C, however, exports a lot to country B, which in turn exports to country A; the arrows in the diagram indicating the predominant direction of trade. Obviously, if bilateral trade were the only possibility, world trade would be cut down in volume severely; imports would balance exports (but at a level determined by the export level of the country engaging least in trade), and although total exports and imports would balance, the aggregate volume would be less than under a multilateral system. This is the sort of argument used by free-trade disciples in supporting their case.

The above, then, are the main arguments put forward against the Ricardian analysis, and it can be seen that only the first two are really serious and potentially damaging. The effect of introducing transport costs and multi-country-commodity analysis is simply to modify Ricardo's conclusions.

However, it will be seen later that the introduction of demand into the analysis not only yields a certain determination when considering *the terms* on which trade takes place, it can also create a situation where Ricardo's conclusions concerning the direction of trade will be reversed. In such cases, demand factors play a relatively greater part than the productivities of factor inputs in determining the direction of trade.

The other major attack is that concerning the use made by Ricardo of the labor theory of value – to attempt to overcome this difficulty, Haberler[15] has developed his theory of *opportunity costs*, or marginal opportunity costs, to be more precise. This idea of opportunity costs in international trade is usually represented by *production possibility curves* which show the amounts of goods which all factors of production in combination can produce. We are moving away, therefore, from a model using only one factor, labor, to one using all available factors.

Suppose we construct a two-commodity, two-country model as before.

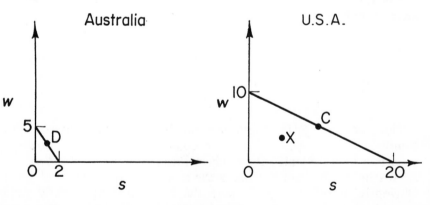

DIAGRAM 1

In the absence of trade, the U.S. production possibility curve shows that its factors of production, in combination, could produce either 10 units of wheat or 20 units of steel, or any combination of wheat and steel represented by any point on its curve.

Any point to the right of the curve is unattainable due to limitations of factor supplies; similarly, any point within the curve (e.g., X) implies that not all of the factors are being used.

In Australia's case, the curve shows possibilities of producing either 5 units of wheat or 2 units of steel, or any combination along the curve. We have here a case of the United States having a comparative advantage in steel production and Australia a comparative advantage in wheat production. Thus, at any point on the United States' production possibility curve, it can produce one more car by giving up a smaller amount of food production than Australia has to give up in order to produce an extra car. Similarly Australia has a comparative advantage in wheat production.

So much for the production conditions, we must now look at the concept of opportunity cost. The opportunity cost of wheat is how much steel has to be given up in order to produce an extra unit of wheat; the opportunity cost of steel is how much wheat has to be given up to produce an extra unit of steel. It makes no difference whether the factors which leave the production of one good to make another are well suited to the new product or not; our definition of opportunity costs is still valid.

Straight line production possibility curves illustrate what is called *constant opportunity costs* – if any resources shift out of wheat production into steel production (in the U.S. case) they can always produce steel in the constant proportion 1:2, no matter what proportion of total resources are so shifted.

Also, it should be noted that with constant opportunity costs, the price ratio domestically will be the same as the opportunity cost ratio (in the U.S. case, one unit of wheat will cost twice as much as a unit of steel). Any higher price of steel will shift resources from wheat into steel production; the supply of wheat will fall and its price rise: the price of steel will fall as its supply increases until the 1:2 price ratio is restored.

The opportunity cost of a product, then, is how much of the other goods have to be given up in order to produce one extra unit of that product.

Going back to our production possibility curves, we cannot tell where a country will be on its production possibility curve before trade. (We need knowledge of domestic demand for this.) Suppose, however, that the United States is at point C consuming 10 units of steel and 5 units of wheat, and Australia is at point D consuming one unit of steel and 2½ units of wheat.

Now, superimpose the two production possibility curves on each other and suppose that trade takes place at the Australian price ratio of 2 units of steel:5 units of wheat.

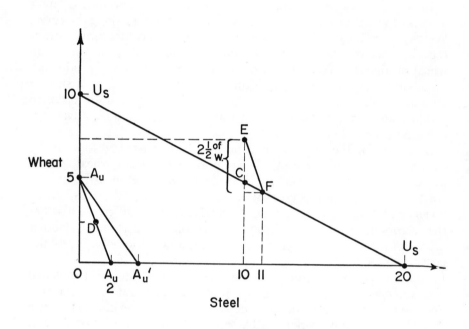

DIAGRAM 2

If Australia were to specialize completely in food production, then its maximum output of wheat would be 5 units which it could trade for steel at the assumed ratio of 5 of wheat for 2 of steel. Assuming that Australia would still like to end up at D, then the United States would be able to import 2½ units of wheat for 1 unit of steel exports and so reach point E by trading along line FE which has the same slope (i.e. represents the same price ratio) as AuAu. In this example, the volume of trade is limited by Australia's relatively small size, but nevertheless the example illustrates two important points:

(1) Trade has benefited the United States by enabling it to reach a point outside its original production possibility curve. Given the trading

price ratio we were using, Australia is no better off, so that all the gains from trade have gone to the United States.

(2) Even although Australia specializes completely in wheat production, the United States becomes more but not completely specialized in steel production.

In spite of the fact that the final price ratio after trade *may* be the same as that obtaining in one (but not both) of the countries before trade, it is more likely that the price ratio will settle somewhere between the two domestic pre-trade price ratios, *both* countries gaining from trade.

Suppose that the post-trade equilibrium price ratio settles down at 20 units of steel for 30 units of wheat as shown by the new price line AuAu'. In this case, the United States will not gain as much as in the previous situation; Australia sharing in the gains from trade.

For the United States the *position* of the price line is not known until we know how much steel Australia wishes to import at the given trading price ratio. Nevertheless, its slope will be the same as AuAu'.

It is obvious, therefore, that Australia will gain, but the actual distribution of the gains will depend on what the final price ratio is; in other words, this depends on demand factors.

However, what we can say is that under conditions of constant opportunity costs, (i.e. straight line production possibility curves), for the maximum benefit from trade, specialization of production after trade will be greater for both countries but may well be incomplete, for a large number of reasons, some economic, some political.

Modifications to Haberler's Analysis

Modifications to Haberler's Analysis consist mainly of altering the assumption of constant opportunity costs; that is, the assumption that the transfer of factors of production between commodities does not affect the relative efficiencies of these factors in either type of activity. This assumption is obviously rather unrealistic, so we will now look at the effects on the analysis of abandoning it.

In the real world, we would expect some resources to be more adaptable to, say, food production than, say, machinery production; other resources will be equally adaptable in different types of activity. The important point to note is that not all resources are equally adaptable in all types of activity.

Under more realistic conditions, then, we can have situations of *increasing* opportunity costs causing the production possibility curve to be concave to the origin.

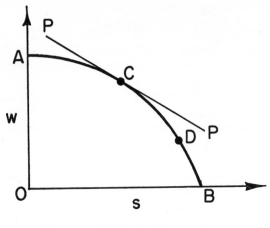

DIAGRAM 3

Over a certain range of possibilities, wheat and steel are fairly substitutable, but as we increase the concentration of production in either of these goods, the factors of production become increasingly nonadaptable. Thus, as we move down the curve from A to B, increasing the production of steel and decreasing that of wheat, the opportunity cost of steel in terms of wheat increases. We must give up more and more wheat in order to gain an extra unit of steel.

Also, another consequence of abandoning our constant opportunity cost assumption is that the price line between wheat and steel ceases to be the same as the production possibility curve; the price ratio domestically between wheat and steel can only be found by reference to demand conditions within the economy. Under conditions of increasing opportunity cost, the *rate* at which wheat exchanges for steel will be determined by demand conditions; that is, the *slope* of the price line will be determined by demand.

Suppose, now, that the demand situation[16] in the economy is such that the slope of PP represents the price ratio between wheat and steel. In equilibrium, production will occur at a point on the production possibility curve where the slope of the curve is the same as the slope of the price line (i.e. at C). At C the rate of transformation of wheat into steel through production (i.e. the slope of the production possibility curve) is the same as the rate of transformation of wheat into steel through trade (i.e. the slope of the price line). When this is the case, the economy will be in equilibrium.

If, for example, production takes place at a point D other than C, then, given the demand conditions, an excess of one good relative to the other will occur, creating a situation in which it would pay to shift resources out of the excessively produced good and into the scarcer good. Thus, there would be a tendency to move towards C. Now, suppose we have a situation in which the domestic price ratios of wheat and steel are not identical in our two countries and the production possibilities can be shown as follows:

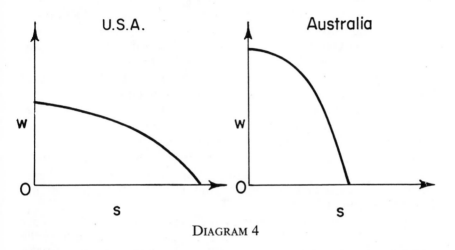

DIAGRAM 4

It is quite obvious from the shapes of the curves that the United States is more efficient at steel production and Australia is more efficient at wheat production.

If we now superimpose our two diagrams, we have the following diagram.

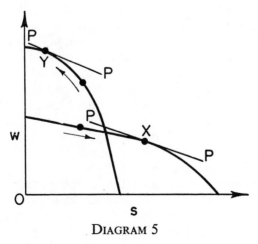

DIAGRAM 5

If trade takes place, an international rate of exchange between wheat and steel will develop, the exact rate again depending on demand conditions in the respective countries. Suppose the final rate of exchange settles down and is represented by the slope of the price line PP; then, in equilibrium, each country will produce at a point on its production possibility curve where the slope of this price line and the slope of its curve are the same (i.e. at X and Y).

The United States will move resources out of wheat production and into steel production, Australia will do the converse; the United States will export steel to Australia and import wheat, the exact amounts traded being indeterminate unless we bring in demand conditions.

The United States will consume at a point along PXP to the left of X, and Australia along PYP to the right of Y. By so doing, both countries will be able to move outside their original production possibility curves and so benefit from trade. The important difference between the case of increasing costs and that of constant costs is that, under constant costs,[17] specialization is more likely to be complete, whereas under increasing costs this is far less likely. Again, however, in real life, specialization even in cases of constant opportunity costs, will not normally be complete.

Haberler's analysis shows that even if we discard the labor theory of value as being invalid and rely on opportunity cost theory the comparative cost theory of trade is still valid – countries will specialize in the production of goods in which they have comparative advantage, so that if the price of one good (A) in terms of another (B) is higher abroad than domestically it will pay a country to shift resources out of the former good (A) and into the latter (B), trading (B) for (A) until the prices of (A) and (B) are equal abroad and domestically.

The student should note that the law of comparative advantage still holds; that is, a country should still trade goods that are relatively cheap to produce at home for those that are not. Now, however, we observe that the differences in opportunity costs that underlie comparative advantage do not alone lead to mutually beneficial trade between countries. Rather, these differences give rise to differences in comparative *prices*, which, in turn, prod countries into engaging in such trade.

The Haberler approach recognizes the existence of many different kinds of productive factors and is a major step forward from Ricardo's simple theory. The opportunity cost doctrine stresses (as the basis of trade) the differences internationally in the production possibility curves of nations – identical absolute amounts of the factor inputs would produce different amounts of a good in different countries. Comparative cost differences arise because of the production function for a given good varying from one country to another and the extent of the variation differing for various goods.

One can also see in the Haberler approach that gains from specialization and trade exist irrespective of *why* a single country has a comparative advantage in one good or a comparative disadvantage in another. In other words, trade is beneficial as long as opportunity costs differ, no matter *why* they differ. This puts to rest immediately the "cheap – foreign – labor" and other naïve protectionist arguments.

The student will now see that this is not the end of the road, there is a further problem; namely, if trade is based on comparative costs which arise out of differing production functions, *what* causes these differences to arise? Why are production possibility curves different in different countries?

It was this question which Ohlin and Heckscher set out to answer.

[1] Adam Smith, *The Wealth of Nations*, 1937, Lerner Edition, Book IV.

[2] *Ibid.*, Book IV, Ch. 2, pp. 423–426.

[3] *The Works and Correspondence of David Ricardo* (Sraffa edition), 1952, Vol. 1. Note that recently a certain amount of controversy has arisen over the logical possibility of *absolute* advantage existing. See R. Brandis, "The Myth of Absolute Advantage," *American Economic Review*, 1967; also comments by R. Anspach, J. Ingram, and Brandis in *American Economic Review*, June 1968.

[4] The rate of exchange here can be defined as the amount of one good given up (i.e. exported) to another country in exchange for a unit of imports of the other good. Thus a rate of exchange of 10 F for 5S can also be expressed as 2 F for 1 S – or 2:1.

[5] It is not so obvious here that world output is bigger after specialization than before, but the student can satisfy himself by comparing the relative values of the products to each country.

[6] Or the value of the total output as in *Case* (c).

[7] A similar sort of calculation can be done for *Case* (c).

[8] J. S. Mill, *Principles of Political Economy*, 1920.

[9] N. Senior, *Three Lectures on the Cost of Obtaining Money*, 1830.

[10] J. E. Cairnes, *Some Leading Principles of Political Economy Newly Expounded*, 1874.

[11] Marshall, *Money, Credit and Commerce*, 1933.

[12] Isard, *Location and Space Economy*, 1956.

[13] Beckerman, "Distance and the Pattern of Intra-European Trade," *Review of Economics and Statistics*, 1956.

[14] R. Jones, "Factor Proportions and the Heckscher-Ohlin Model," *Review of Economic Studies*, Vol. 24 (1956–57); also, "Comparative Advantage and the Theory of Tariffs – a Multi-country, Multi-commodity Model," *Review of Economic Studies*, Vol. 28 (1961).

[15] G. Haberler, *A Survey of International Trade Theory*, 1955.

[16] Students concerned about the way in which the price ratio is determined are referred to Chapter 5.

[17] Note that production-possibility curves may be convex to the origin due to *increasing* returns to scale. Under such circumstances, trade can take place simply due to the existence and exploitation of such scale economies. It has been argued, in fact, that increasing returns to scale may be typical of the real world.

CHAPTER 3

The Theoretical Basis of Trade (ii)

THIS CHAPTER is divided into two sections – the first dealing with the next step forward in our analysis of trade theory, the second section dealing with empirical testing of the various theories of international trade.

SECTION 1 (*a*) THE OHLIN-HECKSCHER THEORY OF TRADE

As we saw in the previous chapter, Classical trade theory argues that the basis of trade lay in the fact that the production function for a given commodity varied from one country to another, and the extent of this variation differed for various goods. But Classical theory made little attempt to explain the causes of such comparative cost differences.

Heckscher[1] and Ohlin,[2] however, developed an alternative formulation of comparative cost doctrine and attempted to explain why comparative cost differences existed internationally.

According to them, the production function for a given commodity was the same, irrespective of the country of production – if absolute identical amounts of factors were applied to the production of a given commodity, then every country would produce an identical amount of output of that good. However, although production functions for a given good behaved like this, they did differ as between different commodities. For instance, one good (X) might require in its production a lot of capital relative to labor, whereas another good (Y) would require a lot of labor relative to capital – thus we had capital-intensive and labor-intensive commodities. It was this difference in *factor intensities* in the production functions of goods along with *actual* differences in relative factor *endowments* of the countries (i.e. one country might possess a lot of capital relative to other factors; another country might possess a lot of land relative to other factors) which explained international differences in comparative costs of production.

In a nutshell, this is the basic idea lying behind the Ohlin-Heckscher Theory of Commodity Trade, which can be restated thus – a country will specialize in the production of and export the good whose production requires a relatively large amount (i.e. relative to other factors of production) of the factor with which the country is relatively well endowed (i.e. again, relative to other factors).

We shall now proceed to examine the theory and assumptions lying behind this statement.

The basic model is constructed from a number of explicit and implicit assumptions using a "double" model system (i.e. two goods, two countries, and two factors of production):

Assumptions
   (i) Perfect competition exists in both the product and factor markets in each country.
  (ii) Factor mobility within a country is complete but factor mobility between countries is nonexistent.
 (iii) Factors are identical qualitatively in both countries.
  (iv) Factor supplies in each country are fixed and fully employed.
   (v) Trade is free and costless – no barriers of any sort and no costs of transport.
  (vi) The physical amounts of each productive factor possessed by each country can be measured.
 (vii) Techniques of producing identical goods are the same in both countries – the same amounts of factor inputs in each country, applied to the production of a given commodity will yield exactly the same output.
(viii) Goods can be classified according to their factor intensity. We are able, therefore, to talk of labor-intensive and capital-intensive goods. This assumption, plus assumption (vii), implies that if one good is relatively capital-intensive in one country, it must be relatively capital-intensive in the other. Also, when one good is classed as being capital-intensive, it must remain so, irrespective of the price of capital relative to the price of labor. Relative factor *prices* must have no bearing, therefore, on whether a good is classified as being labor- or capital-intensive.
  (ix) Constant returns to scale applies to the production functions for the goods, and the production possibility curves are concave to the origin (i.e. factors of production are only partly substitutable).

Ohlin also argues that once we know from assumption (vi) what the relative factor endowments are for each country, we can infer from this what the relative factor-price structures will be for each country. Thus, a country relatively well endowed with labor will have a factor-price structure such that capital will be more expensive (i.e. earn a higher return) relative to labor.

In other words, supply outweighs demand in the determination of relative factor prices. If, however, demand for factors were to play an important role in fixing factor prices, we would have to talk in terms of *economic* scarcities rather than simple physical quantities and physical scarcities.

It should be realized that when considering the Ohlin-Heckscher model we must constantly think in terms of relative quantities – all comparisons made are relative; thus, we cannot say simply because one country X has a greater physical amount of one factor, labor, than another country Y, that country X is relatively well endowed with labor – we must also know the capital endowment of each country. Then, only if the ratio$\left(\dfrac{\text{Labor}}{\text{Capital}}\right)$ in country X is greater than the $\left(\dfrac{\text{Labor}}{\text{Capital}}\right)$ ratio in country Y, can we say that X is relatively well endowed with labor.

$$\text{Thus,} \quad \left(\frac{L}{K}\right)X \text{ may be } \frac{10 \text{ units}}{5 \text{ units}} = 2$$

$$\left(\frac{L}{K}\right)Y \text{ may be } \frac{8 \text{ units}}{2 \text{ units}} = 4$$

In this example, country Y, though it possesses a smaller absolute amount of labor than country X, is nevertheless *relatively* (i.e. relative to capital) well endowed with labor; and although the wage level in Y may be higher than that in X, it will be lower, relative to the return on capital in Y, than the wage level in X.

We must now consider how Ohlin derives from his assumptions, his theory of international trade. The important assumptions in the model are those concerning the production conditions. Assumption (vii) concerning identical production techniques for a given good in each country means that the isoquant map for a given good will be the same in both countries, so that if relative factor prices in both countries were the same, each country would produce the two commodities using identical factor proportions.

Thus, if in the following diagram AA represents a unit isoquant in the production of good A, then a country with a relative factor-price structure as represented by the slope of LC, will combine its factors to produce good A in the proportions Ol of labor to Oc of capital.

If our other country has the same factor-price structure, then since by assumption (vii) the isoquant map it faces for good A will be identical to the above, it too will combine its factors in the same ratio Ol:Oc.

But according to Ohlin, the factor-price structure will be the same in both countries, only if the relative factor endowments are identical (i.e. only if $\left(\dfrac{L}{K}\right)$ in country X $= \left(\dfrac{L}{K}\right)$ in country Y).

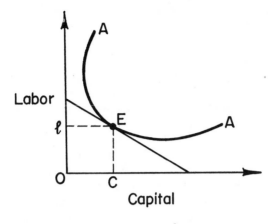

DIAGRAM 6

Otherwise, factor-price structures will differ between countries and so each country will combine its factors in differing proportions, the labor abundant country using labor-intensive production methods, the capital abundant country using capital intensive production methods.

Assumption (viii) means that the isoquant maps for different goods are different, though the isoquant map for a *given* commodity will be the same irrespective of nationality. Also, since, if a good is classified as being capital intensive, it must remain so for all factor-price ratios, this means that the isoquants for two different goods can only cross each other once.

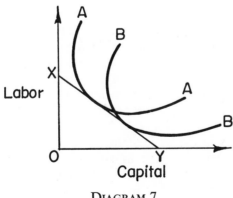

DIAGRAM 7

Thus, in Diagram 7, at any given factor-price ratio (e.g. that ratio represented by the slope of XY), good A will *always* be relatively labor intensive in production, relative to good B, which will be capital intensive. We can also say that a commodity can only be judged to be capital or labor intensive *relative* to the production requirements of another good, *at the same factor-price ratio*.

If the isoquants intersect more than once, good A will not *always* be capital intensive relative to good B. The effects of this will be considered later when we criticize the model.

So far, goods A and B are being produced in each country using identical production techniques, but with goods A and B requiring, individually, different production techniques. Now, if we accept assumption (i) (perfect competition in both factor and product markets), then Euler's Theorem will hold – that is, each factor of production will be paid the value of its marginal physical product. Therefore, under Ohlin's assumptions, the actual *price* of a commodity must, in equilibrium, be equal to its unit costs of production (i.e. the sum of the capital and labor inputs per unit of output valued at their respective market prices).

Now, according to the law of comparative advantage, trade will only take place if *relative* commodity prices differ internationally – that is the price of A relative to the price of B in country X must differ from the price of A relative to the price of B in country Y. Given Ohlin's assumptions and Euler's Theorem, this is the same thing as saying that the cost of producing A relative to the cost of producing B in country X must differ from the cost of producing A relative to the cost of producing B in country Y.

Suppose in our two-country, two-good, two-factor model that country X is relatively well endowed with capital and that, for all factor price ratios, good A is relatively capital intensive in production. According to Ohlin, since country X is capital abundant, the price of capital relative to the price of labor will be low. It follows, therefore, that country X will be able to produce good A relatively cheaply and country Y will be able to produce good B relatively cheaply (simply because factor endowments differ between the two countries). The price ratio between goods A and B will differ between the two countries, therefore, and trade will take place, each country exporting the good in whose production a relatively large amount of its relatively abundant factor is required.

This then, is how in the basic Ohlin-Heckscher model, comparative advantages arise – they are due to the existence of differing international factor-endowment ratios and differing commodity factor intensities.

If relative factor endowments were identical and commodity factor intensities the same, no comparative cost differences (and therefore, under Ohlin's assumptions, no comparative price differences) would arise, and so there would be no theoretical basis for trade. Only if there is a difference in relative factor endowments and commodity factor intensities, can trade take place, the trade pattern being such that the relatively capital abundant country exports the relatively capital-intensive good and imports the relatively labor-intensive one. Thus, in our model, the *only* difference between the two countries was that they had different relative factor endowments and this determined production and trade patterns.

As we have seen, however, the basic Ohlin-Heckscher model relies for its construction on a number of highly simplified and unrealistic assumptions, and it is precisely these assumptions which have been attacked by the critics of Ohlin and Heckscher. We must now consider the criticisms which have been made.

Criticisms of Ohlin-Heckscher

(i) Firstly, it was assumed that factors of identical quality existed in the two countries and that these factors were capable of being measured, in order to calculate factor-endowment ratios. Suppose we consider the factor "capital" of which, let us suppose, there is but one type – type "A." If the quality of type "A" capital varies internationally, then it would be extremely difficult to devise a measuring rod which would allow comparisons to be made of different countries' "capital" factor endowments. However, if quality is invariant with respect to country, but there exists more than *one* type of capital, then we run into problems of aggregating these different *types* in order to get an aggregate measure of a country's capital endowment. Thus, if we are to be able to measure factors on the same basis so as to allow inter-country comparisons of factor supplies to be made, we must postulate that each factor has but one *type* and that the *quality* of this type does not vary.

In the real world of course, it is obvious that (*a*) factors are not identical in quality between countries and (*b*) more than one type of each factor exists.

Therefore, real problems of measurement and comparison would arise in the real world. Not only this, but once we allow factor-type quality to vary between countries, then this variation in itself could be a determinant of trade patterns. On *a priori* grounds one might expect that differing factor qualities would be a powerful influence on factor productivities, thus leading to differing international costs of production and therefore trade possibilities.

(ii) Secondly, Ohlin argued that relative factor prices would reflect exactly relative factor endowments. As mentioned before, this means that in the determination of factor prices, supply outweighs demand (i.e. physical factor abundance is the same as economic factor abundance). However, if demand factors are important in the determination of factor prices, then it is quite possible for the labor abundant country (in the physical sense) to export the capital intensive good. This is so, because if the labor abundant country is such that the demand for labor (and therefore, indirectly, for the labor intensive good) is high enough, then the price of labor relative to capital will also be high and the factor price ratio $\left(\dfrac{L}{K}\right)$ will exceed the $\left(\dfrac{L}{K}\right)$ price ratio in the capital abundant country.

Also, countries with identical factor-endowment ratios could engage in trade, so long as relative production costs (and therefore relative commodity prices) differed. This would be the case if demand conditions for the factor supplies differed between the countries. Thus, unless we can assume that relative factor prices will reflect relative factor endowments, we cannot derive the basic Ohlin-Heckscher Theorem as being the *sole* explanation of trade. If demand is an important variable in the determination of relative factor prices, as it could well be in the real world, then other explanations of why trade takes place are possible – differing factor endowments become but one explanation among many.

(iii) Thirdly, as we saw earlier, Ohlin specifically assumed, in direct contrast to earlier Ricardian Analysis, that production techniques for a given commodity are the same in all countries (i.e. the production surfaces for goods A and B individually are identical). Suppose we drop this assumption and have a situation where production techniques of the two goods taken individually are not identical as between countries.

Consider commodity A – *different* production techniques means that the isoquant map for A facing each country is different. Suppose Diagrams 8 and 9 show a representative isoquant for good A in countries X and Y.

Then, at an identical factor-price ratio in each country represented by the slope of BB, country Y will combine its factors in the ratio Ol:Oc; country X will combine its factors in a different ratio $Ol_1:Oc_1$. It can be seen in this example from the way the diagrams have been constructed that good A will be relatively labor intensive (i.e. relative to the production of A in country Y) and relatively capital intensive in country X. Similar diagrams could be constructed for good B.

Let us now construct what are called factor-intensity curves for good A. To do this, we measure the factor ratios used in production

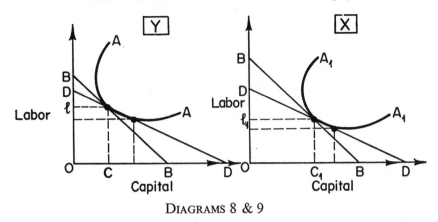

DIAGRAMS 8 & 9

at differing factor price ratios. To construct the curves, measure the $\left(\dfrac{L}{K}\right)$ ratio along the Y-axis and the $\left(\dfrac{L}{K}\right)$ price ratio along the X-axis. Re-

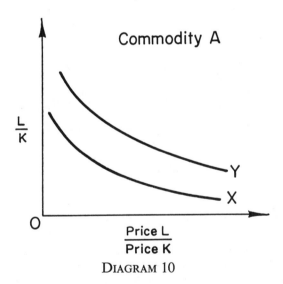

DIAGRAM 10

ferring back to our previous diagram, we can vary the factor-price ratio for each country and note how it combines its factors of production at each factor-price ratio. Thus, in the original situation, the factor ratios in countries Y and X respectively were $Ol:Oc$ and $Ol_1:Oc_1$. It is apparent that $Ol:Oc > Ol_1:Oc_1$ so the $\dfrac{L}{K}$ ratio for country Y will be higher than the $\dfrac{L}{K}$ ratio for country X. Similarly, as we vary the factor-price ratio, e.g. by shifting BB to DD, it can be noted how the $\frac{L}{K}$ ratio varies for each country. As $\frac{LP}{KP}$ increases, the $\frac{L}{K}$ ratio falls in each country. Now, so long as we maintain our assumption that isoquants can only cross once, then a country whose $\frac{L}{K}$ ratio is higher at a *given* factor-price ratio, will *always* have a higher $\frac{L}{K}$ ratio.

In our example, the factor-intensity curve for country Y is higher than that for country X. Similarly, factor-intensity curves for good B could be constructed.[3]

Suppose that the factor-intensity curves for good B in countries X and Y coincide, so that production techniques for good B are identical, but techniques for good A are not. We have assumed that good A is relatively capital intensive in both countries, therefore the factor-intensity curve for good B must lie, everywhere, above the factor-intensity curve for good A in country Y.

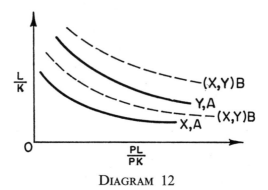

DIAGRAM 12

Now, at any factor-price ratio, X will prefer to produce good A and Y will prefer to produce good B – in harmony with Ohlin's conclusions. What will happen, however, if good B is labor intensive in country X but relatively capital intensive in country Y (the labor abundant country)? In this case, the factor-intensity curve for good B will lie between these for good A. Country X will still prefer to produce good A, but country Y will prefer to produce good A since good A in this case requires less of its scarce factor (capital) than does good B. Will trade take place? The answer to this depends on the actual position of the factor-intensity curve for good B relative to the curve for good A – at any given factor price structure; the closer the "B" curve is to country Y's "A" curve, the less difference will it make to Y whether it specializes in good A or good B. However, the closer the B curve is to Y's "A" curve, the bigger the difference it makes to country X, – X will have a comparative cost advantage in the production of A (relative to B). At some intermediate position between X_A and Y_A comparative cost differences will cease to exist and so trade will not take place.

In this example, then, depending on the position of the "B" curve, comparative cost advantages may arise and lead to trade. However, the trade which takes place will not all correspond to the Ohlin-Heckscher proposition – one of the countries will be exporting the good whose production requires a lot of the relatively abundant factor; the other country will export the good which requires a relatively large amount of its *scarce* factor.

Similar conclusions can be reached when we allow the production techniques for *both* goods to differ between countries – trade may or may not take place, but the necessary condition for trade to occur is still that comparative cost differences must exist. However, when trade does take place, not all of the trade will follow the basic Ohlin-Heckscher theorem.

Suppose the factor intensity curves for A and B are as shown in

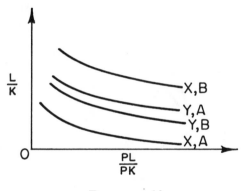

DIAGRAM 13

Diagram 13. Good A is capital intensive in country X; and good B is capital intensive in country Y.

However, the diagram is so constructed that the relation between the curves gives rise to comparative cost differences such that country X will export good A and country Y will export good B.

In the production of good A, the $\frac{L}{K}$ ratio for country X will be lower than the $\frac{L}{K}$ ratio for good B, in country Y the $\frac{L}{K}$ ratio in the production of good A will be higher than the $\frac{L}{K}$ ratio for good B.

$$\text{So,} \quad \left(\frac{L}{K}\right)\text{A,x} < \left(\frac{L}{K}\right)\text{B,x}$$

$$\text{and,} \quad \left(\frac{L}{K}\right)\text{B,y} < \left(\frac{L}{K}\right)\text{A,y}$$

It might appear from this that Y should produce A, since this uses less of its relatively scarce factor. But, from the construction of the example, country X has a relative advantage in the production of A, compared with country Y, and will therefore export good A.

It can be shown, therefore, that once we drop the identity of production techniques assumption, trade patterns need not follow the directions indicated by the basic factor-endowment patterns (i.e. need not follow the directions indicated by the Ohlin-Heckscher theorem).

(iv) Suppose we now retain the Ohlinian assumption of identical international production techniques but allow a situation to arise in which the factor intensity of a good is not invariant with respect to the factor-price structure of the country.

As we saw earlier, if the isoquants for two commodities intersect more than once, we can no longer say that a good will be, for example, capital intensive, no matter what the factor-price structure may be.

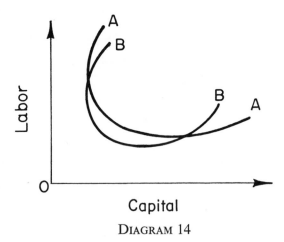

DIAGRAM 14

Ford[4] has demonstrated that if the isoquants intersect twice, good A will be capital intensive over a certain factor-price range and labor intensive over another. Using our factor-intensity curves this can be represented as follows.

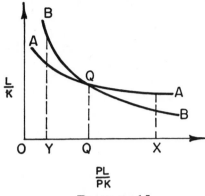

DIAGRAM 15

Q represents what is called the *factor-intensity reversal* point – at any factor-price ratio up to Q, good A is relatively capital intensive, after Q, good B becomes relatively capital-intensive. Since country X is assumed to be the country with relatively large supplies of capital, we could represent its factor-price structure at X. Point Y, correspondingly, represents country Y's factor-price structure. Country X would seem to prefer to produce good B (capital intensive) and Y also would seem to prefer to produce good B (labor intensive), at their given factor-price ratios. However, given the shapes of the curves in the diagram, it is obvious that country Y has a comparative advantage in the production of B and X has a comparative advantage in the production of A. When trade takes place, then, the specialization and exports of Y will correspond to the basic Ohlin Heckscher theorem, but those of country X will not.

Again, once we relax the Ohlinian assumption concerning the relation between factor-price structures and commodity-factor intensities, the trade pattern which is possible need not follow the basic theorem. This is the factor-intensity-reversal criticism.

(v) Another criticism of Ohlin was that he assumed that constant returns to scale were present. However, if a country starts trading, then its industry will have to produce for a bigger market consisting of domestic and foreign purchasers. This will mean that the possibility arises of reaping economies of scale. Consequently, the prices of the goods purchased by these industries will be higher than actual cost, so that production costs are no longer a direct reflection of price.

Also, if we had a situation before trade in which factor endowments differed but no comparative cost differences occurred, it is quite possible that if one of the countries were to specialize in the production of goods requiring its relatively abundant factor, it could reap economies of scale and so *create* comparative cost differences. Trade could then take place, where previously it seemed impossible. It is also conceivable that if scale economies were sufficiently powerful, a country with dearer factors of production could produce a given article cheaper than the country with the relatively cheap supply of factors. In this case, the influence of factor prices has been overshadowed, and trade could occur, purely on the basis of increasing returns to scale.

(vi) It is also possible that, due to demand preferences for the goods being produced, the commodity price ratio will fail to reflect cost ratios and so we can have situations in which the trade pattern does not correspond to the basic theorem.

Ohlin has also been criticized due to the unrealism of his assumption of perfect competition in product and factor markets and complete immobility of factors internationally.[5] The important point is that once we replace the Ohlinian assumptions by more realistic ones, we are faced with a number of possible explanations of why trade takes place:

(i) Differing relative factor endowments;
(ii) Differing factor qualities;
(iii) Differing production techniques;
(iv) Increasing returns to scale;
(v) Consumer demand preferences.

Ohlin himself recognized the unrealism of his assumptions and attempted to modify them in constructing a subsidiary theory in which he concluded that though there were a number of reasons why commodity prices could differ internationally, factor endowments were the predominant factor in any explanation. The *cause* of trade for Ohlin was no different from the Classical theory of Comparative Advantages – trade is caused by differences in relative commodity price ratios. The *basis* of trade is given, however, by the factors which cause these commodity price-ratio differences to emerge – unequal international factor endowments.

So far as the relative simplicity of the model is concerned (two goods, two factors, two countries), Jones[6] has shown that the theorem is valid for a multi-commodity model as well. Given factor supply and production technique data, goods can be ranked in terms of factor ratios and therefore in terms of comparative advantage. However, as was the case when the Ricardian system was extended, demand must be introduced into the analysis in order to determine which goods are exported and which imported.

The model, however, has not as yet been extended to cover a multi-commodity, multi-country analysis. This is, of course, unfortunate, since the real world consists of a multi-commodity, multi-country international economy.

Having considered the Ohlin-Heckscher model, and the criticisms made of it, we shall now go on to look at various attempts which have been made to test empirically the Ricardian and Ohlinian models.

SECTION 2. EMPIRICAL ANALYSES OF COMPARATIVE COST THEORIES

It would appear as if the simple theoretical explanations for trade as given by comparative cost doctrine would be fairly easily testable in the real world – verification of comparative price and cost differences would be based on an examination of comparative factor endowments.

Empirical studies can be divided for convenience into two classes: (a) these concerned with testing whether or not real world trade corresponds to comparative advantage theory and (b) those concerned with the relative factor-endowment theory as an explanation of comparative cost differences.

(a) *Comparative Advantage Testing* – Work in this field has been undertaken chiefly by MacDougall,[7] Stern[8] and Balassa.[9]

It is possible, on certain assumptions, to derive two hypotheses concerning trade from the Ricardian-type analyses.

If we can substitute labor productivity measures for pre-trade prices of traded goods, then the condition for trade is that

$$\frac{P_i B}{P_i A} < \frac{P_j B}{P_j A}$$

where $P_i A$ is the productivity of labor in industry i and $P_j A$ is the productivity of labor in industry j. Similarly, for country B. The commodity produced and exported by country A is i, that by B is j.

However, it is also possible to bring wage rates into the picture and state the hypothesis in terms of unit labor *costs* instead of labor productivity –

$$\frac{P_i B}{P_i A} \cdot \frac{w_i A}{w_i B} < \frac{P_j B}{P_j A} \cdot \frac{w_j A}{w_j B}$$

If one bears these Ricardian hypotheses in mind when considering empirical attempts at verifying then, one will have little trouble in following the analyses of MacDougall, Stern and Balassa. MacDougall was essentially attempting to investigate three hypotheses which he expected should hold if Ricardian analysis was valid in the real world:

(i) The hypothesis that a positive correlation should exist between export shares of a given commodity and the ratio of labor productivities in producing that commodity. What this means is that a country should have a bigger share of the export market, for a given commodity, compared with its rival, the higher the ratio of the productivity of its labor in the production of the good to the productivity of the other country's labor.

MacDougall, Stern and Balassa all produce data which moderately support this hypothesis.

(ii) The hypothesis that the export share of a country in a given good will exceed unity if the product of relative wage rates and inverted labor productivities is greater than unity.

This can be represented as –

$$\text{if } \frac{P_i^B}{P_i^A} \cdot \frac{w_i^A}{w_i^B} > 1, \quad \text{then } \frac{Ex_i^A}{Ex_i^B} > 1$$

Thus, so long as a country's productivity advantage is not affected by excessive wages in the industry concerned, then that country will be able to gain a large share of export markets.

Using *average* wage levels in Britain and the United States, Mac-Dougall found that the U.S. wage level was more than twice the British level. However, where the U.S. productivity was more than twice the British level, the United States had the bulk of the export market. Where productivity was less than twice as high, Britain had the bulk of the export market. Stern found similar confirmation of the hypothesis.

(iii) The hypothesis that a positive correlation should exist between export shares of a given commodity and the wage productivity product used in hypothesis (ii).

$$\text{i.e. } \frac{P_i^B}{P_i^A} \cdot \frac{w_i^B}{w_i^A}$$

Balassa and Stern both found that fairly strong correlations do exist, and Balassa goes farther and argues that the introduction of wage ratios does little to improve comparative productivities as an explanation of export shares.

It would appear that these studies tend to support the Ricardian hypotheses. It should be remembered, however, that the so-called support rests on the assumption that productivity ratios are a good substitute for price ratios. Bhagwati[10] has questioned this approach and finds that "contrary to the general impression (based on the MacDougall, Balassa and Stern results), there is as yet no evidence in favor of the Ricardian hypothesis."

However, in spite of the difficulties which Bhagwati emphasizes, it is difficult to dismiss completely the empirical evidence of Ricardian supporters. We are left in a position where one must judge for oneself the weight to attach to the empirical data so far collected. The student is therefore strongly advised to consult the articles mentioned and attempt to form his own opinion on the subject.

(b) *Factor-Endowment Theory Test* – Several studies have been made of Factor-Endowment Theory the most famous being these of MacDougall,[11] Leontief[12] and Bharadwaj.[13] MacDougall was one of the first to attempt to discover whether the Ohlin-Heckscher model was applicable to the real world. He compared U.S. and U.K. export shares of relatively capital intensive commodities and found that, contrary to expectations, the United Kingdom did not export to the United States goods with low capital intensity relative to labor.

However, this test which seems to refute Factor-Endowment Theory has been severely criticized on statistical grounds and on the grounds that MacDougall's measure of capital intensity (horsepower used at prevailing factor prices) is unsatisfactory.

Leontief's attempt at measuring and comparing the factor intensities of U.S. exports and imports is probably the best known of all, since it comes out with the paradoxical conclusion that the United States exports *labor*-intensive goods and imports capital-intensive ones. Because of this his conclusion is often referred to as the *Leontief Paradox*; a paradox since one would normally accept without question that the United States is a relatively capital abundant country and should, therefore, according to factor-endowment theory, export relatively capital-intensive goods.

Leontief undertook this analysis by considering the effects on the release of resources of a reduction of $1 million worth of U.S. exports and imports.

Without going into the details of his calculations, there is one major methodological criticism which has been made of Leontief's study – Leontief was concerned with export industries and competitive import *replacements*, not actual imports. The Ohlin-Heckscher theorem applies to *actual* exports and imports and, because of this, Ford[14] argues that Leontief's conclusion is not applicable to the basic Ohlinian theorem and cannot therefore invalidate it; not only this, but one could expect U.S. import replacement production to be more capital intensive than export production, simply because U.S. production methods are directed toward using a relatively large amount of capital and a fair proportion of the United States' raw material imports (since they may not exist in the United States in economic quantities, etc.) would require, if the United States were to produce them itself, relatively large amounts of capital.

All we can say, then, is that the United States exports capital-intensive products and "imports products, which if it were to produce them, would require relatively more of its abundant factor."[15]

This is a similar sort of argument to Jones[16] who concluded that it was possible that *both* U.S. export and import-competing goods were produced with more capital-intensive methods than abroad, since the Ohlinian theorem cannot be put into reverse, that is, one cannot conclude from trade patterns what relative factor endowments are, and Leontief made no attempt to measure or compare relative factor endowments.

A number of defenses of the Ohlin-Heckscher theorem have been put forward, and we can now consider them briefly:

(i) Foreign labor is less efficient than U.S. labor. This, essentially, is the argument Leontief himself uses to rescue Ohlin and Heckscher. What we should do is adjust our measure of labor supply by an efficiency factor (Leontief thought the factor should be three, though he does not state how this figure is arrived at). If we do this, we would find that U.S. capital per "worker" (equal to $\frac{1}{3}$ of a "real" worker) turns out to be comparatively smaller than that of many other countries. This would imply, therefore, that the United States is *relatively* labor abundant and so her trade pattern conforms to the basic Ohlin-Heckcher theorem. Diab[17] also appears to arrive at the same conclusion as Leontief, but both Diab's and Leontief's attempts at rescuing Ohlin are unacceptable because, firstly there is no logical reason to choose labor as the more efficient factor and reduce it to "standard" units. If we were to choose capital as being the more efficient factor, we would, of course find that the United States was exceptionally well-endowed with capital. Secondly, even if labor is more efficient, so also may be capital, which means that the adjustment effect on factor-intensity calculations may be reduced or even offset completely.

As we shall see, other explanations of the paradox are available.

(ii) Factor intensities for the same goods may be completely different between the United States and the countries which export these goods to the United States. This means that we have a case of factor-intensity reversal with the result as we noted before, that we cannot tell, simply from the factor endowments, which country will export which product. This could explain the Leontief findings.

(iii) More likely, in the real world, we would have situations in which the production techniques for a given commodity will differ between countries. As we saw before, this can give rise to one of the countries exporting a product which requires for production a relatively large amount of its scarce factor. Thus, we could accept the Leontief findings without necessarily having to reject the Ohlin-Heckscher theorem.

(iv) Demand conditions in the United States may be such that domestic production of capital-intensive goods is insufficient to satisfy this demand, with the result that the United States is forced to import capital-intensive commodities. However, according to Brown,[18] it appears as if the United States consumes relatively more of goods such as services which are relatively labor-intensive.

(v) Hoffmeyer[19] argues that the Leontief paradox is due to his failure to deal adequately with natural resources. If commodities which require a relatively large amount of natural resources are excluded from the calculation of capital-labor ratios, then Leontief's conclusions would be reversed – the United States would be found to import labor intensive goods and export relatively capital-intensive ones. Since *actual* U.S. imports have an important natural resource element, and since Leontief was concerned only with import replacements, we would be better to exclude natural resources commodities from the calculations. We then have no paradox to explain.

Bharadwaj[20] undertook the application of Leontief-type studies to Indian trade, but instead of comparing the trade of one country with the rest of the world, he studied *bilateral* trade between India and the United States. When this was done, it was found that for India-U.S. trade, the factor intensities were the reverse of those which applied to total Indian trade – India exports capital-intensive goods to the United States and imports from the United States labor-intensive goods. Similar studies[21] of bilateral trade are not wholly in support of the rejection of the Ohlin-Heckscher theorem, although the majority certainly fail to support the theorem.

In conclusion, once we have considered the empirical evidence against the Ohlinian theorem and the defenses put forward to rescue it, it would on balance seem reasonable to say that the Ohlin-Heckscher theorem has not been refuted. However, this is mainly because the assumptions on which it is built are so unreal and restrictive that it would be virtually impossible to devise a real world test of the theory. The theory is for all practical purposes irrefutable and is, therefore, to that extent a bad theory. Empirically, the theory holds up only if definitions and data are twisted and tortured until it finally "explains" the observed data. But the explanation is by then useless, since the supposed theory has become a tautology – a country will export those goods using relatively large amounts of those factors used in its exports.

We can see earlier that once we relax the assumptions of the theory, then trade can quite easily take place which does not conform to the basic theorem – Ohlin himself recognized this possibility. It would seem reasonable to expect that, in the real world, production techniques are not identical internationally, that factor qualities do differ, that factor-intensity reversals are a distinct possibility[22] and so on.

Once we allow for this, the Ohlin-Heckscher theorem becomes but *one* of many explanations of why trade takes place. It is not necessarily factor endowments or factor intensities which determine trade, but rather, as we shall see in Chapter 5, it is the whole complex of forces operating through supply *and* demand which determine whether or not trade takes place and on what terms.

APPENDIX

Recent Approaches to Trade Theory

Two attempts have been made recently to throw new light on the old question of why trade takes place between nations – those of Kravis[23] and Linder.[24]

(i) Kravis, in his article, showed that wages in export industries tend to be higher than wages in import competing industries and in all industries together. However, the differences in wage levels are not large in manufacturing industry, and service industries are omitted. In a later discussion, he argues that the composition of trade is not greatly influenced by varying wage structures. In considering the Leontief position, he doubts that the United States is short of capital rather than labor – in particular, he cites the U.S. export of large amounts of capital to foreign countries. According to Kravis, this does not suggest a shortage of U.S. capital. Kravis argues that the commodity composition of trade is primarily determined by "*availability*" and productivity (in relation to wage ratios). By "availability," Kravis means that trade tends to be confined to commodities which are not available at home (i.e. goods such as minerals which are not available for physical reasons; and goods whose output can only be increased at high cost – in other words, where inelasticity of supply exists). Unavailability exists, he argues, due to lack of natural resources relative to demand, or technological advance and product differentiation which allow the innovating country to have temporary monopoly powers. Natural and artificial scarcities create this unavailability therefore.

Although Kravis does not state so explicitly, one would expect from his discussion that the elasticity of supply of foreign export industries will be higher than that of domestic import-competing industries. One would also expect that a country's export industries would have a higher rate of technical progress than the same industries in rival countries.

Kravis, however, does not state these hypotheses in so specific a form; nevertheless, his arguments have a certain common-sense appeal and it would be of interest to actually put these ideas into testable form and discover how the real world treats them.[25]

(ii) Linder distinguishes between trade in manufactures and trade in primary products which is of course, natural resource intensive and can be explained in terms of relative factor endowments. However, Linder argues that trade in manufactures can't be explained in such terms, and in fact, we cannot really predict the exact pattern and composition of trade. What we can do, however, is develop a theory about the *volume of trade* (expressed as a proportion of national income) between pairs of nations – this volume according to Linder, will be higher, the greater the similarity in the demand patterns of the trading countries.

However, again, Linder's thesis, although he attempts some empirical analysis, still requires vigorous analytical formulation and empirical testing.

These, then, are two recent attempts to develop new theories of the basis of trade and, though not brilliantly successful, they are significant and also typical of the recent trend towards empirical testing of hypotheses.

[1] E. Heckscher, "The Effects of Foreign Trade on the Distribution of Income," *Ekonomisk Tidskrift*, 1919.

[2] B. Ohlin, *Interregional and International Trade*, Harvard University Press, 1933.

[3] Note that under strict Ohlinian assumptions, the factor-intensity curves for goods A and B individually will differ, but the curve for any good taken alone will be identical as between countries since production techniques are *identical*. Given

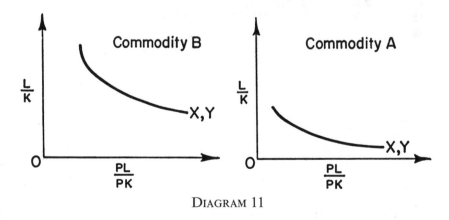

DIAGRAM 11

that good A is relatively capital intensive (i.e. the factor-intensity curve is always below the B curve) country Y will concentrate on production of good A and country X on good B.

[4] J. L. Ford, "The Ohlin-Heckscher Theory of the Basis of Commodity Trade," *Economic Journal*, 1963.

[5] For a complete and detailed examination of these and the previous points, the student is referred to Ford's book *The Ohlin-Heckscher Theory of Commodity Trade*, Asia Publishing House, London, 1965.

[6] R. Jones, "Factor Proportions and the Heckscher-Ohlin Model," *Review of Economic Studies*, Vol. 24 (1956–1957).

[7] G. D. A. MacDougall, "British and American Exports: a Study Suggested by the Theory of Comparative Costs, Part I," *Economic Journal*, 1951; and Part II of the same study, *Economic Journal*, 1952.

[8] R. Stern, "British and American Productivity and Comparative Costs in International Trade," *Oxford Economic Papers*, 1962.

[9] B. Balassa, "An Empirical Demonstration of Classical Comparative Cost Theory," *Review of Economics and Statistics*, 1963.

[10] J. Blagwati, "The Pure Theory of International Trade: a Survey," in *Surveys of Economic Theory*, Vol. II (Macmillan 1965).

[11] G. D. A. MacDougall, *op. cit.*

[12] W. W. Leontief, "Domestic Production and Foreign Trade; the American Capital Position Reexamined," *Economia Internazionale*, 1954; also, "Factor Proportions and the Structure of American Trade: Further Theoretical and Empirical Analysis," *Review of Economic Statistics*, 1956.

[13] R. Bharadwaj, "Structural Basis of India's Foreign Trade" (Series in Monetary and International Economics, No. 6); also "Factor Proportions and the Structure of Indo-U.S. Trade", *Indian Economic Journal*, 1962.

[14] J. L. Ford, *The Ohlin-Heckscher Theory of Commodity Trade*, Ch. VI.

[15] *Ibid.*, p. 60.

[16] R. Jones, "Factor Proportions and the Heckscher-Ohlin Theorem," *Review of Economic Studies*, 1956.

[17] Diab, *The U.S. Capital Position and the Structure of its Foreign Trade*, North-Holland Publishing Co., 1956.

[18] A. J. Brown, "Professor Leontief and the Pattern of World Trade," *Yorkshire Bulletin of Economic and Social Research*, 1957.

[19] E. Hoffemeyer, "The Leontief Paradox Critically Examined," Manchester School, 1958. See also, B. Swerling, "Capital Shortage and Labour Surplus in the U.S.," *Review of Economics and Statistics*, 1954.

[20] R. Bharadwaj, "Factor Proportions and the Structure of Indo-U.S. Trade," *Indian Economic Journal*, October 1962.

[21] See, for example, M. Tatemoto and S. Ichimura, "Factor Proportions and Foreign Trade: the Case of Japan," *Review of Economics and Statistics*, Vol. 41, 1959.

[22] See B. S. Minhas, "The Homohypallagic Production Function, Factor-Intensity Reversals and the Heckscher-Ohlin Theorem," *Journal of Political Economy*, Vol. 70, 1962. See also, P. A. Samuelson, "International Trade and Equalisation of Factor Prices," *Economic Journal*, Vol. 58, 1948; and "International Factor Price Equalisation once Again," *Economic Journal*, Vol. 59, 1949.

[23] I. Kravis, "Wages and Foreign Trade," *Review of Economics and Statistics*, Vol. 38, 1956.

[24] S. Linder, *An Essay on Trade and Transformation*, New York, John Wiley and Sons, 1961.

[25] See also, I. Kravis, "Availability and Other Influences on the Commodity Composition of Trade," *Journal of Political Economy*, 1956.

CHAPTER 4

The Effects of Trade on Factor Prices

IN CHAPTERS 2 and 3 we looked at the fundamental economic explanations of why trade takes place between countries, and analyzed how this trade could benefit those countries taking part in it. We must now consider a most important aspect of international trade; the effects which it can have on the *prices* of the productive factors used in the countries concerned. Obviously, since the relative prices of the productive factors will be a major determinant of businessmen's decisions about what to produce and how to produce it, and since relative factor prices are also important in determining the relative shares of the national product which each factor receives, it is necessary to analyze any forces operating via international trade which might tend to *change* relative or absolute factor returns. Given that changes in factor prices, other things remaining unchanged, will alter factor incomes or returns, we will now look at how trade between countries can alter factor prices.

When trade takes place internationally, the prices of the commodities being traded must, in equilibrium (and assuming perfect competition, no transport costs or other impediments to trade) be identical in the countries concerned. This is exactly what the analysis of the last two chapters has shown – the opening up of trade tends to eliminate comparative cost differences and this continues until the relative costs of the commodities are identical in each country. When this has happened, trade flows will stop increasing and trade will continue at a constant level.

Now, it is possible to show that under certain rather restrictive assumptions, international trade in commodities can act as a substitute for the movement of *factors* between countries, to the extent that if goods are perfectly free to move internationally, but factors of production are completely immobile internationally, then a tendency will exist for the prices of these factors to become equal (both relatively and absolutely) in the countries concerned.

Of course, if factors of production were perfectly mobile between countries (i.e. no costs of movement or barriers to free movement), then differences in the price of a factor internationally would create forces causing that factor to move from the low-return country to the high-return country. The factor concerned would thus tend to become scarcer in the low-return country and more abundant in the high-return country, so causing the price of the factor to correspondingly rise and fall. In other words, the prices of this factor internationally would tend to become equal and factor movement would take place until the prices were equalized, after which there would be no further incentive for movement to take place. So, with complete mobility of factors internationally, factor price equalization would occur.

Ohlin[1] realized this and integrated into his analysis of international trade theory a study of factor markets, arguing that trade (the exchange of commodities) would have a tendency to make factor prices equal internationally, even if factors were immobile between countries.

In his analysis, Ohlin concluded that factor prices, after trade, would only be partially equalized, so that trade in commodities could only act as a *partial* substitute for the free movement of factors. However, as Ford[2] has shown, Ohlin was mistaken on this point and it can be demonstrated, using Ohlin's model, that *complete* factor price equalization will occur.

In this chapter, we shall build a model to show complete factor price equalization and, having done this, we shall look at the criticisms which have been made of the model and its basic assumptions.

(a) DEMONSTRATION OF COMPLETE FACTOR PRICE EQUALIZATION

To begin with, let us state the *Factor Price Equalization Theorem* – trade in commodities, like factor movements, will cause absolute returns to productive factors to be identical in each country taking part in trade (under certain specified conditions). If absolute factor returns can be shown to be identical, then *relative* factor returns must also be identical. The conditions under which the theorem holds are specified below.

(i) We are dealing with a double model (i.e. two countries, two factors and two products). The factors and products are homogeneous internationally and each country, both before and after trade, produces some of each product (i.e. incomplete specialization in production).

(ii) Trade between the countries is absolutely unhampered by tariffs, quotas or any other impediments to free trade; and is also costless (i.e. transport costs, insurance costs, etc., do not exist).

(iii) The total supply of each factor in each country is physically fixed and cannot be altered by factor emigration or immigration. This means, in effect, that productive factors are completely immobile internationally, but we will allow them to be perfectly mobile domestically.

(iv) Perfect competition within both the product and factor markets exists in each country.

(v) Consumer tastes within each country are identical and do not change; thus at any given commodity price ratio, the two goods will be demanded in the same proportion in each country because the commodity demand patterns are the same.

(vi) The production relationships between inputs of factors and outputs of products are identical in each country. This means that the production function for a given good is the same in each country, but the production functions of the two different goods are different. This may seem confusing but, taking a specific example, it simply means that if, say, cotton is produced by a certain technical process in one country, it can only be produced in the other country by using exactly that same production process. The same will hold for another commodity, say, food. However, the production techniques used in producing food and cotton will not be the same.

The production functions for each good are also assumed to be linear homogeneous production functions and will therefore exhibit constant returns to scale (due to the linearity property of the functions). Also, due to the homogeneity property, the relative prices of the factors used will depend solely upon the actual ratio in which the factors are used.

It is also convenient to assume that the isoquants which represent the production functions are convex to the origin – that is, display diminishing marginal rates of substitution between factors;[3] and that the law of diminishing returns applies, so that the marginal product of each factor falls as increased amounts of it are employed with a fixed amount of the other factor.

Taken together, these assumptions concerning the circumstances of production means that Euler's Theorem can be applied. Euler's Theorem[4] states that the total product will be completely used up if each factor is paid a return equal to the value of marginal product. This will be important later when deriving *absolute* factor price equalization.

(vii) Goods can be classified according to their factor intensity – that is, on whether one is produced using a lot or a little of one factor relative to the use of that factor made by the other product. We must also assume that goods so classified retain their classification irrespective of relative factor prices. In other words, factor intensity reversals are ruled out.[5]

(viii) Finally, we shall assume that the relative factor endowments possessed by each country differ. On the basis of the Ohlin-Heckscher Theorem, we shall have therefore a trade creating force operating.

Using basically the above assumptions, there have been two major approaches to the proof of the Factor Price Equalization Theorem, notably those of Samuelson[6] and Johnson,[7] and a third fairly recent proof given by Vanek.[8] Since the Johnson[9] treatment relies fundamentally on a relationship between commodity prices and factor prices established by the traditional approach of Samuelson, and since it is worthless without this, it will be preferable to concentrate on the Samuelson/Vanek type treatment. The Johnson approach is elegant in its simplicity, however, and his model can be gainfully used when analyzing the effects of abandoning some of the assumptions of the basic model as listed above.

To build our model, suppose that our two countries are Australia and the United States, that the two factors used are Labor (L) and Capital (K), and that the two products being produced are cars and food. Let us suppose, finally, that Australia is relatively labor rich (the United States being, therefore, relatively capital rich), and that the commodity "cars" is relatively capital-intensive in production (the commodity "food" being, therefore, relatively labor-intensive in production).

Before we can even start, however, we should clear up a problem which has been submerged in one of our assumptions – that concerning relative factor endowments. What *measure* are we to use in deciding whether a country is relatively well endowed with a particular factor? Ohlin himself used the ratio of pre-trade factor prices as his measure of relative factor endowments. Thus, if in the United States the price of say, capital, relative to the price of labor, were less than the same factor-price-ratio in Australia, then the United States would be judged to be relatively capital rich.

Now, assuming it is possible to prove the factor-price equalization theorem, then the relative and absolute factor prices in both countries will be identical in post-trade equilibrium conditions. According to Ohlin's measure of relative factor endowments, the two countries will now also possess identical relative factor endowment ratios *and yet trade will be taking place*. The Heckscher-Ohlin theorem would thus seem to be invalid. In order to avoid such a paradox, it is preferable to measure relative factor endowments in terms of actual *physical* terms. This is why it is necessary to assume that factors of production are homogeneous – so that comparable measures of factor possession can be obtained which do not lead to apparent paradoxes of the Ohlin type.

Returning to our model building, the first step is to derive *a production transformation curve* for each country. This is a curve which shows all the various possible combinations of our two products (cars and food) which *could* be produced by a country using all of its available factor resources. The shape and position of such a curve will be determined by two things; firstly the relative factor endowments of the country and, secondly, by the relationship between the inputs and outputs of the goods capable of being produced (i.e. the production functions relevant to these commodities).

Now, using the information given about the factor intensities of our two products (assumption vii) we can draw isoquant maps for each commodity, as shown.

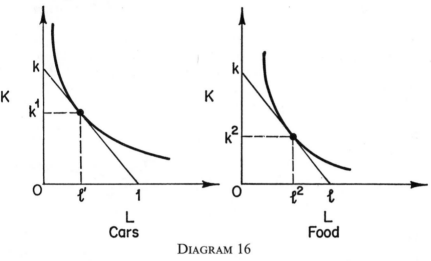

DIAGRAM 16

Since cars are capital intensive in production, then, for a given factor-price ratio (e.g. that represented by kl), a higher capital labor ratio will be used in car production than in food production $\left(\text{i.e. } \dfrac{Ok^1}{Ol^1} > \dfrac{Ok^2}{Ol^2}\right)$. Also, since by assumption (vii), factor intensities do not change

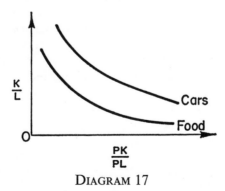

DIAGRAM 17

For a similar diagram, see Ch. 3, Diagram 10.

with factor-price ratios, the factor intensity curve for cars will lie above the factor-intensity curve for food, for all factor-price ratios.

Having derived the isoquant maps for the two goods, and remembering that these maps in fact represent the production functions for the goods, we can combine this information with our knowledge about the relative factor endowments for each country (the United States "capital rich" and Australia "labor rich," relatively). To do this we must construct what are known as *Edgeworth-Bowley Box Diagrams*. The sides of such boxes measure *absolute* factor endowments and the *relative* dimensions of the sides (length:width) will show *relative* factor endowments. Suppose for example, that the United States has O_cL' of labor and O_cK of capital and that Australian has O_cL' of labor and O_cK' of capital. To complete the box, draw LO_f parallel to OK

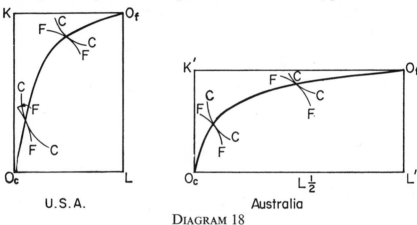

U.S.A.   Australia

DIAGRAM 18

and equal in length to it, and draw KO_f, parallel to O_cL and equal in length to it. Do the same for Australia. Now, by observation, O_cL : $O_cK' > O_cL : O_cK$. Therefore, Australia is *relatively* well endowed with capital. Also, even if Australia were somehow shrunk to one half of its size so that it possessed only $O_cL\frac{1}{2}$ of labor and $O_cK\frac{1}{2}$ of capital, it would still, relative to the United States, be *labor* abundant (i.e. even although the actual physical amount of labor which Australia possessed were less than the absolute amount of labor possessed by the United States). Within the boxes we can now place our isoquant maps for each product; O_c referring to the origin for cars, O_f to the origin for food. To get the isoquant maps for both products on the same diagram, then, we have to turn one set of isoquants upside down. Thus, isoquants for cars will radiate from O_c and isoquants for food from O_f. Remember that these maps will be the same for *both* countries. It should be noted that *every* CC isoquant as shown in the diagram will be tangential at some point to an FF isoquant. Now, if we join up these points of tangency between CC and FF isoquants, we will get a curve (for the United States) like O_CO_f. We can do the same for Australia and get a curve like O_CO_f in Australia's diagram. These curves are called *Contract Curves* and show all points of maximum possible efficiency for each country.

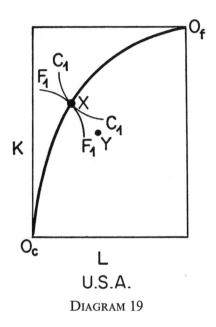

U.S.A.

DIAGRAM 19

Suppose, for example that the United States were at point X on its contract curve producing an amount of cars represented by C_1C_1, and an amount of food represented by F_1F_1. It would be impossible for the United States in this case to increase the output of one good without decreasing the output of the other good – any movement away from X in *any* direction along the contract curve must involve a higher output of one good and a lower output of the other. However, if the United States were at a point *off* the contract curve (e.g. Y), then it could increase the outputs of *both* goods, by moving to a point (e.g. X) *on* the contract curve. Thus all points *on* the contract curve represent efficient points relative to all points off the contract curve.

The movement from the contract curve to the production transformation (production possibility) curve is now relatively simple. Consider the U.S. contract curve shown in Diagram 20. We know that every

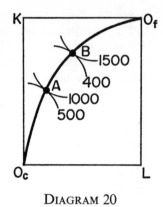

DIAGRAM 20

point in this curve (O_CO_f) represents a point of tangency between a "car" isoquant and a "food" isoquant and that these isoquants will reflect certain outputs of these two commodities. Point A, for instance, might represent an output combination of 1,000 cars plus 500 units of food. Point B, on the other hand, might represent 1,500 cars plus 400 units of food. Every point on the contract curve will thus represent specific output combinations of cars and food. If we now construct a diagram showing outputs of cars along the x-axis and outputs of food along the y-axis, we can show the output combinations corresponding to each and every point on a country's contract curve.

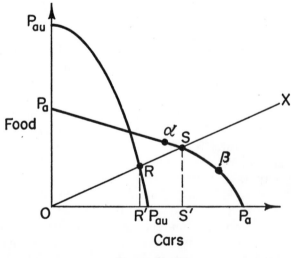

DIAGRAM 21

Thus, point A on the United States' contract curve corresponds to point a on the diagram above; point B corresponds to β. Doing the same for each point on the United States' contract curve, we would get a curve PaPa as above. Taking Australia's contract curve, we could similarly derive a curve PauPau. These curves now show the possible output combinations which each country could produce using all its available factor supplies – in other words they are the countries' production, transformation curves. They are called "transformation" curves because they show how each product could be "transformed" into the other by reallocating the factor supplies between the producing sectors. They also show (as does the contract curve) that more of one product can only be produced by giving up some of the other product.

The different shapes of the transformation curves for the two countries is attributable *solely* to their differing relative factor endowments. The curves also show that the United States has a comparative advantage in the production of cars and Australia a comparative advantage in the production of food.[10] Any straight line (e.g. OX) through the origin will cut PauPau at R and PaPa at S. The slope of OX (RR': OR' = SS':OS') represents the ratio in which the two goods are produced at R and S, and since OX is a straight line, R and S represent identical production ratios in the two countries. Now, if the United States wants to expand car production by one unit, it would have to sacrifice fewer units of food than Australia would if Australia wanted to expand car production by one unit. Thus, the United States has a comparative production advantage in car production relative to Australia; and Australia a relative production advantage in food production.

The amount of one product which has to be given up in order to produce another unit of the other product is technically known as the *marginal rate of transformation* and is represented at any point on a production transformation curve by the slope of the tangent to that point. At point S, therefore, the marginal rate of transformation (i.e. slope of tangent to PaPa at S) is less than the marginal rate of transformation at R. At any given output ratio in both countries, the marginal rate of transformation between cars and food will be lower along the United States' production possibility curve relative to Australia's.

Since it was assumed that tastes were identical in both countries (assumption v), it is possible to represent these tastes in both countries by the same set of community indifference curves[11] and superimpose this indifference map on the production transformation diagram, see over.

Now, the equilibrium conditions for a system of production and consumption are –

(*a*) The marginal rate of transformation in production (i.e. slope of

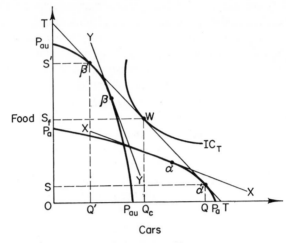

Cars

DIAGRAM 22

production transformation curve) must equal the commodity price ratio (i.e. slope of price line between cars and food).

(b) The marginal rate of substitution in consumption (i.e. slope of indifference curve) must equal the commodity price ratio (i.e. slope of price line).[12]

Thus, in equilibrium for each country –

$$MRS = MRT = \frac{Pcars}{Pfood}$$

Given the above indifference map and production transformation curves, each country will be in equilibrium, before trade takes place, at points α and β, producing and consuming the amounts of food and cars corresponding to such points.

Since the commodity price ratio in the United States (slope of XX) differs from the commodity price ratio in Australia (slope of YY), a basis for trade exists and, since we have assumed that trade is free and unfettered, it will come about that in post-trade equilibrium, the commodity price ratio will be the same in both countries. The United States will specialize in car production and Australia in food production such that the MRT in each country equals the MRS in each country, and both these ratios are equal to the commodity price ratio after trade. These are the equilibrium conditions of trade and will be fulfilled, in our example, with a commodity price ratio of TT, tangential to IC_T at W, to PauPau at β', and to PaPa at α'. The United States will produce OQ of cars and OS of food. Australia will produce OQ' of cars and OS' of food. The United States will consume OQ_C of cars and OQ_f of food and Australia will do likewise.

This is a special case where each country achieves the same level of welfare and consumption corresponding to W on IC_T. Depending on the terms of trade (i.e. the rate at which exports and imports exchange for each other) the production, consumption and welfare levels might have been as shown.

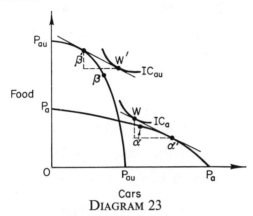

DIAGRAM 23

No matter, however, the marginal rates of transformation and substitution must, in equilibrium, always equal the commodity price ratios. Suppose, in our example, that the outcome after trade is as represented in Diagram 22. The United States exporting Q_cQ of cars to Australia and importing SS_f of food from Australia, thus giving a zero trade balance with exports value = imports value. The final step in the demonstration of factor price equalization is to move back from Diagram 22 to the contract curves, since Diagram 22 cannot show what is happening to factor prices as the two countries specialize in production.

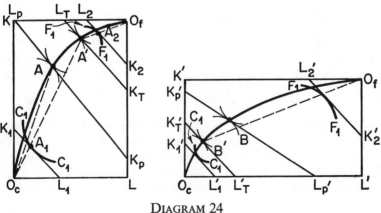

DIAGRAM 24

We can read off Diagram 22 the pre- and post-trade outputs of the two commodities in each country. Corresponding to points α and β (pre-trade equilibrium outputs) and points α' and β' (post-trade equilibrium outputs) there will be points on the contract curves of each country – A, B, and A′, B′, respectively.

Since the factor-price ratios at these points will be given by the slopes of the isoquants tangential to each other at these points, we can read off from the above diagram, the pre- and post-trade factor price-ratios (i.e. relative factor prices).

Before trade, $\dfrac{P_K}{P_L}$ in the United States is equal in both the car and food industries, as shown by the common slope to the isoquants at A, $-L_pK_p$. $\dfrac{P_K}{P_L}$ in Australia is also the same in both industries as shown by slope of $L_p'K_p'$. *But,* $\dfrac{P_K}{P_L}$ is not the same as $\dfrac{P_K}{P_L}$ in Australia (slope of L_pK_p is not equal to slope of $L_p'K_p'$). In other words, in the pre-trade situation, relative factor prices differ between the two countries. Absolute factor prices must also differ, therefore.

Once trade takes place, things change. Each country becomes more specialized in production and moves from A to A′ and from B to B′ (corresponding to movements from α to α' and from β to β' along the production transformation curves). Points A′ and B′ now represent not only equilibrium commodity output proportions, but also equilibrium factor input proportions and *prices*.

As the United States specializes in car production, the $\dfrac{K}{L}$ ratio falls as shown by the fact that O_CA' has a smaller slope than O_CA. Because of this change in factor proportions, the marginal product of capital rises and that of labor falls in accordance with the law of diminishing returns. Similarly, in Australia, the $\dfrac{K}{L}$ ratio rises and the marginal product of capital falls and that of labor rises. Now, since in equilibrium the factors will earn a return equal to their marginal products, the opening up of trade is thus seen to lead to a tendency for relative factor returns to be equalized, $\dfrac{P_K}{P_L}$ in the United States is rising and $\dfrac{P_K}{P_L}$ in Australia is falling relative to their pre-trade values. This is also shown by observing that as the United States moves from A to A′ and Australia from B to B′, the *slopes* of the tangents to the isoquants along AA′ and BB′ become gradually closer together.

To demonstrate complete relative and absolute factor-price equalization, consider the lines $O_C A'$ and $O_f A'$ in the United States and $O_C B'$ and $O_f B'$ in Australia.

Now, it is a property of any straight line through the origin (given that we have assumed linear homogeneous production functions), that it will cut all the isoquants drawn with reference to that origin, at the same angle. Suppose that $C_1 C_1$ and $F_1 F_1$ are the isoquants representing unit outputs of cars and food respectively. We know, then, that the tangent to $C_1 C_1$ at A_1 and the tangent at A' will have the same slope. Similarly, the tangent to $F_1 F_1$ at A_2 will have the same slope as the tangents to the food isoquant at A'. But the food and car isoquants at A' have the *same* slope (since A' is on the contract curve). Therefore, the slopes of $C_1 C_1$ at A_1 and $F_1 F_1$ at A_2 and $L_T K_T$ are all equal.

Now since $C_1 C_1$ and $F_1 F_1$ are unit isoquants, the segments $O_C L_1$ and $O_f L_2$ represent the *marginal costs* of the two goods respectively, expressed in terms of one factor (labor). Similarly, $O_C K_1$ and $O_f K_2$ represent the marginal costs of the two goods in terms of the other factor (capital). Now, from our assumption of perfect competition in the product markets, we know that in equilibrium, the prices of the goods will equal their marginal costs; therefore the ratio of the product prices will equal the ratio of their respective marginal costs. That is,

$$\left(\frac{\text{Pcars}}{\text{Pfood}}\right)_{\text{U.S.}} = \left(\frac{\text{MCcars}}{\text{MCfood}}\right)_{\text{U.S.}} = \frac{O_C L_1}{O_f L_2} = \frac{O_C K_1}{O_f K_2}$$

We also know that in post-trade equilibrium, the prices of the goods traded will be the same in both countries. Therefore the ratio of marginal production costs must be the same in both countries in post-trade equilibrium. That is,

$$\left(\frac{\text{Pcars}}{\text{Pfood}}\right)_{\text{U.S.}} = \left(\frac{\text{Pcars}}{\text{Pfood}}\right)_{\text{Aust.}} = \left(\frac{\text{MCcars}}{\text{MCfood}}\right)_{\text{U.S.}} = \left(\frac{\text{MCcars}}{\text{MCfood}}\right)_{\text{Aust.}}$$

or,
$$\frac{\text{Pcars}}{\text{Pfood}} = \frac{O_C L_1}{O_f L_2} = \frac{O_C L_1'}{O_f L_2'} = \frac{O_C K_1}{O_f K_2} = \frac{O_C K_1'}{O_f K_2'}.$$

Now, using very elementary geometry, it can be shown that, given these relationships, $K_1 L_1$ will be parallel to $K_1' L_1'$ and therefore $L_T K_T$ will be parallel to $K_T' L_T'$. In other words, *relative* factor prices are completely equalized after trade. However, since $K_1 L_1$ is parallel to $K_1' L_1'$ and since both these lines are tangents to the unit car isoquant, it follows that $O_C K_1 = O_C K_1'$ and $O_C L_1 = O_C L_1'$. Similarly, $O_f L_2 = O_f L_2'$ and $O_f K_2 = O_f K_2'$. The marginal costs of each product will be the same in both countries therefore. Also, since $K_1 L_1$ and $K_1' L_1'$ are parallel and tangents to the unit car isoquant, it follows that $O_C A_1$ and $O_C B'$ must have the same slope which means that cars will be

produced in each country using the same factor ratio—$\left(\dfrac{K}{L}\right)$ is identical at
A_1 and B'). Since the marginal productivity of a factor in our model is
determined by this ratio, it follows that the marginal product of each
factor will be the same in both countries.

That is,

$$\left.\begin{array}{l}(MP_L)_{U.S.} = (MP_L)_{Aust.} \\ (MP_K)_{U.S.} = (MP_K)_{Aust.}\end{array}\right\} \text{ in car production.}$$

Similarly, for food production.

Thus, since in perfect competition the return to a factor is equal to its
marginal product, it follows that the *absolute* factor prices are completely equalized.

We have demonstrated, therefore, that equality of goods prices
leads to the equality of factor prices, both relatively and absolutely.

We must remember and stress that this demonstration has emerged
from a model relying on many unrealistic assumptions and is therefore
no more realistic than these assumptions. Once we relax these assumptions we will find that complete factor-price equalization need not follow.
In fact, we can show that factor prices may even move apart as trade
takes place.

This does not mean to say that the factor-price equalization theorem
is worthless. It may have little or no practicality (as the original
theorists realized) but what it does do is provide a basis for the further
analysis of forces affecting factor prices in international trade. In fact,
it is the analysis of such forces (rather than the fundamental theorem
itself) which has provided great interest to theorists in the recent past;
and it is to their furtherance of our understanding of the forces operating
here that we now turn our attention.

(b) Criticisms of Basic Theorem and Qualifications to it

Since the production assumptions are so important for the model,
let us concentrate our attention on the effects of relaxing these assumptions. It is possible to note, however, that the relaxation of some of the
other assumptions in the model will have important consequences for
the theorem – for example, if transport costs exist and as a result
commodity prices after trade are not equalized, then relative factor
prices will not be equalized; if production after trade becomes completely specialized, again factor prices will not become completely
equalized, though they may move closer together.

Let us now recall that in the above demonstration of factor price
equalization, it was assumed that the factor intensities of the commodities was invariant with respect to the factor-price ratios (i.e. no

factor intensity reversals). Studies by Arrow, Chenery, Solow and Minhas[13] suggest that factor intensity reversal may be important in practice and therefore we shall look at the implications of such reversal for the factor-price equalization theorem.

Suppose that the production functions for the two products are such that for every "car" isoquant there will be a "food" isoquant which is tangential to it. The diagram below will therefore depict a representative pair of such isoquants.

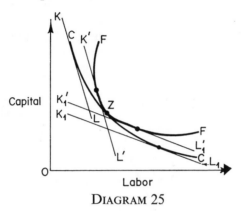

DIAGRAM 25

Now, for certain factor-price ratios (e.g. as given by slopes of KL and K'L') cars will be relatively capital intensive in production. At other factor price ratios (e.g. as given by slopes of K_1L_1 and $K_1'L_1'$), food is relatively capital intensive. At point Z where the two isoquants are tangential, the factor intensities of the two products will be identical. The slope of the line tangential to CC and FF at Z will represent a certain factor price ratio which is termed the *critical* ratio since it is the ratio at which the factor intensities of the products reverse.

If we draw the factor intensity curves for the products corresponding to Diagram 25, they would be as below –

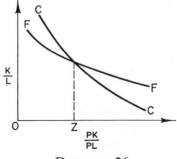

DIAGRAM 26

OZ indicates the critical factor-price ratio at which reversal takes place.

If, of course, the factor-endowment ratios of the two countries are not too divergent, so that their factor-price ratios both lie on the same side of the factor-intensity reversal point, then the factor-price equalization theorem will still hold. If the factor-price ratios before trade lie on opposite sides of the critical point, however, the implications for the theorem are important and require analytical clarification.

Going back to the box diagrams, we will find that with a single factor-intensity reversal, the contract curves for the two countries, will lie on opposite sides of the box diagonals. (When no reversal took place, they lay on the same side of the diagonal as in Diagram 18.) We will therefore have a picture like Diagram 27.

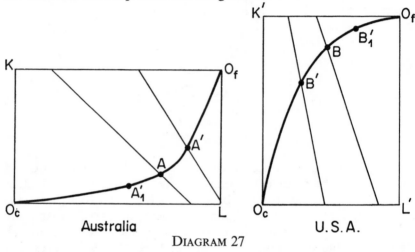

DIAGRAM 27

Let us assume that cars are relatively capital intensive in the United States, food being labor intensive; and that food is relatively capital intensive in Australia, cars being labor intensive. The contract curves will then appear as shown. Suppose now that the pre-trade equilibrium positions of the two countries are represented by points A and B, at which the factor-price ratios will be given by the slopes of the common tangent to the two isoquants. Labor is relatively cheap in Australia compared with the United States, in the pre-trade situation. Assume, now, that the pre-trade commodity price ratios are such as to give Australia a comparative advantage in car production and the United States a comparative advantage in food production. Australia will expand car production and the United States food production, moving from A to A' and B to B' respectively (these representing the points on the production transformation curves at which the commodity price ratio after trade is the same in both countries).

Now, at A′, the $\frac{K}{L}$ ratio is higher than at A; therefore the marginal product of capital will have fallen and so will its price. The slope of the factor price line at A′ will become steeper as shown. Similarly at B′, the $\frac{K}{L}$ ratio is higher and so the price of capital will have fallen. The slope of the factor price line at B′ will therefore be steeper as shown. Since the price of capital has fallen, relative to labor's price, in both countries whether factor prices after trade are equalized at all will depend on the relative slopes of the pre- and post-trade factor price lines in each country. Depending on these relationships there may or may not be a tendency for factor prices to become equal after trade takes place. Johnson[14] has shown that if the *number* of factor-intensity reversals interposed between the pre-trade factor-price ratios in the two countries is odd, then the effect of trade will be to move factor prices in the same direction in both countries (i.e. as in above example) and the difference between them may either widen *or* narrow depending on the circumstances. Note in the above example that if Australia had found its comparative advantage in food production and moved from A to $A_1′$ (the United States moving from B to $B_1′$), the price of labor in both countries would have fallen.

If the number of intervening factor-intensity reversals is *even*, the effect of trade is to move factor prices in the two countries in opposite directions but this may lead to either convergence or divergence of relative factor prices. When the number of reversals is even, a commodity is either labor-intensive or capital-intensive in both countries, so that if the labor-rich country has a comparative advantage in the labor-intensive product, the relative price of labor will rise and factor prices will move towards each other. If the labor-rich country has a comparative advantage in the capital-intensive good, the relative price of capital will rise there and factor prices will diverge.

Thus, once we allow for factor-intensity reversal, trade may have *any* effect on relative factor prices and the production of both goods in both countries is consistent with widely different factor price ratios. Trade, therefore, may or may not act as a partial substitute for factor mobility.

We also assumed that the production functions exhibited constant returns to scale. Once we drop this assumption the model becomes exceedingly complex and little can be said positively about the effect of trade on factor prices. Kemp,[15] however, shows that whatever else, the possibility of complete *absolute* factor price equalization is ruled out. He also demonstrates that so far as relative factor prices are concerned, there may be convergence or divergence with the ratios moving in the same or opposite directions. In addition, ratios may converge and then diverge, thus overshooting a position of equality. Thus, the opening up of trade in these circumstances does not necessarily lead to convergence of relative factor prices.

Finally, we can look at the assumption that specialization of production after trade is not complete. Suppose that the pre-trade equilibrium positions of two countries A and B, producing two products X and Y using capital and labor are as shown.

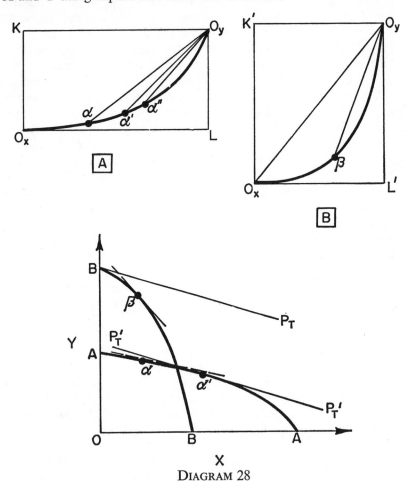

DIAGRAM 28

The pre-trade equilibrium commodity price ratios in A and B respectively are given by the slopes of the tangents at α and β, such that $\dfrac{P_x}{P_y}$ in A is less than $\dfrac{P_x}{P_y}$ in B. In B, the slope of $O_y\beta$ is greater than the slope of $O_y a$ in A. Therefore, the $\dfrac{K}{L}$ ratio in B will be greater than the $\dfrac{K}{L}$ ratio in A and correspondingly the ratio of the prices of capital and labor in B will be less than that in A. Let trade take place and allow the post-trade equilibrium commodity price ratio settle down at a level given by the slope BP_T, parallel to $P_T'P_T'$. A will produce at a', producing more X and less Y than previously, but B will specialize completely in Y production since the point on the y-axis where B's production possibility curve cuts it is the point on B's curve which has a slope as near as possible to the slope of BP_T. The production points in the box diagrams are as indicated by a' and O_x.

Now, since the slope of $O_y a'$ is greater than the slope of $O_y a$, the capital to labor-price ratio will have fallen. Similarly, since the slope of $O_y O_x$ is less than the slope of $O_y \beta$, the capital to labor-price ratio in B will have risen. The relative factor-price ratios at a' and O_x will thus be closer than they were at a and β before trade took place (i.e. a certain amount of factor price equalization has taken place). However, since the slope of $O_y O_x$ is not the same as the slope of $O_y a'$, complete factor-price equalization will not occur. For points between O_x and a'' on A's contract curve there will be no corresponding points on B's contract curve and so relative factor prices cannot become fully equalized if A is at a point along $O_x a''$. There will also be a section of B's contract curve, the points on which have no corresponding points on A's contract curve.[16]

In such cases, then, there will be no equality of relative factor prices, although there may be a tendency *towards* equality.

We can say in conclusion, therefore, that once we abandon the assumptions on which the theorem is founded, the effect of this is to make the complete equalization of factor prices impossible, but the tendency towards equalization may still exist, or it may be completely obliterated and replaced by a tendency for factor prices to move even farther apart. Of course, when we look at the real world, we find that factor prices are not equal; that production functions do differ internationally, as do demand conditions; that transport costs are often very important and that restrictions to the free movement of goods do exist. Why waste time on such a practically irrelevant piece of theorizing? The answer is that such a theory can act as a basis for explaining factor-price differentials – we can look at each assumption in turn and see what effect its removal has on factor prices. It can act as a focal point from which our minds can move in creating more realistic (and necessarily more complex) models of the international economy. It would seem likely that the future will see a growth of such models.

[1] B. Ohlin, *op. cit.*

[2] Ford, *op. cit.*, p. 36.

[3] The marginal rate of substitution between factors is the amount of one factor which can be given up in order to offset the effect of employing an extra unit of the other factor and so maintain output constant along the isoquant

[4] See, C. L. Allen, *Elementary Mathematics of Price Theory*, Ch. 10, Wadsworth, 1962.

[5] See Ch. 2.

[6] P. A. Samuelson, "International Trade and the Equalisation of Factor Prices," *Economic Journal*, 1948; also "International Factor Price Equalisation Once Again," *Economic Journal*, 1949; and "Prices of Factors and Goods in General Equilibrium," *Review of Economic Studies* (1953–54).

[7] H. G. Johnson, "Factor Endowments, International Trade and Factor Prices," Manchester School, 1957.

[8] J. Vanek, "An Alternative Proof of the Factor Price Equalisation Theorem," *Quarterly Journal of Economics*, 1960.

[9] See also, Harrod, "Factor-Price Relations Under Free Trade," *Economic Journal*, 1958.

[10] R. Jones, "Factor Proportions and the Heckscher-Ohlin Theorem," *Review of Economic Studies*, 1956–57.

[11] See, W. J. Baumol, "The Community Indifference Map: a Construction," *Review of Economic Studies*, Vol. 17, No. 44.

[12] If the student is unfamiliar with these conditions, consult any basic textbook on Price Theory.

[13] K. J Arrow, H. B. Chenery, B. S. Minhas and R. M. Solow, "Capital–Labour Substitution and Economic Efficiency," *Review of Economic Statistics*, 1961.

[14] H. G. Johnson, "Factor Endowments, International Trade and Factor Prices," Manchester School, 1957.

[15] M. C. Kemp, *The Pure Theory of International Trade*, 1964.

[16] $O_y a''$ is parallel to $O_y O_x$ in $\boxed{B}$. On "corresponding points," see K. Lancaster, "The Heckscher-Ohlin Trade Model: a Geometric Treatment," *Economica*, 1957.

CHAPTER 5

Equilibrium in International Trade

So FAR in our analysis of trade, we have concentrated mainly on the supply side of the system by trying to explain why trade takes place (i.e. why supplies of exports exist) and what effect this trade will have on the productive factors. The Demand side of the system has only been referred to in passing and brought into our consideration solely to round off the analysis. In Chapter 2, for instance, we said that the rate at which exports were traded for imports would be determined by demand conditions, and left it at that. In Chapter 4 we brought demand into the analysis in the form of a given post-trade commodity price ratio, but did not explain how this price ratio was achieved. In this chapter, we will look at the factors working on the Demand side and see how they interact with the Supply side of the system.

Let us return to an example of comparative cost differences between two countries and suppose that the table below represents the output possibilities for given factor inputs (as in Chapter 2).

TABLE 1

	U.S.A.	U.K.
Cars	10	5
Food	4	3

Before trade, cars will exchange for food in the ratio 10:4 in the United States, and at 10:6 in the United Kingdom. These ratios will set the limits beyond which the post-trade price cannot settle. If the trading price ratio were 4 units of food for 10 units of cars, then the United States would be completely indifferent as to whether she produced both goods herself or specialized. Britian, however, would be only too willing to specialize in food production and export 4 units of food for 10 units of cars.

In this case, Britain would be the sole gainer from trade. Similarly, the United States would alone gain if the price ratio were 5 of cars for 3 of food. *Where* will the price settle after trade? What is required is information concerning demand – how strong is the U.S. demand for the products compared with the corresponding British demand?

The price at which foreign trade will take place is determined then by the *"law of reciprocal demand"*[1] as Mill termed it. Neither Ricardo nor Smith had dealt with this problem, and Mill was one of the first Classical economists to approach the problem. According to Mill, the exchange value of the two products being traded would be adjusted by the demand conditions in both countries such that the exports of each country would just pay for its imports.

In our simple two-country, two-commodity world, this must, of course, be the case, otherwise unsold stocks of one product may build up and the price accordingly reduced to get rid of these stocks.

However, as Kindleberger[2] points out, if the two countries are of unequal economic size, it is possible that the demand effects of the smaller country will be dwarfed by those of the larger in such a way that the price ratio in the larger country will prevail and the small country will be able to export as much of its product as it wishes and so make large gains from trade. Mill also recognized this and showed how a small country whose products were in great demand in the world market (e.g. a small country producing coffee and exporting it to the United States) could gain considerably from trading even although the demand for its imports from the rest of the world was high. This is so because, although its demand for imported U.S. cars, say, is strong, it will be insignificant in relation to the world demand for cars and so the law of reciprocal demand will be irrelevant in this instance.

Mill was also among the first to show that the existence of transportation costs in trade will modify the effects of reciprocal demand on price and could, in certain cases, eliminate the potential gains from trade.

Bearing these considerations in mind, we can analyze the theory behind the law of reciprocal demand as portrayed by Marshall[3] and Edgeworth with what are termed *"offer curves."* Their analysis has subsequently been refined by Scitovsky,[4] Meade,[5] and Lerner.[6] Following Meade's device, we can build up the offer curve from the production possibilities curve and the consumption indifference map for a country.

In Diagram 29, measure the amount of U.S. importables (food) consumed in the United States along the y-axis; and along the x-axis, to the left of O, measure the amount of U.S. exportables (cars), consumed in the United States. We can then draw in the North-West quadrant the U.S. production possibilities curve along with a set of consumption indifference curves representing the tastes and preferences of the U.S. community.[7]

If the United States is a closed economy, it will produce and consume at E, reaching a level of welfare indicated by IC_1. Now slide P_aP_a' *along*

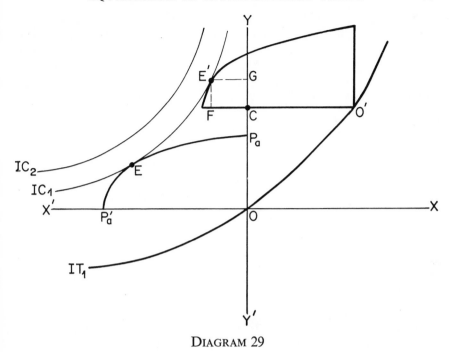

DIAGRAM 29

IC_1, in such a way that $P_a'O$ is kept horizontal and P_aP_a' is tangential to IC_1. When this is done, O will trace out IT_1 U.S. *Trade Indifference curve* corresponding to IC_1. For each consumption indifference curve there is a corresponding Trade Indifference curve obtained as above. Taking one such curve, IT_1, then at every point on this curve, the United States will be indifferent whether it trades or not. At E, it will produce and consume the amounts of food and cars corresponding to E; at E', it will produce O'F of cars and FE' of food. It only consumes CF of cars, however, and OG of food; trading O'C of cars for OC of food. Since E and E' are on the same consumption indifference curve, the United States is indifferent as to whether it stays at O (no trade) or moves to O' and trades as above. This applies to any point along IT_1. Since there is a trade indifference curve corresponding to each community indifference curve, we can construct a trade indifference map. Now, a country will be better off the higher the trade indifference curve which it can reach, so we may assume that a country will try to reach the highest possible trade indifference curve.

Suppose that before trade, the price ratio between cars and food is $\dfrac{T_x}{O_x}$ as given by the *slope* of the price line OT in Diagram 30. If we increase the price of cars (U.S. exportables in terms of food

(U.S. importables), OT will rotate about O in an anti-clockwise direction. We will, then, get points of tangency between these price lines and the trade indifference curves as shown. If we now join up these points of tangency we will get the curve OA which is, in fact, the U.S. offer curve – a curve showing how many cars the United States is willing to offer at various prices for a given amount of food. Expressing the same thing oppositely, the offer curve shows how much food the United States will buy at given prices for food in terms of cars.

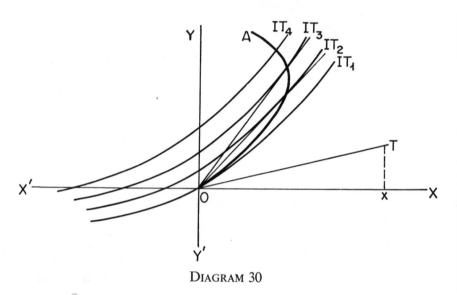

DIAGRAM 30

The slope of the offer curve illustrates that as more and more food is available, it will offer less and less cars per unit of food; reflecting the marginal utility elements intrinsic in the shape of the community indifference curves. The offer curve is a special type of demand curve, expressing the demand for importables *in terms of the supply of exportables*, instead of in terms of money.

An offer curve for Australia can be derived similarly, putting its production possibility curve and community indifference map in the South-East quadrant. The two offer curves are shown in Diagram 31. At P, the price ratio (OP) between exportables and importables will be the same in both countries and equal amounts of food and cars will be exported and imported by the two countries (i.e. zero trade balance). The slopes of OA (PT) and OB (PT) represent the pre-trade price ratios in each country and set the limits within which the post-trade price ratio can settle. The slope of OP represents the equilibrium ratio because at any other slope (e.g. OQ), Australia would be willing

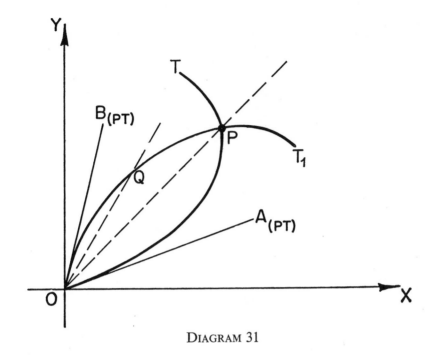

DIAGRAM 31

to offer slightly less food than at P for considerably fewer cars. But, for this amount of cars, the United States is willing to accept a great deal less food. (See the U.S. offer curve.) This will not represent an equilibrium situation, nor will any other situation except that represented by P. At P, the slope of OP will be the same as the slopes of the U.S. and Australia's trade indifference curves which will be tangential to each other.

It is possible to use Meade's diagrams, to illustrate the gains from free trade, in the following way. Diagram 32 over is the same as Diagram 31 except that the production blocks for the two countries have been added and the relevant trade and consumption indifference curves.

At P, the United States will produce PR of cars and RA of food; and consume CR of cars and BA of food, importing BR of food in exchange for PC of cars. Australia will produce at E, EF of cars and PF of food; and consume GE of cars and FS of food, importing GF (= PC) of cars for PS (= RB) of food.

Under this free trade situation, the international price ratio (slope of OP) is the same as the internal price ratios in the two countries (slopes of C and C_1, at A and E respectively).

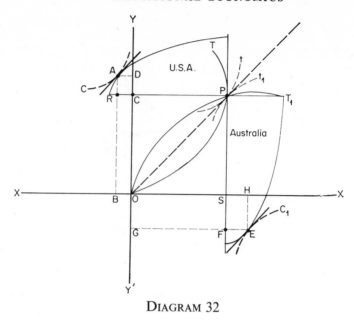

DIAGRAM 32

If we now take the pre- and post-trade equilibrium price ratios in the United States we can measure the gains from trading either in terms of pre- or post-trade prices.

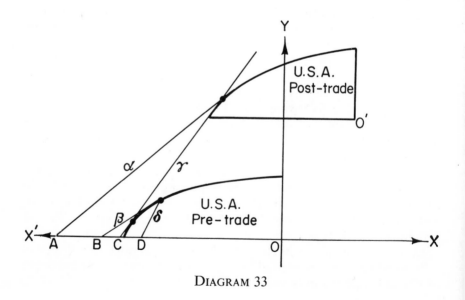

DIAGRAM 33

The slopes of α and β in Diagram 33 represent the pre-trade price ratios; the slopes of γ and δ represent the post-trade price ratios.

Using the pre-trade measure of the U.S. national income, this is OB. After trade, but at pre-trade prices, its income has increased to OA (i.e. a gain of AB). At post-trade prices, the gain is CD. A similar calculation can be made for Australia.

The situation at P in Diagram 32 is also a welfare maximization position in the sense that it is impossible to increase the welfare of one country without reducing the welfare of the other.[8] By using the offer curve technique which brings together the supply and demand sides of the system, it is possible to exhibit the conditions of free trade equilibrium. Thus, in Diagram 32 we will have a new trade balance and identical prices in each country of the two goods being traded. The equilibrium price ratio between exports and imports will be given by the slope of OP, since at this ratio exports and imports exactly balance (i.e. the slope of a straight line from the origin will express the price ratio between Y and X). The prices at which the goods are traded is what is normally termed the *Terms of Trade* and it can be observed from the offer curves that a lowering of the slope of the price line (i.e. the *Terms of Trade* line) will result in a deterioration in the Terms of Trade for the United States and an improvement in the Terms of Trade for Australia. What this means in volume terms is that the United States, for a given volume of exports (OS), would receive in return a smaller volume of imports (< SP). The reverse holds for Australia.

Thus, the resulting relative welfare gains from trade will depend on the equilibrium terms of trade. In general, the closer a country's pre-trade price ratio is to the post-trade terms of trade, the smaller will be its relative gains from trading.

At the limit, if the terms of trade are the same as the pre-trade domestic price ratio is in a country, then that country cannot reach a higher indifference curve by trading, it simply produces more of one commodity (its exports) and reduces production of the other (its imports). For this to happen, the production possibilities curve must (over the relevant part) be a straight line with a slope equal to the terms of trade. It has been suggested that this might be the case for a large country trading with a very small country.

Since changes in the terms of trade may take place in both the short and the long run, it will be important to consider which factors may cause such changes. This is so, because changes in the terms of trade can have a big impact on income levels when trade is large relative to output (e.g. small underdeveloped primary producing countries). Changes in the terms of trade may also help in explaining differing income levels internationally (and changes in economic welfare).[9] As we saw earlier, the terms of trade can be defined as the ratio of export prices to import prices, but since, in the real world, there are more export and import goods (and therefore prices) than in our model, we must use an *index* of export prices and an *index* of import prices.

This ratio is then expressed as a percentage; it has been called the *Net Barter Terms of Trade* (or Commodity or Merchandise Terms of Trade). A rise in this ratio shows that a *given* volume of exports exchanges for a *larger* volume of imports than previously; a fall in the index shows the opposite. However, changes in the Net Barter Terms of Trade do not tell us *why* the relative prices of exports and imports have moved as they have, nor do they tell us what has happened to the physical volume of exports and imports, or to the Balance of Payments. All that changes in the Net Barter Terms of Trade do is tell us *how* relative export and import prices have moved.

However, it would be reasonable to assume that changes in export and import volumes are apt to accompany changes in the Net Barter Terms of Trade.

The *Gross Barter Terms of Trade* is the ratio, expressed as a percentage, of an export quantity index and an import quantity index. These quantity index numbers are derived by dividing index numbers of value (price X quantity) by index numbers of price. However, as with the Net Barter Terms of Trade, changes in the Gross Barter Terms of Trade are unambiguous, only if the Balance of Payments is balanced in both periods under consideration. Since the Net Barter Terms of Trade may mislead if the volume of exports has changed significantly, it may be desirable to modify the Net Barter Terms of Trade by means of a quantity index. This concept is called the *Income Terms of Trade*[10] $\left(\dfrac{PxQx}{Pm}\right)$ and a rise in this index means that a country can obtain a larger quantity of imports for its exports than previously.

This measure has also been called a country's "capacity to import," but this is misleading, since import capacity will depend on factors which do not come into the calculation of the Income Terms of Trade but are nevertheless important in determining import capacity (e.g. capital transfers).

There are two other relevant concepts to consider – the Single Factoral Terms of Trade and the Double Factoral Terms of Trade as developed by Viner,[11] according to whom any significant changes in productivity in export sectors should be allowed for in calculating changes in a country's terms of trade.

The Single Factoral Terms of Trade is the Net Barter measurement adjusted for changes in productivity in exports. Thus, if export prices fall, the Net Barter measurement would show a deterioration in the terms of trade. However, if productivity in export manufacture has at the same time risen more, then the country is better off in real terms, and this will be reflected in a rise in the Single Factoral Terms of Trade. This means that the country receives more imports per unit of productive factors incorporated in exports than previously.

The Double Factoral Terms of Trade takes changes in productivity in domestic and foreign export sectors into account. Thus, in the above example, if productivity in imports had also risen, then the Double Factoral Terms of Trade could show a decline.

Suppose, for example, that export prices fell by 15%, export productivity rose by 25%, import prices stayed constant and import productivity increased by 10%.

Then the Single Factoral measurement would show a rise in the terms of trade, whilst the Double Factoral measurement would show a fall. The Double Factoral Terms of Trade shows the change in the rate of exchange between a unit of domestic productive factors in exports and a unit of foreign productive factors in imports.

However, as Devons[12] argues, it is virtually impossible to define or measure a unit of inputs and so we are forced to fall back on the use of the Net Barter Terms of Trade. However, in using this measurement, we must at all times bear in mind that we cannot move directly from changes in the Net Barter Terms of Trade to changes in a country's economic welfare. To analyze welfare changes, we would have to take into consideration any productivity changes; changes in the volume of trade; changes in capital flows; changes in invisible earnings, etc.

Having decided on our measure of the terms of trade, we can now go on to look at the various factors which can influence a country's terms of trade.

The major factors which could affect the terms of trade are

(*a*) Economic development and growth affecting demand and supply;
(*b*) Capital transfers from one country to another;
(*c*) Demand shifts independent of economic growth;
(*d*) Tariffs (i.e. changes in commercial policy);
(*e*) Depreciation or appreciation of the country's currency.

Consideration will now be given to each of these factors in turn, but note that the last section should be left until students have mastered Chapter 10 on exchange-rate changes.

(*a*) EFFECTS OF ECONOMIC DEVELOPMENT AND GROWTH ON THE TERMS OF TRADE

Economic growth may be defined simply as an increase in a country's gross national product over time, or one may wish to refine it and define it in terms of increasing income per head over time.

However, for our purposes, it will suffice to regard growth as referring simply to increased output. Using the usual double model of previous chapters, we can show how growth (whether caused by an increased labor supply, capital accumulation or advanced technology) may affect the terms of trade, by which from now on we shall mean the Net Barter Terms of Trade. To simplify the analysis, assume that growth does not lead to a change in tastes. Suppose that growth moves a country's production possibilities curve outwards to P_1P_1 (see Diagram 34).

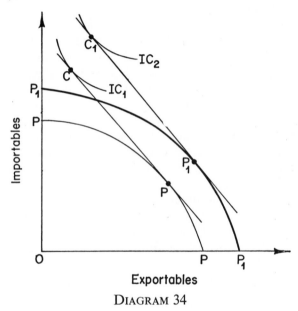

DIAGRAM 34

Before growth, production was at p and consumption at C on community indifference curve IC_1. The terms of trade are given by the slope of pC. If, after growth, the terms of trade are unchanged, then production will move to p_1 and consumption to C_1. If the terms of trade improve, the slope of pC will increase and consumption will be on a higher indifference curve than IC_2. If the terms of trade deteriorate, then consumption will take place on a lower curve than IC_2. However, so long as the gains from growth exceed the losses from worsening terms of trade, the country will find itself better off after growth than before. If the terms of trade deteriorate sufficiently, the country may find itself on a lower curve than IC_1, indicating that real income would have fallen due to the increased output being more than offset by the worsened terms of trade. Bhagwati[13] calls this situation "immiserising growth" and, although it is a theoretical possibility, the probability of its happening is fairly low.[14] The *direction of change* of the terms of trade with growth will be determined by what happens to the net demand for imports. Growth will probably lead to an increased demand for imports, it may also lead to increased production of importables in the growing country. It will be the net effect of these demand and supply factors which determines the directions in which the terms of trade move. These forces have been analyzed in the literature in terms of output elasticity of demand and output elasticity of supply. *Output elasticity of demand* (oEd) is the percentage change in consumption of importables divided by the percentage change in the total output. *Output elasticity of supply* (oEs) is the percentage change in production of importables divided by the percentage change in total output. Both are measured at constant relative commodity prices.

The degree of elasticity has also been categorized in terms of trade biases:[15]

If oEd is $= 1$ this is a neutral demand effect.
If   „   is > 1 this is a pro-trade demand effect.
If   „   is < 1 this is an anti-trade demand effect.
If   „   is negative this is an ultra-anti-trade demand effect.
If oEs is $= 1$ this is a neutral supply effect.
If   „   is > 1 this is an anti-trade supply effect.
If   „   is < 1 this is a pro-trade supply effect.
If   „   is negative this is an ultra-pro-trade supply effect.

The net effect of growth is the combined result of the production (supply) and consumption (demand) effects. Note, however, that a neutral demand effect combined with a neutral supply effect will cause an *adverse* shift in the terms of trade (this is because there has been a *net* rise in the demand for importables). The terms of trade will improve for the growing country only if the combined effect is ultra-anti-trade biased (i.e. a *net* fall in the demand for importables).

A fuller treatment of the terms of trade effects of growth would require consideration of what happens (*a*) if growth is taking place in the rest of the world as well (i.e. our other country),[16] (*b*) if technical progress is non-neutral with respect to foreign trade.[17] Also, since the effects of growth will be very important for developing countries, a number of economists have put forward various ideas concerning the direction of movement of the terms of trade for such countries.[18] However, neither the hypotheses nor the evidence all point in the same direction – Kindleberger, Prebish, Myrdal and others argue that theory and empirical data suggest that a downward trend in the terms of trade for underdeveloped countries is probable and has, in fact, happened. On the other hand, Haberler, Meier and Morgan[19] claim that the empirical evidence is faulty and does not indicate a downward trend, and that the hypotheses on which such predictions are built are inadequate.

Because of the divergence of opinion on this subject, the student is advised to gain some understanding of the issues involved and come to his own conclusions.

(b) EFFECTS OF INTERNATIONAL CAPITAL TRANSFERS ON THE TERMS OF TRADE

The transfers considered could take the form of a grant, an interest payment, war reparations, a loan or a loan repayment; it makes little difference to the analysis. The problems which arise under transfer payments are:

(1) Will the way in which the payment is raised and the way in which it is spent take place without disequilibrating the balance of payments? The country making the transfer will wish to create an offsetting export surplus; the receiving country may spend part of the transfer on imports, but will the extra import bill equal the export surplus of the other country?

(2) If the post-transfer balance of payments is no longer in equilibrium, how will the adjustment mechanism work? In what direction will the terms of trade move in order to restore equilibrium? The Classical economists argued that the transferring country suffered a *primary burden* in having to raise the transfer (e.g. by increasing taxes); it might also suffer a *secondary burden* if the terms of trade turned against it as a result of the transfer. The Classical view, in fact, was that the terms of trade would turn against the transferring country. However, modern theoretical analysis shows that, under certain circumstances, the terms of trade can move in either direction.

Suppose that country X makes a transfer payment to country Y. In order to make the transfer, X must reduce domestic incomes and expenditure and as a result, spending on imports will fall. Conversely, Y will now have a bigger income and will therefore increase its spending on imports. Both these effects of the transfer will improve X's balance of payments. However, whether or not the improvement in the balance of payments is sufficient to offset the deterioration due to the capital transfer will depend on the size of the marginal propensities to import of the two countries. If the sum of the two marginal propensities is equal to unity, the balance of payments will balance after the transfer has been made. If the sum is greater than unity, then X will have a net export surplus and so, to restore equilibrium, the terms of trade will move in favor of the transferring country. Similarly, if the sum is less than unity, X will have a net import surplus and so, to restore equilibrium, the terms of trade will move against country X.

Thus, for the Classical view to hold, the sum of the elasticities would have to be less than unity; a condition which may not be fulfilled in practice. The above description is too naïve and simple, however. We must take into account the possibility that the transfer may be financed out of savings,[20] with the result that aggregate expenditure may not fall by as much as the size of the transfer. On the other side, the receiving country may simply add to its savings (at the individual or central bank level) and therefore not increase its expenditures on imports. Also, we must allow for the fact that the transfer will have multiple effects on income and therefore on the balance of payments. Thus, if the transfer comes from and goes into savings, then exports and imports will be unaffected and the country making the transfer will finish up with a deficit in its balance of payments.

To eliminate the deficit, the terms of trade will have to change against the country making the transfer. This will take place if deflation is followed or devaluation takes place. It would be relatively easy to construct various situations involving variations in the effects of the transfer on savings and spending directly and induced changes in savings and spending through the multiplier. Johnson[21] has developed such a model showing that any outcome so far as the terms of trade are concerned is possible and there is no reason *a priori* to expect them to move in one direction rather than another. The outcome will depend on the net effects of income changes in the two countries, the relative propensities to spend on domestic and imported goods and the elasticity of supply of the two categories of goods in the two countries. Johnson's analysis is in terms of two countries operating on fixed exchange rates with the transfer being "effected" via income and price adjustments.

Kemp has studied the problem under conditions of flexible exchange rates; that is, where the balance of payments is always in equilibrium and changes in the terms of trade are represented by changes in the exchange rate between the two currencies. Under such conditions Kemp analyzes the effect of raising the transfer in various ways (by, means of borrowing from the central bank, by raising income tax or by imposing a tax on imports) and also looks at how the way in which the receiving country distributes the transfer affects the outcome, so far as the rate of exchange (i.e. the terms of trade) is concerned. Again, depending on the sizes of the relevant marginal propensities and income changes, the rate of exchange may either depreciate (i.e. a deterioration in the terms of trade) or appreciate (i.e. an improvement in the terms of trade).

To discover the probable movement of the terms of trade in any specific instance, one would have to analyze empirically the determinants of the system. This has been attempted (e.g. Kindleberger) but the results are inconclusive; although it might be reasonable to argue that capital transfers from advanced industrialized countries to small underdeveloped ones are likely to cause shifts in the terms of trade in favor of the capital-importing country. This would be so because increases in demand for the advanced countries goods will be relatively small and supply elasticities of their exports will be fairly high. Also, the supply elasticities of the underdeveloped country may well be low. In spite of this general hypothesis, one feels that generalizations regarding the effects of transfers on the terms of trade are apt to be highly misleading. One must simply take each case on its own merits and analyze the forces operating there. This same criticism can be made of analyses of historical movements in the terms of trade, whatever their cause.

(c) THE EFFECT OF DEMAND SHIFTS ON THE TERMS OF TRADE

Since the terms of trade express the balancing of the forces of demand and supply which operate in the international economy, one would expect that a rise in the demand for a country's imports would, other things remaining equal, cause a rise in the price of these imports relative to the price of exports; that is, a deterioration in the terms of trade of the country concerned, and vice versa. Similarly, one would expect that a rise in the demand for a country's exports would lead to a rise in the price of exports relative to imports; that is, an improvement in the terms of trade. This assumes, of course, that there is some elasticity in the relevant supply curves. If supply curves were infinitely elastic then changes in the demand for imports or exports would not result in price changes and so the terms of trade would remain unchanged.

These effects can be seen by means of our offer curve analysis. Suppose the pre-demand-shift situation is as depicted over with OX and OY being the offer curves of countries X and Y respectively; and let country X's demand for imports from Y rise. Then X's offer curve will shift to the right, as shown, to OX_1.

As a result, the terms of trade will change from the slope of OT to the slope of OT_1 – a deterioration for country X. If the supply of Y's exportables were infinitely elastic, the terms of trade would remain as the slope of OT. The actual degree of deterioration of the terms of trade will depend on three factors:

(i) *The extent of the shift.* Obviously, the more the demand for Y's exportables increases, the more will the terms of trade deteriorate for country X (i.e. the farther will OX drift to the right).

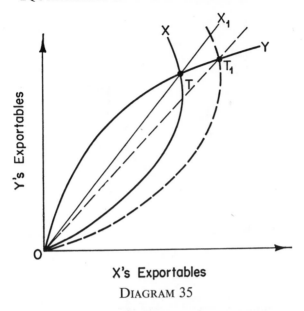

X's Exportables

DIAGRAM 35

(ii) *The elasticity of Y's offer curve.*[22] The more elastic is Y's offer curve, the less will the terms of trade deteriorate, and *vice versa.* If Y's offer curve were infinitely elastic, it would be a straight line OT through the origin and no shift in demand for Y's exportables would change the equilibrium terms of trade.

(iii) *The elasticity of X's offer curve.* Other things remaining equal, the more elastic is X's offer curve, the more will its terms of trade deteriorate as its demand for Y's exportables increases. Kemp[23] has examined the effect on the terms of trade of various types of demand shift and comes to the conclusion that a country's terms of trade will worsen irrespective of the way in which this demand for imports increases, provided that its offer curve has an elasticity greater than unity.

(*d*) EFFECT OF TARIFFS ON THE TERMS OF TRADE

To illustrate the effects of imposing tariffs we shall again use the offer curve technique. The specific effects of a tariff will depend on the way the tariff is imposed and on the elasticities of the offer curves. In general, the analysis is similar to that used for demand shifts. Suppose the offer curves before the imposition of the tariff are OX and OY and the slope of OT is the terms of trade. Let country X impose a tariff of x% on imports so that, to pay the duty, traders in X now have to give up to the government x% of their import purchases. Country X's offer curve will therefore shift upwards to OX′ as shown.

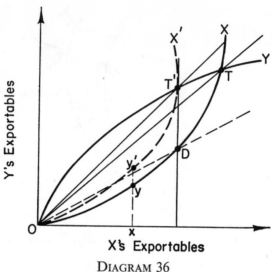

X's Exportables

DIAGRAM 36

Previously, country X was willing to offer Ox of its exports in exchange for xy of imports. However, if it received xy of imports for Ox of exports, it would have to pay over x% of imports to the government. Because of the tariff, country X will be willing to offer Ox of exports in exchange for a larger quantity of imports (xy'), paying over x% of xy' (equal to yy') of imports to the government. Thus, OX shifts upwards to OX'; and the terms of trade become equal to the slope of OT', that is, an *improvement* in X's terms of trade. Domestically, however, the price ratio between exports and imports changes from the slope of OT to the slope of OD, that is, a rise in the price of imports relative to exports. Similarly, if the tariff is imposed on the export commodity, the terms of trade will improve and the domestic ratio of export and import prices rise. However, for an equivalent size of tariff, the terms of trade will improve more and the domestic price ratio rise less, for a tariff imposed on the export goods. The student is left to work this out for himself.

The above conclusions depend on two basic assumptions:

(i) That the offer curve of country Y is not infinitely elastic. If this were the case, the terms of trade would not change but the domestic price of imports would rise by the amount of the tariffs.

(ii) That country Y does not retaliate by imposing a tariff on X's exports. If retaliation takes place, the final terms of trade can move in either direction, depending on the size of the tariffs. However, the domestic prices of imports in both countries will rise and therefore the *volume* of trade must fall. Thus, it has been argued that the imposition of tariffs and consequent retaliation will mean that both countries lose.[24] This is what lies behind the reciprocal tariff removing aims of bodies like G.A.T.T. and the Kennedy Round.

This might be a convenient point at which to digress for a little while to consider the role of tariffs in U.S. commercial policy, especially since changes in such policy could have an important effect on the domestic economy of the United States and on the welfare of other countries in view of the size of the United States as a trading nation.

In 1930 as the effects of the Depression were being felt in the United States pressure for tariff protection reached its height and gave birth to the Hawley-Smoot Law. Under this piece of legislation very high rates of duty on imports were imposed in the belief that they would protect domestic industry (and therefore employment) from foreign competition. However, with a new administration in 1933 and a growing realization that tariffs were not having the depression-dampening effects hoped for, a new Act was passed in 1934, The Trade Agreements Act, whose aim was to expand international trade, employment and welfare by moving towards freer trade. Negotiations between the United States and other trading nations were to take place and were to incorporate "unconditional most-favored nation treatment" which meant that any concessions granted by the United States to another country were to be automatically extended to all third countries, whether or not equivalent concessions were made in return. Also, any concessions granted to a third country by a country with which the United States had negotiated a trade agreement were to be unconditionally and automatically extended to the United States. In order to achieve significant trade liberalization, the President was granted powers such that tariffs on dutiable imports could be cut by as much as 50% of the 1934 levels, and by 1945 the duty on many commodities had in fact been reduced to 50% of their 1934 levels.

In the 1940s to early 1950s, however, pressure for increased protection was growing and as a result various obstacles were placed in the way of extending the 1934 trade liberalization program, "escape clauses," for example, were added to post 1947 agreements giving the United States the right to withdraw or modify a tariff concession if it caused or threatened "serious injury" to competitive domestic producers. In 1955 it was decided that duty reductions would not be allowed if the reduction threatened the domestic production necessary to projected national defense requirements. (The main example relevant here is the petroleum industry – in 1959 quotas were placed on imports of crude oil and petroleum products in order to safeguard "national defense requirements.")

The outcome of the 1936 program was that by 1953, more than 50%

of U.S. dutiable imports were subject to tariffs of 10% or less (*ad valorem*), although there was still a large number of cases where tariffs were completely protective (for instance, the duty on scientific instruments was 50%, on clocks 60–172%). However, between 1953 and 1962 no significant tariff reductions took place, partly due to the lessened scope for such reductions, and partly due to the strengthening of "loopholes." This slowing down in U.S. progress towards freer trade, together with the formation of a competitive European Community in 1957 meant that in 1962, when the Trade Agreement Act expired, the United States had to decide whether it was going to follow a similar policy of trade liberalization or combat European competitiveness with protectionism. Viewing the new Europe not only as a competitor but also as an expanding market for U.S. exports, it was decided to follow a course of action conducive to the expansion of trade. This decision found expression in the Kennedy inspired Trade Expansion Act of 1962 which authorized the President to cut tariffs by up to 50% of the 1962 rates and in some cases remove them completely (where the United States and the E. E. C. together accounted for 80% or more of world trade; in the case of tropical agricultural and forestry products, and finally in the case of so-called "nuisance duties" of 5% or less). Although the loopholes of previous legislation remained in a modified form, the chief aim of the new legislation was to expand and liberalize trade. An important point to note is that after 1958 the United States was experiencing severe balance of payments deficits and the way it chose to remedy this was through export expansion rather than import restrictions.

By 1967, after the "Kennedy Round" of tariff negotiations, the industrial countries had made reductions on 70% of their dutiable imports, excluding cereals, meat and dairy products. Two thirds of these cuts were of 50% or more, another fifth being between 25 and 50%.

The United States, however, should not rest on its laurels since it would be very easy to slip backwards into protectionism, especially if this could be excused on balance-of-payments grounds. Also, it is only recently that any progress has been made in eliminating nontariff barriers to trade (quotas, etc.) so that scope exists here for future trade liberalization.

Now, to return to the theoretical analysis, suppose that a country imposes a tariff but that no retaliation takes place. Can we say definitely that the terms of trade will improve? We cannot, because the final outcome will depend to some extent on what the tariff imposing government does with the tariff proceeds. The government may sterilize the receipts or it may distribute them (e.g. by means of reducing taxation). This redistribution of the proceeds will tend to raise the demand for

imports to an extent depending on the size of the marginal propensity
to spend on imports out of increased income. Thus, we have two forces
operating in opposite directions. The price effect of the tariff will tend
to reduce the import demand to an extent depending on the price
elasticity of demand for imports. The income effect of redistribution
will tend to raise the demand for imports. Depending on the size of the
marginal propensity and the price elasticity of demand, the outcome
can either be an improvement or a deterioration in the terms of trade.
Once we allow for possible distribution of tariff proceeds, the effect
of imposing a tariff may be to shift the terms of trade in either direction.

The terms of trade will also be altered by the imposition of import
quotas since such quotas, by limiting the extent of importation, will
tend to cause a rise in the price of the imported commodity. To some
extent then, quotas are similar to tariffs. Tariffs, however, may not
prove completely protective in that the imports concerned can still
come into the country (although at a higher price). Quotas, on the
other hand, limit imports to a fixed amount, with the result that the
increase in price following quota impositions is more indeterminate
than the price increase following tariff impositions. This is because, in
general, the price rise due to a tariff will be no greater than the amount
of the tariff. What we can say, then, is that with a tariff, the price rise
is circumscribed, whilst the volume of imports is not; on the other
hand, with quotas, the volume is circumscribed whilst the price rise is
not. Since both quotas and tariffs are similar in their effects, one can
say that a quota could do everything that a tariff can do – that is,
reduce the volume of imports, raise their price, and even collect revenue
if a tariff-quota is used (a tariff-quota is a flexible system designed to
gain the advantages of quotas and tariffs).

Finally, let us consider the problem of whether or not a tariff which
improves the terms of trade leads to the country concerned being better
off. This is important because, given some price elasticity in the demand
for imports, the *volume* of trade must decline as the result of a tariff
imposition and the welfare effects of the tariff will depend on whether
or not the decline in trade volume is more than offset by the gains from
improved terms of trade.

Mill and the Classical economists argued on this point that a country
could improve its welfare as compared with the free-trade position by
imposing a tariff. However, as we saw, the possibility of retaliation
may reduce the likelihood of this happening. Suppose, however, that
retaliation is ruled out. Then what tariff should a country improve in
order to maximize the gains from doing so? In other words, what is the
optimum tariff?[25] The optimum tariff can be defined as that tariff any
increase in which would lead to a loss in trade volume which more

than outweighs the gains from improved terms of trade. Short of this tariff, the terms of trade can be improved without being offset by greater losses from lower trade volumes.

Let the pre-tariff offer curves be OX and OY and the terms of trade be the slope of OT. Suppose, also, that the relevant trade indifference curves for country X are as shown – TI_1 and TI_2. Thus, country X is

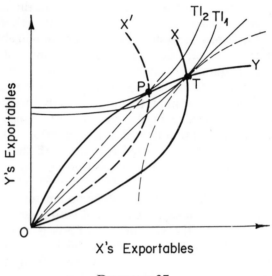

DIAGRAM 37

at a position T on trade indifference curve TI_1. At p, OY is tangential to X's trade indifference curve TI_2 which is the highest curve which X can reach in these circumstances. Thus X will impose a tariff such that her new distorted offer curve will pass through P (i.e. OX'), the new terms of trade becoming the slope of OP. The tariff which brings this about will be the optimum tariff for X to impose.[25]

(*e*) EFFECT OF DEPRECIATION OF THE CURRENCY ON THE TERMS OF TRADE[26]

One might expect at first glance, that a depreciation of one's currency would lead to a deterioration in the terms of trade, because import prices will rise and export prices fall. This is not necessarily so, however, because when measuring the terms of trade we must stick to measurements of prices either in terms of foreign currency or the domestic currency. Thus, with depreciation, import prices rise in domestic currency but stay unchanged in foreign currency; export prices fall in foreign currency but stay unchanged in domestic currency. However, taking account of secondary effects (e.g. higher cost of raw material imports into the depreciating country) it is probably more correct to say that depreciation will raise the domestic currency price of both imports and exports. Similarly, the foreign currency price of both imports and exports will tend to fall. Thus, which way the terms of trade go will depend on the relative sizes of the price changes, given that both will move in the same direction.

To determine the direction of change of the terms of trade, we must consider the forces which in turn determine the sizes of the relative price changes of imports and exports; that is, the elasticities of demand and supply for exports and imports.

Joan Robinson[27] has analyzed the role of elasticities and has shown (expressing prices in terms of the depreciating country's currency) that depreciation will worsen the terms of trade if the product of the supply elasticities is greater than the product of the demand elasticities. Although the method of proving this is somewhat complex, it is relatively simple to demonstrate the importance of demand and supply elasticities.

Suppose, for example, the demand of the depreciating country for imports were perfectly inelastic and the demand for its exports were elastic. On the supply side, suppose that the supply of imports to the depreciating country were elastic and the supply of its exports were also elastic.

This situation is shown below –

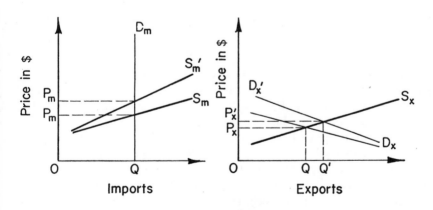

DIAGRAM 38

Before depreciation, the prices of imports and exports are OP_m and OP_x. Now let the currency depreciate by say 10%; then the supply curve of imports will shift upwards to S_m' and the demand curve for exports shift outwards to D_x'; giving new equilibrium prices of OP_m' and OP_x'. The price of imports will have risen by a greater percentage amount than the price of exports $\left(\dfrac{P_m P_m'}{OP_m} > \dfrac{P_x P_x'}{OP_x} \right)$ and so the terms of trade will have deteriorated. (Also note that the product of the supply elasticities is greater than the product of the demand elasticities.)

Suppose, on the other hand, that the demand for imports were elastic and the supply of imports were very inelastic, the supply and demand elasticities for exports remaining unchanged.

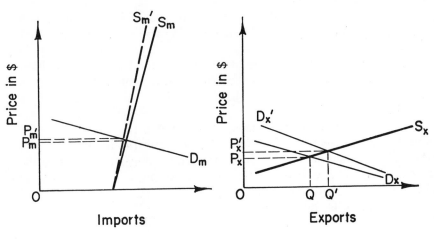

DIAGRAM 39

In this case, the price of exports rises proportionately more than the price of imports and the terms of trade improve (the product of the supply elasticities is less than the product of the demand elasticities).

We can see, therefore, how important demand and supply elasticities are in determining in which direction the terms of trade move.

The above analysis is too simple, however, in that it takes no account of income changes brought about by depreciation, or of the importance of cross elasticities of demand. Depreciation may cause relative price differences to emerge between traded and non-traded commodities, with the result that the demand for imports may shift due to the effect of cross elasticities. Also, real incomes may change as a result of these relative price changes and this, in turn, will affect the demand for imports. Because of these repercussions, the "final" elasticities may differ from the partial ones used above.

On these complexities, the student is referred to a model developed by Kennedy[28] and another by Kemp[29] who takes money and monetary policy into account.

In conclusion, it must be emphasized again that although the analysis used in this chapter may be of some use in determining in which direction and by how much the terms of trade may move in different circumstances, one cannot infer directly from these movements and their degree what has happened to the economic welfare of the country or countries concerned.

More information is required before conclusions regarding welfare changes can be reached, information concerning changes in the volume of trade, changes in the quality of traded goods, changes in productivity, changes in other sections of the balance of payments and so on. It is particularly important to bear these considerations in mind when attempting to analyze the historical movement of the terms of trade for a country or groups of countries.[30]

[1] J. S. Mill, *Principles of Political Economy*, 1920.

[2] C. P. Kindleberger, *International Economics*, third edition, p. 107.

[3] A. Marshall, *The Pure Theory of Foreign Trade*, 1930.

[4] T. Scitovsky, "A Reconsideration of the Theory of Tariffs," *Review of Economic Studies*, 1942.

[5] J. E. Meade, *A Geometry of International Trade*, Allen and Unwin, 1952.

[6] A. P. Lerner, "The Symmetry Between Import and Export Taxes," *Economica*, 1936.

[7] On community indifference curves, see Baumol, *op. cit.*

[8] See Meade, *op. cit.*, Ch. 3, pp. 24–26.

[9] See W. W. Rostow, *The Process of Economic Growth*, Chs. 8 and 9.

[10] Dorrance, "The Income Terms of Trade," *Review of Economic Studies*, 1948–49.

[11] J. Viner, *Studies in the Theory of International Trade*, 1937.

[12] E. Devons, "Statistics of the U.K. Terms of Trade," Manchester School, 1954.

[13] J. Bhagwati, "Immiserising Growth: a Geometrical Note," *Review of Economic Studies*, 1958.

[14] See, G. M. Meier, *International Trade and Development*, 1963.

[15] For a fuller treatment of these effects, see, H. G. Johnson, *International Trade and Economic Growth*, Ch. III, 1958.

[16] J. Bhagwati, "Growth Terms of Trade and Comparative Advantage," *Economia Internazionale*, 1959.

[17] R. Findlay and H. Grubert, "Factor Intensity, Technological Progress, and the Terms of Trade," *Oxford Economic Papers*, 1959.

[18] S. G. Triantis, "Economic Progress, Occupational Redistribution and International Terms of Trade," *Economic Journal*, 1953.

[19] See Meier, *op. cit.*; also, T. Morgan, "The Long-Run Terms of Trade Between Agriculture and Manufacturing," *Economic Development and Cultural Change*, 1959.

[20] Note that by introducing savings we have moved from a static "real" theory to a monetary theory of transfer.

[21] H. G. Johnson, "The Transfer Problem: a Note on Criteria for Changes in the Terms of Trade," *Economica*, 1955; also, "The Transfer Problem and Exchange Stability," *Journal of Political Economy*, 1956.

[22] For a definition of offer-curve elasticity, see J. Vanek, *International Trade: Theory and Economic Policy*, 1962.

[23] M. C. Kemp, "The Relation Between Changes in International Demand and the Terms of Trade," *Econometrica*, 1956.

[24] See, C. P. Kindleberger, *International Economics*, 1963.

[25] For a fuller discussion of the "optimum tariff," see Meade and Johnson. Note also that, according to Johnson, even with retaliation a country may gain by imposing a tariff. The outcome, as so often is the case, depends on the particular circumstances of each case.

[26] Note again that by introducing a currency we are, *ex definitione*, making the problem a monetary and not a "real" one.

[27] J. Robinson, *Essays in the Theory of Employment*, 1937. See also, G. Haberler, "Currency Depreciation and the Terms of Trade," in *Wirtschaftliche Entwicklung und Sociale Ordnung*, 1952, for a geometric treatment.

[28] C. Kennedy, "Devaluation and the Terms of Trade," *Review of Economic Studies*, 1950–51.

[29] M. C. Kemp, "The Rate of Exchange, the Terms of Trade and the Balance of Payments in Fully Employed Economies," *International Economic Review*, 1962.

[30] See G. Haberler, "Terms of Trade and Economic Development," in *Economic Development for Latin America*, edited by Howard S. Ellis, 1961; G. M. Meier, *International Trade and Development*, 1963, and "Long-Period Determinants of Britain's Terms of Trade, 1880–1913," *Review of Economic Studies*, 1952–53; T. Morgan, "Trends in Terms of Trade and Their Repercussions on Primary Producers," in *International Trade Theory in a Developing World*, edited by Roy Harrod, 1963; J. Viner, *International Trade and Economic Development*, 1952.

CHAPTER 6

The Theory of Customs Unions

IT IS appropriate that a theoretical treatment of customs unions follow on from a discussion of the effects of tariffs on the terms of trade, since in the formation of trade blocs, such as customs unions, discriminatory tariffs arise. This is because, by definition, a customs union is an agreement between members of a group of countries to abolish all tariffs levied by each member on imports from the other members, whilst, at the same time, establishing a tariff at common rates on imports into the member countries from non-member countries (the so-called Common External Tariff or C.E.T. for short). Note also that there are various meanings given to the terms "customs union"; it may be very limited, involving only one commodity, or it may be complete, encompassing the abolition of all restrictions on the movement of goods *and* factors, and the adoption of common fiscal and monetary policies as well. This complete form of customs union is normally called an economic union. The setting up of a customs union results in the preferential treatment of goods imported from member countries and therefore discriminates against goods coming from the outside world. Because of this change in the tariff structure, economic relationships within the union change, with the result that consumption and production patterns may alter, the terms of trade may be affected and the rate of growth may change. It is important, therefore, that we study the way in which the formation of a customs union will act on these variables before we can reach any sort of conclusion regarding the desirability or otherwise of such groupings.

Unfortunately, however, the theory of customs unions is rather complicated; it is a special case of the theory of international discrimination which, in turn, is part of the theory of imperfect markets. Customs union theory is also relatively young, the first major breakthrough coming with Viner's book *The Customs Union Issue*, published in 1950, and followed in 1955 by Meade's *The Theory of Customs Unions*. These two books have had such an impact on thought concerning this subject that they can be regarded as classics in this field. Perhaps the most thorough theoretical treatment of customs union theory is to be found in Vanek's book, *General Equilibrium of International Discrimination*, published in 1965.

Before Viner's contribution, it had usually been thought that a customs union would raise world welfare since it was a step towards a more ideal situation (free trade). However, as Viner pointed out, a customs union, because it combines elements of freer trade with elements of increased protection, can have both beneficial and detrimental effects. Thus, although freedom of trade between the members is increased, more protection for member producers against outside competition is increased because the member countries not only have a protected domestic market, they also have protected markets in the other members' countries. The net effect of a customs union on welfare depends, therefore, on whether the beneficial effects outweigh the detrimental effects. Since, by definition, tariffs must exist between a customs union and the outside world, we must be dealing with an imperfect market; but, since a customs union is a mixture of freer trade and more protection, it cannot be analyzed by orthodox welfare theory which concerns itself with *the optimum conditions* for welfare maximization. Assuming a perfectly competitive world economy, the best situation is free trade, because this will satisfy the Pareto optimum conditions which are defined by the equality of all marginal rates of substitution and transformation for any pair of products and for all individuals.

However, the existence of tariffs will make it impossible to achieve such optimum conditions – tariffs distort prices – so a theory is required which will deal with the conditions for *improving* welfare rather than achieving the best possible (i.e. a constrained maximization problem). Such a theory dealing with sub-optimum conditions was developed by Meade[1] and later restated and generalized by Lipsey and Lancaster[2] – the *"theory of the second best"*. Viner himself realized that the formation of a customs union, though it is a step toward freer trade, does not necessarily increase total welfare because we are dealing with sub-optimum conditions. This rudimentary form of the theory of second-best is perhaps Viner's major contribution to customs union theory and our understanding of the issues involved. The second-best theorem can be stated thus – if in an economy *all* the optimum conditions for welfare maximization are not fulfilled simultaneously, then a change which increases the number of conditions fulfilled does not necessarily increase the welfare of that economy. The effect on welfare of fulfilling one more condition will depend on the circumstances of each case.[3]

Interest in the customs union issue is, of course, of great practical importance and has obvious relevance to the post-war proliferation of such types of union as the European Economic Community formed in 1957 after the organization of the Benelux Customs Union and the

European Coal and Steel Community; the European Free Trade Area[4] and the Latin American Free Trade Area.[4]

Also, following the success of such bodies as the E.E.C. and E.F.T.A., considerable interest has been shown in the possibility of forming customs unions for the less developed countries in the world.[5]

Turning now to the analysis of the effects of a customs union on welfare we are immediately faced with the problem of the second-best; how can we determine whether the beneficial aspects outweigh the detrimental ones and so judge if the customs union would be desirable? This is extremely difficult, whether we are concerned with only the welfare of an individual member country, all the member countries together or the whole world, because welfare theory does not permit inter-personal comparisons of utility to be made. Thus, if the formation of a customs union makes one or more persons better off, but also makes one or more persons worse off, then we cannot say whether the *net* effect on aggregate welfare is good or bad. We can reach a conclusion concerning welfare only if all the welfare changes are in the same direction or if it is known whether or not the gainers can compensate the losers fully.

This is extremely relevant to customs union theory, because the formation of a customs union will change the pattern of production, consumption and trade between and within the member countries. Also, it is likely that changes will take place in the distribution of income between and within member countries leading to alteration in the distribution of economic welfare. It is possible to see briefly how consumption, production and trade are affected before making a more detailed analysis of the forces involved:

(i) Consumption will be affected because the existence of discriminatory tariffs under the customs union will alter the previously existing price structure in such a way as to make imported commodities from the member countries relatively cheaper compared with domestic commodities and with imports coming from the outside world (i.e. relative to the initial pre-customs union situation). Because of this altered relative price structure, consumption will shift towards imports from members and away from domestic goods and imports from non-members, so altering the efficiency of consumption and causing welfare changes.

(ii) Production will be affected as well by the changes in relative prices. Some industries will find that the demand for their products has increased due to the elimination of inter-member tariffs and they may be able to increase output and gain economics of scale, thereby increasing the efficiency of production. On the other hand, inefficient domestic production of certain goods may be stimulated by the existence of a C.E.T. higher than the previous tariff level, and this will have detrimental effects on productive efficiency. As a result, changes in the level of welfare and its distribution will take place.

(iii) Trade will be affected in the short run in such a way as to increase the scale of intra-union trade and decrease that between the union and the rest of the world. In the long run the volume of trade between the union and the outside world will probably increase and may even rise faster than if the union had not been formed. This would be the case if, for example, the formation of the union led to faster growth rates amongst the member countries, leading in turn to a rising demand for imports from non-members. Increases in intra-union trade may raise the economic welfare of the members but cause a fall in that of non-members. In spite of this, the long run effects may be to raise world welfare to a higher level than that which would have existed had the union not been formed. It will be an extremely complex problem to decide whether the long run gains are great enough to offset the short run effects on world welfare, assuming, for the sake of argument, that the losses in welfare suffered by the rest of the world are greater than the increases enjoyed by the union members.

These union effects on trade, discussed above, were termed by Viner "*trade creation*" and "*trade diversion*," and are descriptive of the facts that the abolition of tariff barriers between members will stimulate or create intra-union trade (which is generally regarded as being good) whilst, at the same time, remove or divert trade from outside countries to member countries (which is generally regarded as being bad). The words "good" and "bad" are used here deriving from the assumption that trade is desirable (or "good") because it increases world income by allowing goods to flow in accordance with the principles of comparative advantage (i.e. from high to low and cost regions). Trade creation and trade diversion have become the fundamental phenomena associated with the customs union issue and are the main contributions to the problem of assessing the net welfare effects of the union. As Meade points out, even if we accept the welfare connotations of trade diversion and creation, we still have the problem of deciding how to combine the two in arriving at an index of overall "goodness" (this is similar to the problem of comparing the long- and short-run effects on welfare of the union). Meade's main point in constructing such an index is that different types of trade created or diverted will affect society with different degrees of harm, and so some sort of weighing is required. However, Vanek[6] is critical of Meade's approach, pointing out that it depends on assuming that individual utilities be measurable and comparable (which Vanek calls a "cardinalist" method). Vanek prefers the "ordinalist method," which relies on the "compensation criterion" as suggested by various writers,[7] because, by using this method, we can move into imperfect markets with our welfare analysis and, also, the ordinalist method is based on more realistic assumptions.[8]

However, in our analysis of this chapter, we shall not be concerned with the intricacies of welfare economics and shall assume that if a customs union leads to short-run improvements in the efficiency of production and consumption, then welfare will have increased.

We can look now at the effects of a customs union on production and consumption and then consider more complex general equilibrium models.

(i) EFFECT ON PRODUCTION

As mentioned earlier, a customs union may allow member countries to specialize in production according to the principles of comparative advantage and so increase their efficiency. It may also permit the enjoyment of scale economies due to a larger union market being created as a result of tariff removals. According to Viner's analysis of production effects, if the union shifts production from a higher-cost source to a lower-cost source, it creates trade, and this constitutes a movement towards freer trade. On the other hand, if production is shifted in the reverse direction from lower cost to higher cost sources, this constitutes trade diversion and is a movement away from free trade. Given that such shifts may take place, the efficiency with which resources are utilized will be altered and the overall effect may be to increase or decrease productive efficiency. (In general, trade creation will give a more efficient allocation of world resources and trade diversion a less efficient allocation.) The meaning of trade creation and diversion can be shown very easily by means of a simple numerical example:

Suppose we have three countries – the United States, France and Germany – and their respective costs of production for a certain good are 100 dollars, 80 dollars and 90 dollars.

Suppose the United States has a tariff of 40 dollars on imports from France and Germany, who in their turn have tariffs of 20 dollars on imports. In this situation the United States will produce the product itself, as will France and Germany, since it would cost more to import from any source. However, let us consider what would happen if the United States and Germany combine in a customs union with an external tariff of 30 dollars. In this situation, the United States will import the product from Germany, who will now supply it at a cost of 90 dollars instead of the previous 130 dollars. No imports will come from France into either the United States or Germany since the cost of doing this (110 dollars) is higher than the cost of producing in Germany, and the United States will not produce the product since she can get it on better terms from Germany. This represents a case of trade creation where the place of production is moved to a lower-cost source (Germany).

TABLE 1

	Production Cost	Lowest Cost of Imports
U.S.A.	100	120
France	80	110
Germany	90	100

However, if the original tariff imposed by the United States were 15 dollars and that imposed by France and Germany were the same as before (20 dollars), then the United States would import the commodity from France at a price of 95 dollars, whilst France and Germany would produce for themselves and import none. Again, let the United States and Germany unite in a customs union with an external tariff of 17 dollars. In this case, the United States will import from Germany at a price of 90 dollars and stop buying from France, since it would now be more costly to do so (97 dollars). This is an example of trade diversion since production is shifted from a low-cost source (France) to a high-cost source (Germany) with a resulting loss in productive efficiency.

If the beneficial effects of trade creation outweigh the detrimental effects of trade diversion, it is usually concluded that productive efficiency will have increased, but we cannot infer from this that welfare will have increased, because some individuals (and countries) will have lost, and others benefited, as a result of the changes in the location of production. Of course, if efficiency has increased, it should be *possible* for the countries or individuals who have gained to compensate the losers and still have some net gain, but this does not mean that such redistribution will, in fact, take place. In the cases discussed above the benefits will all accrue to the union members and any trade diversion may adversely affect *both* the union and the outside world since, within the union, production will shift to relatively high-cost sources, whilst in the outside world resources will either become unemployed or shift to the production of goods in which the outside world has a smaller comparative advantage.

When it comes to trying to evaluate and quantify the gains and losses involved, the difficulties are immense, especially when we allow for the possibility of increasing or decreasing costs in production.[9] However, later in the chapter some attempt will be made to analyze the gains and losses involved diagrammatically.

So far we have concerned ourselves solely with the production effects of a customs union (which was really what Viner did) and neglected any effects which the union might have on consumption. This must now be righted, given that discriminating tariffs will alter the relative prices of commodities and therefore patterns of consumption.

(ii) EFFECT ON CONSUMPTION

It can be seen that, in the numerical example given above, the price of the product fell in the United States after the formation of the union between the United States and Germany (from 100 dollars to 90 dollars). Accordingly, one would expect that the consumption of the product in the United States would increase, assuming that the demand curve possesses *some* elasticity. Even in the second case where trade diversion occured, imports into the United States rose and, providing that the member country from which the imports are obtained has a lower production cost than the importing member, some gain will accrue to the United States. However, as Lipsey shows,[10] Viner implicitly assumed that goods were consumed in some fixed proportion which was invariant with respect to relative prices. But, once we abandon this assumption and allow relative price changes to alter consumption patterns, then obviously economic welfare will be affected, just as economic welfare is affected by changes in production patterns.

Meade[11] has formulated an analysis of the effects on consumption in a model where production patterns are assumed to be rigid and only consumption and trade can vary. Suppose, for example, our three countries can each only produce one product and that the tariffs imposed by each country on imports from the others are as given in the table below –

TABLE 2

	Product	Tariff
U.S.A.	Cars	10%
France	Wine	20%
Germany	Tools	30%

Let the United States and Germany form a customs union. Then, according to Meade,[12] we can to some extent gauge the potential gain in living standards in these two countries through increased trading by comparing ratios of the marginal utilities of the products. Before the formation of the union, the ratio of marginal utilities in the United

States between Tools and Cars was higher than the same ratio in Germany, because the U.S. tariff raised the price of Tools by 10%, whereas Germany's tariff raised the price of Cars by 30%. The ratio of the marginal utility of Tools to the marginal utility of cars is approximately 33% higher in the United States than in Germany, giving some idea of the gain to be had initially from increased trade. As trade expands, the additional gain declines as the ratios of the marginal utilities in the two countries approach each other. In the union, the United States removes its tariff on Tools and will probably increase consumption of Tools and lower consumption of Cars and Wine. In Germany, imports of Cars and consumption of Tools and Wine falls. Thus, to offset the gains from increased intra-union trade, there will be world losses corresponding to the lower level of trade between the union and the third country (France).

According to Meade, the net effect on welfare will depend on the initial tariff structure and the elasticities of demand for the products. The higher the original tariffs of members relative to outside country tariffs, the greater the extent of trade creation and the corresponding consumption gains for members; and the lower will be the losses from trade diversion. Also, the net gains will be greater, the higher the degree of substitutability between member countries products, and the lower the degree of substitutability between products of members and non-members. This would mean that demand elasticities are high for members' products and low for non-member products, thus tending to cause a large amount of trade creation but little trade diversion.

Having examined the production and consumption effects of a union, we are now in a position to attempt to combine the two and get an overall picture. It should be realized, however, that the following analysis is only *partial* in that secondary and further effects of the changes in relative prices and production are not taken into account. Obviously, shifts in production patterns will affect consumption and changes in consumption patterns will affect production – phenomena which we shall examine in more detail in a later discussion of general equilibrium models. Let us now consider[13] what happens for a single commodity when a union is formed, assuming, for the sake of simplicity, that all demand and supply curves are linear, that the domestic country faces increasing costs in production whilst the foreign supply curves are infinitely elastic, and that exchange rates are fixed so that prices in foreign currency can be converted into prices in domestic currency. Domestic demand for the product is represented by DD and domestic supply by SS, with foreign supply curves for two countries A and B being AA and BB. (A represents a potential union member and B represents the rest of the world.)

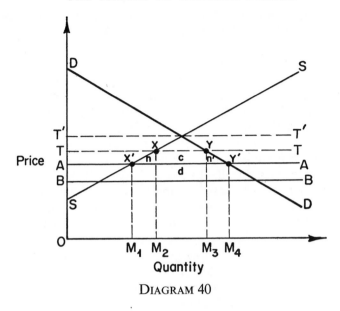

DIAGRAM 40

Now, let a tariff of BT be imposed by the home country on imports from A and B. In this situation, imports of M_2M_3 will come from country B with no imports from country A (because A is a relatively high-cost producer), and OM_2 being produced domestically. Total consumption is OM_3 and the domestic price is OT; with the level of economic welfare domestically being represented by the sum of consumers' surplus (DYT), producers' surplus (SXT) and tariff revenue (BT $\times M_2M_3$). Now suppose the tariff BT is abolished for trade between the domestic country and country A; then AA becomes the relevant foreign supply curve since country A is now a relatively cheap source of the product compared with B. Price in the home market falls to OA with M_1M_4 being imported from A and OM_1 being produced domestically. Total consumption of the product is now at a higher level, OM_4, than previously. It can be seen that in forming the union a certain amount of trade creation and diversion has taken place – trade between the members has increased, whereas trade between the home country and country B has ceased, constituting trade diversion, since B is a low-cost *producer* relative to A.

The size of trade created is equal to the cut-back in domestic production (M_1M_2) plus the increase in import volume (M_3M_4) whilst the extent of trade diverted is equal to M_2M_3.

Bearing in mind the limitations of Meade's analysis, we can also measure the welfare gains and losses. Due to trade creation, consumers' surplus increases from DYT to DY'A (i.e. by TYY'A) whereas producers' surplus falls from SXT to SX'A (i.e. by TXX'A), and, of course, the tariff revenue (BT$\times$M$_2$M$_3$) is lost, part of the loss being offset by increased consumers' surplus (area "c"), the remaining loss being due to trade diversion from country B to country A (area "d"). The increase in consumers' surplus exceeds the loss of revenue "c" and the loss of producers' surplus by an amount equal to the area of triangle "n" plus triangle n', this area representing the *net* welfare gain through trade creation. The *overall* welfare effect of the union depends on whether or not the net welfare gain from trade creation exceeds or falls short of the welfare loss from trade diversion, (area "d").[14] On the foregoing analysis it was assumed that the supply curves of external countries were perfectly elastic and, as a result, consumers' and producers' surpluses for these sources do not change. However, if external supply curves are less than perfectly elastic, then as trade is diverted from foreign to union sources, the foreign supply price falls and the home country will gain improved terms of trade on any trade with non-member countries which survives the union. One result of this movement in the terms of trade will be to lessen the degree of trade diversion; the help from this increasing, the more the foreign source is exploited. Also, as imports from members expand, the supply price will tend to rise, thus increasing the losses through trade diversion. This only scratches the surface of the problems, which require very complex treatment, and for a fuller treatment the student is referred to the references given below.[15]

However, despite the limitations of our analysis, certain general points can be made concerning the welfare effects of consumption and production shifts.

(i) The higher the initial tariff level, the greater will be the gains from trade creation. It can be seen from the above diagram that a tariff of BT' would increase the areas n and n', and lower the area of d.

(ii) The more elastic the demand and supply curves, for the home country, the greater will be the gains from trade creation. It can be seen from the diagram that the flatter the curves are, the greater will the areas n and n' become.

(iii) The losses from trade diversion will be smaller, the smaller the difference in cost between the partner and foreign sources of supply. Again, from the diagram, it can be observed that a lessening of such cost differences will reduce area d.

(iv) Trade diversion will be lesser, the lower the elasticity of demand in the union for goods imported from outside the union, and the lower the elasticity of supply of such goods from the outside world. Also, the more inelastic the foreign demand is for union exports, and the more inelastic the supply of foreign exports to the union, the greater will be the terms of trade gains for the union.

(v) The lower the common external tariff imposed after the formation of the union on external imports, as compared with the pre-union tariff, the smaller will be the losses from trade diversion; because it will be less likely under such circumstances that a union producer will displace an outside producer in supplying the union market.

(vi) The larger the union, the lower is the possibility of trade diversion and the greater will be the gains from reallocating production. Also, the union is more likely to raise economic welfare, the lower the proportion of pre-union trade with outside countries.

In addition to these general points, we can also say that trade creation may have beneficial effects on a member's trade with the outside world. This would be the case if some foreign products were complementary to imports from partners, or if the member's exports to partners are substitutes in domestic consumption for foreign goods. In either case, trade with the outside world would increase for such products. Of course, the effects could go the other way and this would accentuate the losses from trade diversion.[16] Given the above relationships, can we say anything about which countries would be most likely to gain from forming a customs union?

Before the publication of Viner's book, it had generally been thought that a union between *complementary* economies (i.e. economies with different patterns of production and little overlap in the types of goods produced) was more beneficial than a union between *rival* economies (i.e. economics with similar patterns of production and much overlap in the types of goods produced). Viner, however, argued that the reverse was the case on the grounds that a union of rival economics would cause greater trade creation.[17] This argument gave rise to great confusion until it was realized[18] that Viner's definitions were ambiguous. Viner was referring to the *range* of products produced, whereas modern usage of complementarity and rivalry refers to differences in *comparative production costs*.

Rival (or competitive) economies are ones with similar cost ratios between products, and complementary economies are ones with dissimilar cost ratios. Once we define the terms in this way, a union between complementary economies (ones producing similar products but at differing comparative production costs) will give rise to greater gains than one between rival economies (producing dissimilar products). If trade creation does occur, then the gains will be greater, the greater the difference in costs of production between the members of the union.[19] One can also say that the more dissimilar the members are to the rest of the world, the more they will gain, because trade diversion will then be less, since members will still have to import such products produced by the outside world, but not in the union (e.g. raw materials, etc.). In the light of all these observations, one would expect that a customs union like the E.E.C. would be highly successful since (a) a high proportion of pre-union trade was with each other, (b) they produce and trade in much the same products, indicating a high degree of rivalry.[20] When one looks at the rate of growth of intra-union trade after the formation of the union, these expectations are borne out. A similar sort of picture is seen when one studies E.F.T.A. trade, though the growth of intra-union trade here has not been so great; probably because the members of E.F.T.A. are more complementary than those of the E.E.C. Some trade diversion will, of course, occur, even for the E.E.C., especially for certain tropical foodstuffs previously imported from Latin America and for temperate agricultural product coming from the United States.[21] In E.F.T.A., the degree of trade diversion will be much higher and will cover a broader range of commodities.

So far as the underdeveloped countries are concerned, a large proportion of their trade is with industrial economies and it is likely that if such countries formed a union, any domestic manufacturing industries would be heavily protected, and as a result a large amount of trade diversion would take place.

Secondary Effects of Integration. So far the analysis has been confined to the primary effects of integration on the allocation of production and consumption, based on pre-unionization costs. However, there are other points which may bring secondary advantages to union members and we shall look at these before going on to discuss general equilibrium models.

The first point is that, as a result of the union being formed, competition may become more widespread as national boundaries are flung open and so lead to increases in productive efficiency in addition to the initial production reallocation effects.[22] Thus, even if monopolists exist in one country before the union, they will have to compete with their counterparts once tariffs between members are removed. Also, by enlarging the market and increasing the spread of information regarding prices, etc., throughout the union, other obstacles to competition should be removed (e.g. lack of initiative on the part of businessmen operating in a protected domestic industry). Scitovsky is the major proponent of such views, arguing that the major gains in productive efficiency will come from the reorganization of production, not so much between countries as *within* countries. Other economists, however, suggest that a customs union will foster the growth of cartels and monopolies, especially if internal economies of scale are important and the market for the product rather limited.

The second point is that the formation of a union may speed up the rate of growth of members' economies due to important large-scale economies releasing resources for other uses, and also the larger market making investment and expenditure on research and development more attractive and safe.[23] However, although larger firms do spend proportionately more on research and development compared with small firms, recent studies do not show a superior performance of large firms so far as innovation goes. Thus, technological advance may not speed up as a result of forming a union. However, if growth does accelerate, this will have beneficial effects on the outside world, since rising real incomes within the union will tend to lessen the degree of any trade diversion which occurred in the short run. This offset will, of course, depend on the rate of growth of income within the union, and the marginal propensities to import of the union members.

The third point is that a union formation may allow firms and industries to exploit more fully large-scale economies. However, even with scale economies, production cost within the union may still be higher than cost outside, and if trade diversion occurs in such industries, then some or all partner countries may suffer a decline in welfare as a result of union formation.[24] Some economists (e.g. Balassa) argue strongly that the formation of a union and the resulting enlarged markets will cause substantial scale economies, and that Western European integration will give rise to such external and internal economies. On the other hand, Johnson argues that if Britain were to join the E.E.C., only small gains from scale economies would result. Kindleberger[25] also argues that European firms, in general, are not too small to be efficient. In fact, firms may become too big and so create inefficiency. In addition, firms, if limited to a small domestic market, are always able to expand the market by exporting and so grow and achieve any economies available. A union is not required for this, though it may make exporting easier. All we can say regarding internal and external economies is that the evidence for advanced industrial countries is inconclusive and cannot give any great support either way so far as customs union formation is concerned.

So far we have concerned ourselves with partial equilibrium analysis and looked briefly at some secondary effects of union formation. Now we shall go on to look at general equilibrium models.

Customs Unions and General Equilibrium Theory. As mentioned earlier, Vanek[26] has developed the most modern and comprehensive analysis of customs unions in terms of general equilibrium theory. Although his method and analysis are greatly extended in his later work, his technique consists essentially of using offer curves to show equilibrium between three countries (two union members and one country representing the outside world) and two products.

Let the United States and France form a customs union, and let "X" represent the rest of the world, with the U.S. exportables being cars, France's exportables being wine. We can represent the pre-union trade set-up between the United States and France by means of their offer curves as shown.

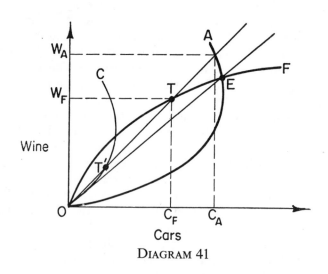

DIAGRAM 41

OA is the U.S. offer curve and OF France's offer curve, the equilibrium terms of trade being the slope of OE. Now, the major step in Vanek's treatment is to construct an *excess offer curve* for the two countries intending to form the union. This will show the net offer curve of the United States and France acting together in trade with the rest of the world "X." To construct this excess offer curve, consider the varying situation for the union countries at different terms of trade. If the terms of trade are the slope of OE, then trade between France and the United States is in balance, with no excess supply or demand for either product. Thus, for terms of trade line OE, the excess offer will be zero and so the excess offer curve must pass through the origin. If the terms of trade are given by the slope of OT, however, trade between the two countries is not balanced since, at such terms of trade, the United States is willing to offer OC$_A$ cars in exchange for OW$_A$ of wine from France, but France is only willing to offer OW$_A$ of wine in exchange for OC$_F$ of cars. We can say therefore, that in this situation there exists for the two countries together an excess supply of cars given by C$_F$C$_A$, or to put it another way, an excess demand for wine, given by W$_F$W$_A$.

This would mean, that at terms of trade given by the slope of OT, the two countries together would be willing to offer CFCA of cars in exchange for WFWA of wine. If such an exchange took place with the two countries exporting cars and importing wine, then trade would balance and OT would become equilibrium terms of trade. Thus, we can plot one point on our excess offer curve corresponding to terms of trade of the slope of OT, this point having an x-co-ordinate given by the length of CFCA and a y-co-ordinate given by the length of WFWA (i.e. point T′ in the diagram). If we do the same for other terms of trade having values greater than the slope of OE, then we will trace out our excess-offer curve OT′C. This offer curve will show how much exports the two countries acting together (i.e. in a customs union free trade area) are willing to offer at different price ratios in exchange for imports from the outside world.

To show the effects of forming a customs union between France and the United States, suppose that both countries imposed tariffs on each other's imports and that the extent of these tariffs is given by the shift of their offer curves to the free trade positions after the formation of the customs union. This is illustrated below where OAc and OFc are the customs union offer curves of the two countries and OAT and OFT are the corresponding offer curves before removal of the tariffs.

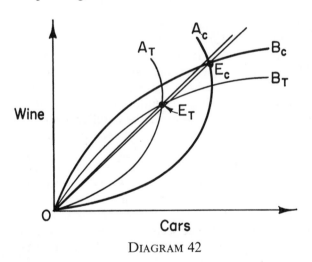

DIAGRAM 42

If the United States and France trade only with each other, then the equilibrium terms of trade before tariff removal would be given by the slope of OE_T; and after tariff removals, the terms of trade would become the slope of OE_C. This shift represents an improvement in the terms of trade for the United States and a deterioration for France.

However, given that the two countries will be trading with the outside world, the equilibrium terms of trade will be determined by the intersection of the free trade excess offer curve of the two countries and the offer curve of the rest of the world. This is shown below, where OC_T is the excess offer curve when tariffs are in force between the two countries and OX is the offer curve of the rest of the world.

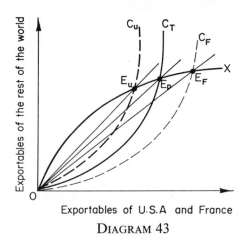

Exportables of U.S.A and France

DIAGRAM 43

E_P is therefore the equilibrium position before the formation of the union. Once the union is formed, trade between France and the United States is free, but a common tariff is imposed on imports from the rest of the world, and so the excess offer curve corresponding to the free trade positions of France and the United States (OCF) shifts leftwards to OCU, the extent of the shift depending on the size of the common external tariff. EU represents therefore the equilibrium position for the world after the formation of the union between France and the United States.

In the above situation the terms of trade for the union have improved in relation to the pre-union situation. (OEU is steeper than OEP). Within the union, the terms of trade, given by the slope of OEF, improve for France and deteriorate for the United States (OEP is steeper than OEF). It can also be seen from the diagram that the higher the tariff imposed by union members on outside imports, the more will OCF shift and the greater will be the extent of trade diversion. Note, also, that although the U.S. terms of trade deteriorate for intra-union trade, it will benefit from trade creation effects, exporting more to France than previously.

Note must be taken of the fact that only one side of the model has been analyzed, since in constructing our excess offer curve in Diagram 41 we only looked at what happened for price lines to the left of OE (i.e. improvements in the terms of trade for the United States). If the relevant price lines in trade with the outside world have slopes less steep than OE, then our excess offer curve will be concave to the x-axis; illustrating that the union would be willing to offer wine to the outside world in exchange for cars, because the outside world is such that they are trying to import wine and export cars.

The same sort of analysis can be used, however, except that the U.S terms of trade will improve and France's deteriorate.

Although the technique used above is very useful for illustrating the effects of union formation on trade with the outside world, it must be realized that it is an extremely simplified model and that too much should not be read into it. For instance, if the union is very small economically, then the offer curve of the outside world will be infinitely elastic, with the result that the union cannot alter the terms of trade by imposing a tariff on outside imports. Also, if the union promotes and allows a faster rise in productivity and output, then real incomes will rise and, depending on the propensities to import of the member countries, the demand for imports will rise and so tend to worsen the terms of trade for the union.[27] If trade diversion takes place, however, this will tend to improve the union's terms of trade by reducing the demand for imports from the outside world and also by lowering the supply of exports from the union to the outside world.

Thus, unless we specify the time period involved and the strengths and directions of the forces operating on the terms of trade, we cannot determine for certain in which direction the terms of trade will move as a result of the formation of a union. Nevertheless, to realize that these problems exist (as they do in most other fields of economic analysis) and to see what the variables are which are operating and being affected, is half the battle. The other half consists of empirically analyzing each case in order to determine the specific magnitudes of the relevant variables.

[1] See Meade, *op. cit.*

[2] R. G. Lipsey and K. Lancaster, "The General Theory of the Second Best," *Review of Economic Studies*, 1956–57.

[3] For an illustrative exposition of the theory of second best, see H. G. Johnson, *Money, Trade, and Economic Growth*, Unwin University Books, 1964, Ch. 3.

[4] A Free Trade Area removes tariffs and other trade restrictions amongst member countries, whilst each member retains its own traiff rates on imports from non-member countries (i.e. no C.E.T.).

[5] See, for example, R. L. Allen, *Integration in Less Developed Areas*, Kyklos, 1961.

[6] J. Vanek, *op. cit.*

[7] See, N. Kaldor, "Welfare Propositions in Economics," *Economic Journal*, 1939; J. R. Hicks, "The Foundations of Welfare Economics," *Economic Journal*, 1939.

Also, Scitovsky, "A Note on Welfare Propositions in Economics," *Review of Economic Studies*, Vol. 9.

[8] For a full discussion of this, see Vanek, *op. cit.*, Ch. IV (i).

[9] See Meade, op. cit., and Vanek, *op. cit.*

[10] R. G. Lipsey, "The Theory of Customs Unions: a General Survey," *Economic Journal*, 1960.

[11] Meade, *op. cit.*

[12] Students should note, as mentioned earlier, that Meade's method of evaluating gains and losses is subject to serious conceptual problems since, amongst other things, it assumes that all buyers and sellers in all countries have the same marginal utility of money income. For further discussion, see Vanek, *op. cit.*

[13] The following analysis follows closely that of Johnson, *Money, Trade, and Economic Growth*, 1964, pp. 53–56.

[14] It must be stressed that the above analysis depends on the assumptions that not only is utility measurable, but that the utilities of different individuals must be additive.

[15] See H. G. Johnson, "The Criteria of Economic Advantage," *Bulletin of the Oxford University Institute of Statistics*, 1957; also D. D. Humphrey and C. E. Ferguson, "The Domestic and World Benefits of a Customs Union," *Economia Internazionale*, 1960.

[16] See Johnson, *op. cit.*, p. 56.

[17] See Viner, *op. cit.*, p. 50, and Lipsey, *op. cit.*, pp. 498–99.

[18] See B. Balassa, *The Theory of Economic Integration*, 1961.

[19] On this complementarity : rivalry argument, see Balassa, *op. cit.*; Johnson, *op. cit.*, p. 57–58; Viner, *op. cit.*

[20] See Balassa, *op. cit.*, pp. 33–34; Johnson, *op. cit.*, p. 58.

[21] See W. Salant and others, *The U.S. Balance of Payments in* 1968, 1963.

[22] See Balassa, *op. cit.*, pp. 164–65; also Scitovsky, *Economic Theory and Western European Integration*, 1958.

[23] Scitovsky, *op. cit.*, pp. 19–48 and 110–135.

[24] For a diagramatic treatment of this point, see Johnson, *op. cit.*, pp. 59–61.

[25] C. P. Kindleberger, "The U.S. and European Regional Economic Integration," *Social Science*, 1959.

[26] J. Vanek, *op. cit.*, 1962 and 1964.

[27] See Scitovsky, *op. cit.*, pp. 70–74. For a theoretical treatment of the effects of a union on the terms of trade, see Mundell, "Tariff Preferences and the Terms of Trade," *Manchester School*, 1964.

CHAPTER 7

Balance of Payments

HAVING CONCERNED ourselves so far with the "real" forces operating in international trade, we must now analyze the effects of introducing monetary factors and see what problems arise. As we saw in Chapter 1, one of the major differences between international and domestic trade is that whereas domestic trade is carried on in a single currency, international trade involves the buying and selling of goods and services, etc., across national frontiers, and therefore necessitates the use of foreign currencies. In this and the following chapters, we shall examine the sort of problems which can arise as a result of this monetary phenomenon – the conversion of one national currency into other national currencies.

As we know, international trade is a two-way affair; countries both export and import, and as a result create a *flow* of goods, services and capital which, in turn, creates a *flow* of currency to pay for these "real" resources. Thus, when Britain exports cloth to the United States), and since this cloth must be paid for, it gives rise to a flow of money in the reverse direction. It is precisely this sort of economic transaction involving the flow of resources which gives rise to a demand for and supply of foreign exchange. The reasons why the people of one country wish to make payments to foreigners and foreigners wish to make payments to domestic residents are many. The export and import of goods and services constitute by far the major source of demand for and supply of foreign currency, but other sources also exist, It is these sources and the way in which the price of a foreign currency (i.e. its rate of exchange) is determined which we shall study in the latter part of this chapter.

Now, although we know that international transactions of the above sort give rise to monetary activities, if we are to build a more complete model of a country's international monetary relations then we require some method of condensing a country's various economic relations with the rest of the world. This can be done by drawing up a country's *Balance of Payments*, which is a summary record of a country's economic and financial transactions with the rest of the world over a certain period of time. Although the term balance of payments is traditionally used, it is an inaccurate title for a tabulation of a country's international transactions since it covers receipts as well as payments. The use of the term also emphasizes the balancing of accounting receipts and payments, and although this is one of the more important uses of a balance of payments, it is not its only use. Like many other tabulations, the balance of payments does not show cumulative totals, but only changes in the various accounts over the specified period which is usually a year. In other words, it is concerned with *flows*, unlike the Balance of Indebtedness which, as we shall see later, is concerned with *stocks* existing at a point in time.

Strictly defined, the balance of payments of a country is a systematic statistical record of all economic transactions during a specified period of time between the residents of the reporting country and those of the rest of the world. To fully understand what this means, we must clarify the terms "economic transactions" and "residents."

Economic transactions is defined by the I.M.F. as the provision of an economic value by one economic unit to another. That is, it is an exchange of value which consists of the transfer of title to an economic good or asset from one economic unit (person, group, firm, etc.) to another, or the rendering of an economic service from one unit to another. We can distinguish five types of economic transactions:

(*a*) the buying and selling of goods and services in exchange for financial assets (monetary gold and short-term liabilities in the form of money);

(*b*) the exchange of one type of financial asset for another (e.g. the sale of securities for money, or the repayment of a debt);

(*c*) the exchange of goods and services for other goods and services (i.e. barter);

(*d*) the provision or acquisition of goods and services without any corresponding exchange (e.g. grants to underdeveloped countries in the form of food or tractors);

(*e*) the provision or acquisition of financial assets without any corresponding exchange (e.g. gifts of money from the residents of one country to the residents of another).

It can be seen, therefore, that not all international transactions give rise to the payment and receipt of money (e.g. (*c*) and (*d*) above). There also exists a certain difference of opinion as to whether or not particular transactions should be included in the balance of payments. For instance, if the overseas branch of a company earns profits on its overseas business which it then ploughs back into the company, should the profits earned by entered in the credit side of the balance of payments and a corresponding debit entry made for overseas investment, thus leaving the overall balance of payments figures unchanged, or should no entries at all be made? As we shall see, the answer to these sorts of question can be affirmative or negative depending on the reason for asking the question in the first place.

Residents are defined by the I.M.F. in accordance with the concept of permanent place of living and general center of interest. For instance, persons are residents of the country where they *normally* reside, so that when on holiday abroad they are still, for balance of payments purposes, treated as being residents of the country where they normally reside. Similarly, the foreign subsidiary of a company resident in another country is a resident, for balance of payments purposes, of the country in which it is located. Inter-governmental organizations such as the I.M.F., I.B.R.D. and U.N. are not regarded as residents of any particular country, regardless of where they actually are located and operate. In the balance of payments, they are treated in a separate classification as international organizations, and transactions with them are considered to be with non-residents. Economically, it makes no difference how we treat such groups so long as we are consistent in our treatment of them.

Basically, the balance of payments is an analytical tool for the study of international economic relationships, although this was not always so, the trade accounts as used by the mercantilists being used to support their own subjective views. It is essentially aimed at providing information for the Government relating to a country's international operations, by showing the size and nature of its overseas economic transactions. The Government can then use this information to support or alter its economic policies. The balance of payments shows the pattern of a country's external economic relationships and, as time passes, it reveals changes which have taken place in them. The magnitudes involved in trade, government overseas expenditure, etc., can be compared with a country's other national accounts and show the proportion of output sent to and received from abroad. This ratio can also be compared with similar ratios for other countries and so arrive at the relative extent to which various countries engage in international economic transactions.

Changes in a country's debtor or creditor position over a year, the extent to which a country is giving or receiving aid and how this compares with the performance of other countries, can be gauged by a study of balance of payments statistics. When adjusted, it may indicate the impact of domestic policy measures on trade, capital flows, etc.; it may, in a crude way, reveal which parts of the balance of payments are giving, or likely to give, trouble. Knowing why the balance of payments is compiled and what can be gained by so doing, we can now study in greater detail the actual contents of the balance sheet.

Balance of Payments Construction. In theory, the balance of payments is constructed on the double-entry book-keeping procedure, every international transaction being classified as *both* a credit and a debit. We can demonstrate this sytem through a simple illustration involving two countries – the United States and Britain. What happens in the balance of payments of each country if the United States imports goods to the value of 1,000 dollars from Britain?

The initial effects can be shown in the table below –

TABLE 1

| | U.S.A. | | U.K. | |
	Debit	Credit	Debit	Credit
Trade	$1000			$1000

This, however, is only the first step. The British exporter must be paid by the U.S. importer; therefore, *offsetting transactions* occur in each country so that the sum of the credit items equals the sum of the debit items in each country. If the importer pays cash or receives credit from the exporter then the payment of credit represents a capital inflow for the United States and a capital outflow for Britain, the balances of payments now appearing as in Table 2.

TABLE 2

| | U.S.A. | | U.K. | |
	Debit	Credit	Debit	Credit
Trade	$1000			$1000
Capital		$1000	$1000	

Thus, the British export of goods is offset by an equivalent export of capital. What is most important to note here, is that capital exports give rise to debits, whereas capital imports give rise to credits. The capital export on Britain's part (i.e. the granting of credit to the United States or the acceptance of U.S. money) represents an increase in claims on foreigners or a reduction in liabilities to foreigners, so far as Britain is concerned. This increase in British *claims* on the United States (or the repayment of old liabilities) can be regarded as an asset which Britain has imported, and therefore must be classified as a debit item. Similarly, the United States has exported debt (which is an asset) and so this is classified as a credit. Thus, a decrease in claims on foreigners or an increase in liabilities to foreigners is a capital inflow and therefore a credit item in the balance of payments.

In practice, it is usually possible to gather information on only one side of a given transaction. So far as exports and imports of visible goods is concerned, there is little difficulty, but when it comes to capital movements, it is much more difficult to get data on both sides of the transactions (e.g. gifts) so that the possibility for errors creeping in is increased.

Thus, although in theory the balance of payments as constructed on the double-entry system must balance out to zero, in practice total debits and credits may differ, and so a balancing item called "Errors and Omissions" is added in order to balance the payments and receipts. In an *accounting* sense, therefore, the balance of payments always balances. This fact will be considered later in the chapter. Now, given that some international transactions which take place during the currency of the balance of payments do not involve any payments or receipts of cash either currently or later (e.g. gifts in kind or export credits), and given that each transaction is nevertheless labeled in the balance of payments as either a payment (debit) or receipt (credit), then whether or not a transaction is entered as a payment or receipt is obviously not determined by whether or not it involves an *actual* international payment. What, then, determines classification? The answer is that a *Payments* transaction is one which, *if it were settled in cash*, would lead to an outflow of money to other countries; a *Receipts* transaction is one which, *if it were settled in cash*, would lead to an inflow of money from abroad. Thus, whether or not *actual* cash settlements are made is irrelevant when classifying transactions. The logic of this system is that if a money payment is not made, then a substitute method of settlement must be found, which involves the international transfer of claims. Thus, payments transactions give rise to the creation of claims on a country, whilst receipts transactions give rise to the creation of claims against other countries.

Having discovered how to classify all transactions, we can now look at the sub-accounts in the balance of payments.

(i) The first main sub-account is the *Current (Goods and Services) Account*, which covers all transactions involving the flow of goods and services between the reporting country and the rest of the world. Thus, all merchandise trade is included, exports and imports of *visible* goods being valued, under present-day I.M.F. procedures, on an f.o.b. or f.a.s. basis. Although some difficulties may arise in the valuation of visible exports and imports (e.g. the values placed on goods moving from a foreign branch of a firm to its domestic patent may be valued rather arbitrarily), generally speaking merchandise trade is fairly easily dealt with. Any difference which exists between the Credits and Debits for Visible Exports and imports is called the *Balance of Trade* – if the debits exceed the credits, this is normally termed an unfavorable balance of trade, if the reverse holds, it is a favorable balance. Though merchandise trade accounts for the major part of the current account for most countries (there are exceptions, such as Norway), the rest of the account can constitute an important element, as in the case of the United States and Britain.[1] This is the so-called *Invisible Account* which covers such items as insurance, freight, royalties on books and films, banking services, tourist payments and receipts, interest on loans, dividends on shares, private transfers, etc. Certain categories of governmental transactions are also included in the invisibles account, such as receipts from foreign armies based in the reporting country, grants to underdeveloped countries, reparations payments, etc. Some economists hold the view that reparations payments and government grants should not be included in the Current Account since they are capital movements; the I.M.F., however, follows the rule that genuine capital movements give rise to or eliminate a claim, whereas reparations and grants are once and for all payments and therefore a special category of transfer payments which should be included in the Current Account.

For various reasons, the Current Account can be regarded as the most basic of all the sub-accounts. Firstly, because of its relative size compared with other sub-accounts; secondly because it contains all transactions which give rise to or use up a country's national income; and thirdly, because even long-term capital movements (which perform an important autonomous role in the international economy) can be effected ultimately only via movement of real goods and services.

(ii) The second sub-account is the *Capital Account*, which covers debts and claims payable in money or themselves constituting money. It contains, gross, all changes in claims on or of a country owed by or owed to the rest of the world. Thus, if a resident invests or loans money abroad, then the rest of the world has a claim against that resident, who, in turn has an equivalent asset (the shares or promise to repay the loan). Similarly, changes in the bank balances held by residents in foreign banks and changes in the bank balances held by foreigners in domestic banks are included in the Capital Account. Thus, the Capital Account is concerned with changes in the claims of residents on overseas residents and changes in the liabilities of residents to overseas residents.

If we use our previously discovered method for classifying all international transactions, then we shall note an important point, since all capital transactions (long or short, governmental or private) involve flows of capital (either actual or potential). Thus we can classify immediately all capital outflows as *debits* and all capital inflows as *credits*. This important point often confuses the student who tends to look at a capital outflow (inflow) as an export (import) which should therefore be classified as a credit (debit). However, as we have seen, it is the direction of potential (or actual) *cash* flows which is important. Another way of classifying transactions is to look at the potential (or actual) effects of the transaction on the quantity of domestic and foreign currencies supplied. Any transaction leading to a rise in the quantity of domestic currency supplied is treated as a debit, and any transaction leading to a rise in the quantity of foreign currency supplied is a credit.

The Capital Account may be sub-divided into *Long-Term* Capital and *Short-Term* Capital: long-term involving all movements of ownership instruments with a maturity of more than one year, short-term involving all movements of ownership instruments of less than one year's maturity. Thus, long-term capital consists mainly of transactions in equities, loans, bonds, real estate, whereas short-term capital is mainly bank deposits, acceptances, drafts. Long-term capital movements involve the international transfer of purchasing power, which provides the means of financing a net flow of goods and services from the lending or investing country to the rest of the world. Short-term capital movements can normally be regarded as being *induced* (i.e. not autonomous) by other balance of payments transactions in the sense that they operate so as to temporarily fill in any gaps between the total receipts and payments on other transactions. Thus, if other imports exceed exports, the difference may be "made up" by drawing down foreign bank balances held by residents, or by paying domestic currency which is added to domestic bank balances held by foreigners, or by obtaining short-term foreign credits (i.e. short-term loans). In each case, a short-term capital movement takes place involving the transfer of claims and debts.

The Capital Account may also be divided into *Official* and *Private* accounts on the basis that private capital flows normally take place in order to make a profit or avoid a loss (e.g. buying and selling of shares), whereas official capital flows may be induced responses to changes which are taking place elsewhere in the balance of payments (e.g. changes in officially held balances of short-term assets).

(iii) The third major sub-account is the *Monetary Gold Account*, which includes all movements of gold between countries out of and into official monetary reserves. Gold exported from the monetary gold reserves are treated as exports and therefore as a credit, whereas gold imports are a debit. A great deal of interest attaches to this account, however, because for most countries, gold stocks (along with convertible currency reserves), constitute a reserve which may be used to buy additional foreign exchange, since gold is readily convertible into any national currency at a fixed price. Gold and convertible currency reserves are normally only drawn upon (or added to) in order to cover a payments deficit (surplus) in all other sub-accounts combined. It may be regarded, therefore, as an official compensating capital-type movement used to settle residual international payments. (Note that the gold need not be physically transferred, earmarking is sufficient.) Note also that if a gold-producing country, such as South Africa sells the gold to the Central Monetary Authorities, the buying is recorded in the balance of payments as a debit on monetary account and the selling as a credit on merchandise account (even although no *international* transactions have taken place). If the gold is later exported (to cover an imbalance in the balance of payments), then the export will be recorded as a credit on monetary gold account. If initially the gold had been sold direct to foreigners, the final effect is the same; South Africa experiences a credit on merchandise account, whilst the recipients of the gold experience a debit on monetary gold account. This means, however, that for the world as a whole, exports exceed imports by the amount of newly mined gold exported from the gold producers.

As we saw earlier, since the balance of payments is constructed on a double-entry based book-keeping system, the sum of credit items must exactly equal the sum of debit items (if the actual and estimated records of transactions fail to match exactly, the "balancing item," Errors and Omissions, will see that they do). Thus, the concept of a *surplus* (credits exceeding debits), or *deficit* (debits exceeding credits) on the balance of payments *in toto* is mathematically impossible – it must always balance. This is not to say, however, that any single sub-account or group of sub-accounts cannot show a surplus or deficit; in fact, it would be highly unlikely that balance *within* the balance of payments should prevail everywhere. Clearly, then, balance in the whole balance of payments tells us nothing about a country's international position, since balance must at all times prevail. To learn of a country's international economic performance, one must look at the individual sub-accounts and analyze the causes of any surpluses and deficits which may be present.

Hence, we can see that the equality of total credits and debits is the same as a zero algebraic sum of the balances in the separate sub-accounts, so that large imbalances can exist within individual sub-accounts, so long as they are exactly offset by imbalances of opposite sign in the other accounts. Thus, a surplus on Current Account may be offset partly or completely by a deficit on Capital Account (e.g. by lending or investing overseas). If the offset is only partial, then the total balance will be achieved by having a deficit on Gold Account of the required size. It is possible, therefore, for the terms "surplus" and "deficit" to be used to refer to any single sub-account or group of sub-accounts – in the latter case above, the Current Account was in surplus, the overall Current and Capital Accounts were also in surplus, whilst the gold account was in deficit. Nevertheless, one tends to regard the U.S. balance of payments as being in deficit (as is the case with the U.K.), whilst Germany, on the other hand, one tends to think of as being in surplus. How can we make economic sense of such views when we know that any country's balance of payments can, *overall*, neither be in surplus nor deficit? The answer is that what is called surplus or deficit is a matter of definition. When we use the terms in the above way (e.g. by saying that the U.S. balance of payments was in deficit in 1967) we are using the terms in a special restricted way; we have consciously selected certain sub-accounts and attributed *their* balance to the *whole* balance of payments. Thus, surpluses or deficits are defined in terms of certain groupings of items within balance of payments accounts.

The measurement of surpluses and deficits is based on a division of the balance of payments into two sections – one *above the line* (or substantive) and the other *below the line* (or balancing). The deficit or surplus is thought of as arising in the accounts above the line, and being *financed* (or balanced) by the accounts below the line. Since, obviously, either the surplus (deficit) above the line or the corresponding deficit (surplus) below the line could be used to describe the overall balance of payments, it is entirely convention that the substantive accounts (i.e. above the line measurements) are used for this purpose. Thus, if a country has a deficit on Current and Capital Accounts taken together, one would normally refer to the balance of payments as being in deficit, and expect to see a corresponding surplus on Monetary Gold Account (i.e. below the line). However, gold is not the only item put below the line; short-term reserve assets used to measure the surplus or deficit include *net* changes in deposits in foreign banks and liabilities of domestic banks, in accumulations of foreign currencies and foreign ownership of domestic currency, in holdings of and liabilities in short-term bank and commercial paper, in drawing rights in the I.M.F., and I.M.F. holdings of domestic currency, etc. Generally such items along with gold are classified as balancing and may be further classified according to type of assets and type of owner. One should note, however, that not all countries measure surpluses and deficits by including exactly the same items, though all include changes in the gold and foreign exchange assets of monetary institutions. The United States, Germany and Japan, for example, do not include below the line changes in foreign exchange assets of private commercial banks; France is unusual in including below the line changes in the holdings of foreign exchange assets of the non-monetary and non-bank sectors. Also, although the United States is normal in including below the line changes in the liquid liabilities of the commercial banks and non-monetary sector, she is unusual in excluding changes in the *assets* of the non-monetary sector.[2] When we come to consider where to put Errors and Omissions we find that, as yet, no general agreement exists on this point, although obviously if errors and omissions are sizeable, where they are put is seriously going to affect the size of the overall balance of payments.[3] To classify them logically would require a study of where exactly the errors and omissions have occurred and then to apportion the account accordingly. Since the size and permanence of a country's balance of payments surplus or deficit will have important implications for economic policy (e.g. large deficits may lead to speculation against a currency and disturbances in the flow of trade; countries highly competitive in export markets may try to minimize the size of their published surpluses, etc.), then the method used of measuring surpluses and deficits is a matter of great national importance. The same sort of considerations apply when trying to determine which assets a country should include in its reserves which are available for the defence of its currency. Thus, if the monetary authorities of a country can get hold of the liquid foreign exchange assets of its commercial banks, it may include them in its reserves; on the other hand, it may, except in times of war, be virtually impossible to acquire non-bank holdings of gold and foreign exchange, in which case these assets will be left out of reserve calculations. Most countries, however, include in reserves gold and official foreign exchange holdings and I.M.F. drawing rights (distinguishing between automatic and conditional rights). An important point to note here is that both the United States and Britain view the liquid liabilities of the commercial banks and non-monetary sector as below the line items, but the United States views the assets of these sectors to be above the line items, since it does not consider it to be easy to acquire such assets, although the liabilities of these sectors do affect the U.S. reserves position.[4] As Poul Høst-Madsen points out,[5] such asymmetries among nations can lead to sizeable differences in the totals of surpluses and deficits for the world as a whole. In fact, during 1959–60, these asymmetries caused the total deficits of U.S.A., U.K., Japan and nine European industrial nations to exceed their total surpluses by up to one billion dollars.

To help overcome such problems and achieve a certain degree of uniformity, more and more economists are using the concepts of *basic balance* and *overall balance*. According to this method, balance of payments accounts are divided into two major groups, one measuring the basic balance, the other the overall balance. In the basic balance are put Current Account and Long-Term Capital Account items, the so-called *fundamental* transactions, whilst the overall balance contains short-term capital, monetary gold and errors and omissions, the so-called financing transactions. The origin of this method lies in the report of the 1961 Kennedy Task-Force on Balance of Payments, which argued that the purpose of so dividing the balance of payments accounts was to discover if the U.S. surplus on Current Account was big enough to cover U.S. loans and grants to overseas countries. Thus, the basic balance is the Current Account surplus (deficit) minus the Long-Term Capital outflow (inflow); the overall balance is basic balance plus errors and omissions and net short-term movements (including gold). The overall balance, therefore, is the net change in gold and short-term liabilities to foreigners required in order to ensure that total credits equal total debits. In recent years, the U.S. Department of Commerce has introduced balance of payments presentations using the basic and overall concepts, although they have included certain types of short-term capital as well as errors and omissions in the basic balance.[6] A great deal of discussion, especially in the United States, has centered round this problem of what is the "correct" measure to use for balance of payments surpluses or deficits.

Such discussion has become increasingly evident since the United States began, in 1958, to run large balance of payments deficits, at least, as reported in official statistics at the time. Certain economists argue that the current method of measuring surpluses and deficits tends to exaggerate the size of the actual deficit which might lead the U.S. Government to adopt corrective measures not really required, and this could have serious repercussions on the domestic economy. Also, exaggeration of U.S. deficits, if they persist, could strengthen any speculative pressures upon the dollar and cause heavy purchases from the U.S. gold stock. The current method used by the United States is based on the idea that the United States must be in a position to maintain the dollar exchange rate and maintain the international liquidity quality of the dollar. According to Lederer of the Department of Commerce, therefore, the U.S. short-term *liquidity* position is the best measure of the ability of the authorities to defend the dollar.[7] We should not, Lederer argues, net out changes in the short-term liabilities of the U.S. to foreign *private* banks and other holders against changes in the short-term assets (claims) of U.S. *private* residents on foreigners, because such assets are not readily available to the authorities for the defense of the currency. *Official* short-term assets should, however, be netted against *official* short-term liabilities; and foreign holdings of U.S. Government bonds should be added to U.S. liquid liabilities, since such bonds are held as reserves, not as long-term investments, and could therefore be cashed in at short notice. The current practice corresponds to Lederer's ideas and can be considered as being a measure composed of two groups of assets and liabilities:

(1) *Liabilities of U.S.* – short-term official and banking liabilities and foreign holdings of marketable U.S. Government bonds and notes.

(*a*) Foreign private holders including banks, international and regional organizations, but excluding the I.M.F.

(*b*) Foreign official holders.

(2) *Assets of U.S. monetary authorities.*

(*a*) I.M.F. position.

(*b*) Gold.

(*c*) Convertible currency holdings.

Some economists dispute that current U.S. practice is ideal and that alternative concepts are superior.[8] For example, as indicated earlier, Hal Lary wants to divide transactions on the basis of *their sensitivity to monetary policy*, putting those items which are sensitive to monetary policy below the line (i.e. essentially, quickly available to combat a potentially enormous movement of liquid claims against the dollar). Using this concept, U.S. short-term private assets are put below the line instead of above the line as with the Department of Commerce liquidity measure, leading to differing magnitudes for surpluses and deficits. Thus, during 1960–61, the liquidity measure gave a deficit of 3.2 billion dollars, whilst the sensitivity measure showed a deficit of only 1.2 billion dollars. Another economist, Walter R. Gardner, formerly chief of the I.M.F.'s Balance of Payments Division, has proposed the use of an *Exchange-Market Balance* concept which comprises the basic balance (defined by Gardner as the Current Account together with direct investments and non-commercial transactions such as government aid, military expenditures, etc.), and Open-Market Capital Account consisting of portfolio securities, short-term capital and errors and omissions. The Exchange-Market Balance, then, measures the surplus or deficit of the United States, this imbalance being offset in the final account (called *Compensatory Financing*), which includes gold, United States loans, I.M.F. dollar assets and other official dollar assets.

Essentially, then, Gardiner wants to divide the balance of payments into two sections, one dealing with autonomous transactions (i.e. ones which take place independently of other transactions in the balance of payments) and the other with compensating transactions (i.e. ones which take place because of other transactions failing to balance out exactly).[9] Another suggestion has been put forward by the

Review Committee for Balance of Payments Statistics,[10] namely that the present liquidity measure be replaced by the "balance settled by official transactions." This official settlements concept differs from the liquidity concept chiefly in its treatment of short-term capital movements, the effect of which is to minimize the deficits and exaggerate the surpluses.

As we saw earlier, the liquidity (i.e. Department of Commerce) measure puts *private* short-term assets of U.S. residents above, and *private* short-term liabilities of U.S. banks and other residents below the line. The official settlements measure puts *all* private short-term transactions above the line. The difference may well be significant, as can be seen by comparing the size of surpluses and deficits as measured by both concepts. Thus, in 1954, both measures showed a deficit of 1.5 billion dollars, whereas in 1959 the liquidity measure gave a deficit of 4.2 billion dollars, whilst the official settlements measure gave a deficit of 2.5 billion dollars, a difference of 1.7 billion dollars. The official settlements measure can be seen to be based on a division of the accounts not according to the liquidity of the assets but according to the nature of the foreign holders (i.e. between the official monetary authorities and private individuals and firms).

No doubt the bewildered student will be wondering which of these various measures is the correct one to use! The problem is that there is no single measure which can be regarded as being *the* correct one which is right for all problems; each measure has its strength and weaknesses which will be more or less important depending upon the questions to which the analyst is trying to find answers. There is no such thing as *the* balance of payments – differences in presenting the accounts, in classifying transactions and in interpreting the results can take many forms (as we have seen), all of which may be valid so long as they are meaningful for the questions being asked about a country's international economic transactions.[11]

A concept related to the balance of payments is the *Balance of Indebtedness* which, however, unlike the balance of payments, is concerned with *stocks* of assets at a point in time. It is a statement of the total claims (assets) of a country's residents on the rest of the world, and the total liabilities (foreign assets) of these residents to the rest of the world. The following table gives some idea of the position of the United States.

As can be seen, the problem which the United States faces is not one of solvency (1964 overall claims exceeded overall liabilities by almost 42 billion dollars) but of liquidity (1964 short-term claims fell short of short-term liabilities by almost 18 billion dollars). Also, if one looks at Britain assets exceeded total liabilities by 5 billion dollars, whereas

TABLE 3

INTERNATIONAL INVESTMENT POSITION OF THE UNITED STATES $M

	1950	1960 ($b.)	1964
U.S. Assets and Investment Abroad	31,539	71·4	98,720
Private	19,004	50·3	75,419
Long-Term	17,488	45·4	64,731
Short-Term	1,516	4·9	10,688
U.S. Government	12,535	21·1	23,301
Long-Term	10,768	18·2	18,772
Short-Term	322	2·9	3,328
Foreign Investments and Assets in U.S.	17,635	44·7	56,842
Long-Term	7,997	18·4	24,979
Short-Term	9,638	26·2	31,863
U.S. Net Creditor Position	13,904	26·7	41,858
Long-Term	20,259	45·2	58,524
Short-Term	−7,800	−18·4	−17,847

Source: Department of Commerce Survey of Business, 1965.

short-term liabilities exceeded short-term assets by 7.2 billion dollars, in 1965.

The balance of indebtedness is, however, a fairly crude measure of a country's international creditor position, because firstly there is no internal check on the size of errors and omissions, due to the fact that the balance of indebtedness is not constructed on a double-entry book-keeping system, and secondly it is extremely difficult to value the assets and liabilities in a rigorous fashion since no method exists for determining whether book-values should be used, market values, or values which could be realized in a quick sale. Thus, although the balance of indebtedness is an interesting concept, it is not a particularly useful tool for analysis of international economic problems.

Now, it should be obvious that the balance of payments is essentially a monetary phenomenon which is largely reflected in foreign exchange markets. In these markets the means of making payments abroad are bought and sold, and prices (i.e. rates of exchange) established, which prices can be regarded as the links between national currencies, enabling price and cost comparisons to be made. A *rate of exchange* is a price – the price of a unit of foreign currency in terms of domestic currency. A rise in the rate of exchange means that more domestic currency is required to purchase a unit of foreign currency, which means that the *international* value of domestic currency has fallen – it has *depreciated*. Similarly, a fall in the rate of exchange means that less domestic currency is required to purchase a unit of foreign currency, which means that the *international* value of domestic currency has risen – it has *appreciated*. The foreign exchange market, then, is a market for the buying and selling of foreign currencies and the prices established will be determined, like all prices, by the interaction of demand and supply. To help us understand the following chapters it might be useful to think of balance of payments transactions as giving rise to a demand for or supply of foreign exchange. Thus visible exports, capital imports, invisible receipts, gold sales, etc., will all give rise to the payment by foreigners of domestic currency to domestic residents. To get hold of this domestic currency, the foreigners will have exchanged their own currencies – in other words, the supply of foreign currencies increases whilst the demand for domestic currency rises. Similarly, visible imports, capital exports, invisible payments, gold buying, etc., all give rise to the payment by domestic residents of foreign currency to foreigners. The domestic residents, to get hold of the foreign currencies, will have exchanged domestic currency – that is, increased the supply of domestic currency and raised the demand for foreign currencies. These effects will react on the exchange rate with consequent policy effects to be discussed later. Two points should be noted: first, not all balance of payments transactions involve the acquisition of foreign exchange or the supply of domestic currency (e.g. gifts) and, secondly, not all foreign exchange transactions appear in the balance of payments (e.g. the sale of foreign exchange by one firm to another).[12] The foreign exchange market operates primarily in the transfer internationally of purchasing power but, for our purposes, the means of effecting the transfer are not important; it is sufficient to remember that these transfers are carried out by the simultaneous clearing, on a multilateral basis, of debts and claims. This is the basic function of the market – the clearing of the demand for and supply of foreign exchange, thus effecting payment into and out of a country.[13]

Now, in order to develop a theory of foreign-exchange rates, let us assume, for the sake of simplicity, a two-country model, where all partial foreign-exchange markets can be merged into a single market with one currency being bought and the other currency acting as "money." Like all prices determined by the market, exchange rates will tend to settle where the aggregate quantity of foreign exchange demanded equals the aggregate quantity supplied. It follows, therefore, that in our theory of exchange-rate determination, we must analyze the sources of supply and demand, and also the effects of changes in the parameters of the supply and demand functions. Initially, let us assume that the monetary authorities do not intervene to artificially fix or alter exchange rates (e.g. by buying or selling gold), and that the only factor affecting the supply or demand for foreign exchange is commodity trade. We therefore rule out, for the moment, foreign lending and borrowing, unilateral transfers, etc. (which we shall reintroduce at a later point), and study commodity trade in isolation.

The *demand schedule for foreign exchange* relates the various quantities of foreign exchange which will be demanded at different exchange rates (i.e. different prices), and since we are considering only commodity trade, we can say that the demand for foreign exchange is a derived demand, derived from the demand for imports.

In turn, the demand for imports will be related in the normal way to the price of imports domestically, which price will be determined by the rate of exchange in conjunction with the price of imports as expressed in foreign currency. We would, therefore, expect changes in the rate of exchange, other things remaining equal, to cause changes in the domestic price of imports and so in the quantity of imports demanded. A rise in the exchange rate (i.e. a rise in the price of foreign currency) makes imports more expensive in terms of domestic currency and, therefore, the quantity of imports demanded will fall. In this way, variations in the exchange rate will be inversely related to variations in the quantity of imports demanded – that is, the demand curve for *foreign-exchange* will be inversely related to the exchange rate and so have the normal shape for demand curves. The elasticity of demand for foreign exchange will be the same as the elasticity of demand for the actual imports, as can be seen from the following example:

Foreign   At a rate of exchange of £1 = $3, domestic price is $60
Currency   ,, ,, ,, ,,   ,,   ,, £1 = $2.5 ,,   ,, ,, $50
Price   ,, ,, ,, ,,   ,,   ,, £1 = $2   ,,   ,, ,, $40
= £20

At a price of $60, suppose 100 units are demanded.
,, ,, ,,   ,, $50   ,,   120 ,,   ,,   ,,
,, ,, ,,   ,, $40   ,,   140 ,,   ,,   ,,

Then, quantity of foreign-exchange demanded when the rate of exchange is £1 = $3   is £2,000
    £1 = $2.5 is £2,400
    £1 = $2   is £2,800

Now, elasticity of demand for imports over range $60–$50 is 1
    ,,   ,, $50–$40 is 9/13
and elasticity of demand for foreign exchange over range $3–$2.5 is 1
    ,,   ,, $2.5–$2 is 9/13

Thus, the elasticity of demand for foreign exchange is an exact reflection of the elasticity of demand for imports.

Turning now to the supply side, the *supply schedule of foreign exchange* has as its source the *foreign demand* for our imports, and therefore the forces which determine the foreign demand for our exports will also determine the supply of foreign exchange. Now,.other things remaining equal, the demand for our imports will be a function of the price (expressed in foreign currency) of these imports. If the exchange rate rises, our exports will become cheaper in terms of foreign currency and so the quantity of exports demanded will rise, giving us again a normal demand curve for our exports. Given this relationship between the price of exports and the quantity demanded, we can see that the derived demand for the exporter's currency (which we are regarding as the domestic currency) will be of the normal type. From this derived demand for domestic currency, the supply of foreign currency can be found by simply multiplying the quantity of domestic currency demanded by the rate of exchange. Note, however, that if the demand for our exports is inelastic over a range, the supply of foreign exchange will *fall* as the exchange rates rises and this will mean that part of the supply curve of foreign exchange will be negatively sloped. The implications of this will be discussed presently.

Having derived the demand and supply curves for foreign exchange, we can bring them together as shown below.

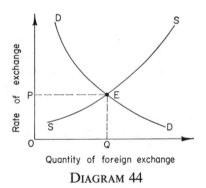

DIAGRAM 44

At E, the market is in equilibrium, OQ foreign exchange being demanded and supplied at the rate of exchange OP. The volume of exports is OPEQ pounds which is also equal to the volume of imports. Thus, in equilibrium, when we rule out everything but commodity trade, the balance of trade must be zero. This will apply even if the supply of foreign exchange were completely inelastic (as it might be in the very short-run). For example, if the demand for imports were suddenly to expand to D_1D_1, the rate of exchange would rise to OP_1.

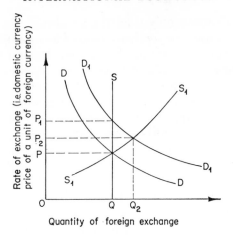

Quantity of foreign exchange

DIAGRAM 45

In the short-run, however, export orders will increase and the relevant supply curve will become S_1S_1, going a higher equilibrium level of exports and imports at a higher exchange rate OP_2.

It should be obvious that the basics of foreign exchange-rate theory lies in the study of the *elasticities* of the demand and supply curves for foreign exchange, which requires a study of the forces affecting the demand for and supply of foreign exchange.

First of all, let us look at the factors affecting the relation between the rate of exchange and the quantity of exports demanded. We know from our analysis above that the more elastic the demand for exports the more elastic the supply of foreign exchange will be, and that an inelastic demand for exports leads to an inverse relationship between the supply of foreign exchange and the exchange rate. However, it is only under exceptional circumstances that the sole factor affecting the supply of foreign exchange will be the demand for exports. For instance, suppose that the product which we export is also produced by the importing country as a very close substitute, so that there is virtually only one price for "the" product. Now, if the exchange rate rises, the price of our exports will fall, and let us assume that the demand for our exports is inelastic so that although there is an increase in the quantity of exports demanded, it is less than proportional to the fall in price. But the price received by foreign suppliers will also have fallen and, therefore, it is likely that they will cut back supply accordingly, depending upon the elasticity of their supply curve. The unsatisfied demand thus created can find expression by operating on *our* exports, so that the more elastic is the foreign supply of the product, the greater will be our gain as a result of the cutback in production. Thus, although the *ceteris paribus* demand for our exports is inelastic, its inelasticity will be reduced through the production effects in the foreign country. We can say, therefore, that the elasticity of supply of foreign exchange (i.e. the elasticity of demand for our exports) will be higher, the higher the elasticity of supply of foreign products which compete with our exports. In this example, the elasticity of demand for our exports would be elastic, anyway, given the closeness in the substitutability of the two products. Two other factors which will affect the elasticity of supply of foreign currency are (*a*) the elasticity of supply of our exports and (*b*) the elasticity of home demand for our export products.

Let us consider the effects of varying the *elasticity of supply* of our exports, ignoring the effects of the elasticity of supply of foreign substitutes.

If the supply of our exports is perfectly elastic, the domestic currency value of our exports will rise following a rise in the exchange rate, but the effect on the foreign currency value of our exports will be determined by the elasticity of demand for our exports.

This can be illustrated in the following way.

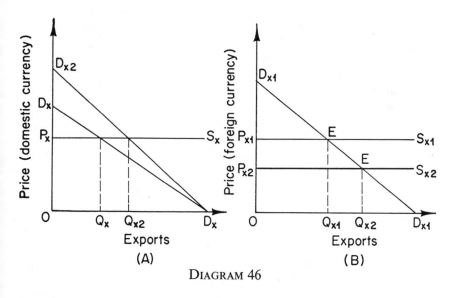

DIAGRAM 46

In (A) DxDx represents the foreign demand for our exports at varying prices expressed in terms of domestic currency and PxSx is the supply curve for our exports. Similarly in (B) Dx_1Dx_1 and Px_1Sx_1 are the demand and supply curves for our exports in terms of foreign currency prices. Now, if the exchange rate rises by x%, then DxDx will shift upwards by x% to Dx_2Dx, but the supply curve will not shift since exporters are only interested in the domestic currency price they get for their exports. Importers, on the other hand, are only interested in the foreign currency price they have to pay for their imports, which means that a rise in the exchange rate will cause the demand for our exports (in terms of domestic currency prices) to shift upwards by a constant percentage amount as shown. Dx_1Dx_1 does not shift (since we have assumed that tastes, etc., remain unchanged throughout this analysis) but Px_1Sx_1 shifts downwards to Px_2Sx_2, since at the higher exchange rate a given price in foreign currency represents a higher price in domestic currency.

At the new equilibrium positions, OQx_2 units of exports are exported bringing in foreign exchange of $OQx_2E_2Px_2$ compared with a previous amount of OQx_1EPx_1. Whether the new quantity of foreign exchange supplied is greater or less than previously will depend upon the elasticity of demand for our exports. If, as in the above example, the demand were elastic, then the supply of foreign exchange would increase as the exchange rate rises. If the demand were inelastic, then the foreign currency value of our exports would fall, following a rise in the exchange rate. Let us assume now that the relevant section of the demand curve for our exports is elastic. What happens to foreign exchange receipts if we vary the elasticity of the supply curve?

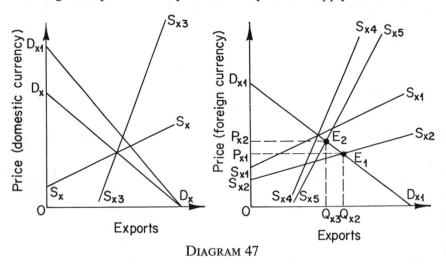

DIAGRAM 47

If the supply curve is elastic ($SxSx$ and Sx_1Sx_1) a given rise in the rate of exchange will lower the curve Sx_1Sx_1 to Sx_2Sx_2 by a constant percentage amount, and foreign exchange earnings will become $OQx_2E_1Px_1$. If the supply curve Sx_3Sx_3, and Sx_4Sx_4 is inelastic, then a rise in the rate of exchange will shift Sx_4Sx_4 downwards to Sx_5Sx_5 and foreign exchange earnings become $OQx_3E_2Px_2$.

Now it can be seen that, because the demand curve is elastic, the new quantity of foreign exchange supplied after the rise in the exchange rate will be greater than originally, no matter what the elasticity of supply is (except that when the supply curve has zero elasticity, the supply of foreign-exchange will be unchanged). However, given an elastic demand for our exports, the supply of foreign exchange, in response to exchange-rate alterations, will be higher, the higher the elasticity of supply of our exports. Following the same sort of argument, it is possible to show that if the demand for our exports is inelastic, then a rise in the rate of exchange will cause a fall in the supply of foreign exchange and that the extent of the fall will be greater the greater the elasticity of supply of our exports. That is, the elasticity of supply of foreign exchange will be greater the lower the elasticity of supply of our exports. We can see, then, how important supply elasticities are when considering the effect of exchange rate variation on the supply of foreign exchange.

It is interesting to note that supply elasticities in the export industries may not be affected solely by production conditions (i.e. the physical ease with which output can be expanded following a rise in the rate of exchange) but will be influenced to some extent by the *domestic* demand (if any exists) for the goods being exported. Thus, let us suppose that the "production" elasticity of supply of exports is inelastic. This means that, following a rise in the rate of exchange, the *domestic currency* price of our exports will rise by a greater amount than had supply been elastic. Now, following the rise in the domestic price of our exports, the domestic consumption of these goods will fall by an amount determined by the elasticity of domestic demand for our exports. If the domestic demand is fairly elastic, the output released by the price increase may be sufficient to turn the inelastic "production" supply curve into an elastic "output" supply curve. We can say, therefore, that the elasticity of supply of foreign exchange will be higher the higher the elasticity of domestic demand for our exports since the greater the elasticity of domestic demand, the greater the elasticity of supply of exports. If the foreign demand for our exports is inelastic, however, then the elasticity of supply of foreign-exchange will be higher the lower the elasticity of domestic demand for our exports.

So far we have analyzed only the supply curve of foreign exchange and so it is now time to turn to a consideration of the factors affecting the *demand curve* for foreign exchange. As we shall see, the demand for foreign exchange will be determined by the same set of forces which determined the supply of foreign exchange. On the supply side we found that the elasticity was determined by four main factors:

(*a*) the elasticity of demand for our exports;
(*b*) the elasticity of supply of foreign articles competing with our exports;
(*c*) the elasticity of "production" supply of exportables;
(*d*) the elasticity of domestic demand for the goods exported (i.e. the elasticity of "output" supply of exportables).

We shall find correspondingly that, on the demand side, the elasticity of demand for foreign exchange is determined by the same class of forces.

Firstly, the higher the elasticity of demand for the goods which we import, the higher will be the elasticity of demand for foreign exchange.

Secondly, the higher the elasticity of supply of domestic goods which compete in the domestic market with the goods which we import, the higher will be the elasticity of demand for foreign exchange. Suppose, for example, that the domestic demand for importables is perfectly inelastic and the rate of exchange falls. The result is that imports become cheaper in terms of domestic currency and therefore, to compete with imports, the price of domestically produced substitutes will have to fall. Now, if the elasticity of supply of domestic substitutes is high, then the market share abandoned by domestic producers will go to imports and so the quantity of imports will rise by more than if the elasticity of supply of domestic substitutes had been low. In this way the elasticity of demand for foreign exchange will be affected to a greater or lesser extent.

Thirdly, the higher the elasticity of "production" supply of imports, the higher will be the elasticity of demand for foreign exchange. If the elasticity of "production" supply is infinite, then a fall in the rate of exchange will make imports cheaper in terms of domestic currency and so the demand for imports will increase. Foreign producers of our imports will be able to meet the increased demand without altering price by expanding along their infinitely elastic supply curve. However, had their supply curve been perfectly inelastic, they would have been unable to expand production and so the price of imports in terms of foreign currency would have risen by an amount sufficient to offset the effects of the lower price of foreign currency. This would have lowered the elasticity of demand for foreign exchange.

Fourthly, the higher the elasticity of the foreign demand for the goods we import, the higher will be the elasticity of demand for foreign exchange. Suppose, for example, that following a fall in the price of foreign currency, foreign producers are unable to expand production, so that, as above, the foreign currency price of the goods increases. As a result the foreign demand for these articles will be choked off to a greater or lesser extent (depending on the elasticity of foreign demand) and thus release some production for *our* market. In this way, the elasticity of "output" supply will be increased and this will influence the elasticity of demand for foreign exchange.

We can see now how the various forces affect the elasticity of demand for and supply of foreign exchange. So far, however, we have concerned ourselves solely with commodity trade. We shall now remedy this to a certain extent by analyzing the effects of introducing long-term capital movements and invisible services.[14]

Initially, let us assume that a demand for foreign exchange on the part of capital exporters (e.g. for overseas investment) does not alter the demand for and supply of foreign exchange due to commodity trade.

Thus, suppose that the commodity trade situation is as depicted below, with DD the demand for foreign exchange and SS the supply of foreign exchange.

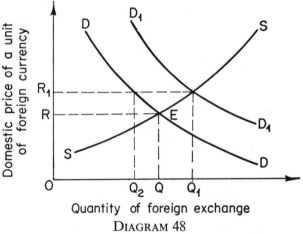

Quantity of foreign exchange

DIAGRAM 48

OR would be the equilibrium rate of exchange and exports would equal imports both in terms of foreign and domestic currencies. Now suppose that a demand for foreign exchange arises in order to invest capital overseas. We can add this demand to the original demand curve to get D_1D_1, the aggregate demand curve. The effect of this is to drive up the rate of exchange to OR_1, but note what has happened.

QQ_2 foreign exchange is no longer demanded by commodity importers and QQ_1, extra foreign exchange is supplied by foreign importers. $QQ_2 + QQ_1 (= Q_2Q_1)$ is exactly the amount of foreign exchange demanded by the capital exporters at the new rate of exchange. The effect of the capital export, then, has been to reduce commodity imports and increase commodity exports so that in our simple model, with only commodity trade and long-term capital movements, the balance of trade is uniquely determined by the balance of capital movements –

Exports (in terms of foreign currency) are OQ_1
Imports (in terms of foreign currency) are OQ_2
Capital exports (in terms of foreign currency) are Q_2Q_1
The balance of trade $(OQ_1 - OQ_2)$ = Net capital exports (Q_2Q_1)

It is quite simple to introduce "invisibles" into the analysis, in the same way as capital movements, without affecting the sort of analysis in any way. It is sufficient to note that the elasticities of the demand for and supply of foreign exchange arising out of invisible transactions may vary from less than zero to more than unity.

Finally, let us abandon the assumption that capital and "invisible" transactions do not influence the demand for and supply of foreign exchange arising out of commodity trade. Let us suppose that, for some reason or other, more people wish to go abroad for their vacations so that the demand curve for foreign exchange arising out of vacation travel shifts outwards to the right.

This may influence the commodity demand and supply curves in various ways. For instance, the people who are now traveling abroad may well plan to spend less on other things, among which are imported articles (for instance the purchase of a new foreign car may be postponed to pay for the vacation). Thus, the increased demand for foreign exchange due to increased travel is partly offset by a fall in the demand due to commodity imports. Also, part of the income now spent on travel may previously have been spent on exportables, so that the domestic demand for such articles will fall. Unless the supply elasticity of such exportables is infinite, a fall in their price will occur, and assuming some elasticity in the foreign demand curve for our exports, increased exports will result. Exporters may also be more willing to look for outlets abroad in the face of a falling domestic demand for their products. The effect will be to shift the supply of foreign exchange out to the right. The effects of capital movements can be analyzed in the same way, the relevant questions being concerned with the source of the funds, how they are used and how they might have been used had the capital movement not taken place.

Note, however, that it is impossible to say, *a priori*, whether the net effect on the demand for and supply of foreign exchange for commodity trade will be in one direction rather than the other. If a capital export, for instance, leads to an increased foreign demand for exports, the workers in the busy export industries may have a higher than average propensity to import, in which case the demand for foreign exchange due to commodity imports may move out to the right. What one *can* say is that it is extremely unlikely that the original situation will remain unchanged once we introduce capital movements and "invisible" transactions.

The important limitations of this analysis are, firstly, that it is a partial analysis abstracted from a monetary general equilibrium model at full employment, so that exchange rate variations are not allowed to react back on the schedules through income or other effects. Obviously, if the foreign sector is large relative to the whole economy, such feedback effects, government policy alterations in the light of exchange rate variations, etc., may well be highly significant, so that the limitations of the analysis would in such cases be severe.

Although the method of analysis used in this discussion of exchange rates is highly simplified, it should suffice to give the student a grasp of the basics of exchange rates theory. For a further fuller treatment, the student is referred to Fritz Machlup's classic article on the theory of foreign exchanges published in *Economica* for November 1939.

[1] See "The Report of the Committee on Invisible Exports," London, 1967. Also, M. Panić, "Britain's Invisible Balance," *Lloyds' Bank Review*, July 1968.

[2] On such peculiarities and similarities, see Poul Høst-Madsen, "Asymmetries Between Balance of Payments Surpluses and Deficits," I.M.F. Staff Papers, 1962.

[3] See W. Lederer, "Measuring the Balance of Payments," American Statistical Association, 1961, Proceedings of the Business and Economic Statistics Section, 1962.

[4] This is the U.S. Department of Commerce view. Hal Lary of N.B.E.R., however, wants to put below the line all items in addition to gold which are responsive to monetary policy (and so include private short-term foreign assets).

[5] *Op. cit.*, pp. 195–197.

[6] See W. Salant *et al.*, "The United States Balance of Payments in 1968," Brookings Institution, 1963.

[7] W. Lederer, "The Balance of Payments in 1963," *Survey of Current Business*, Vol. 144, (1964).

[8] For a fuller discussion of the issues at stake and a critique of the U.S. position, see W. Gordon, *American Economic Review*, 1963; and H. N. Goldstein, *American Economic Review*, 1963; also, W. Lederer, Special Papers in *International Economics No. 5* (1963), and Hal Lary, *op. cit.*

[9] See W. Gardner, "An Exchange – Market Analysis of the U.S. Balance of Payments," *I.M.F. Staff Papers*, 1961, and R. Triffin, in "1961 Proceedings of the Business and Economic Statistics Section," of the American Statistical Association.

[10] "Report of the Review Committee for Balance of Payments Statistics," U.S. Government Printing Office, 1964.

[11] For a most illuminating view of the problem, see F. Machlup, "The Mysterious Numbers Game," Ch. 7 of *International Monetary Relations*.

[12] Note also that balance of payments and foreign exchange transactions may

differ in timing since payments for goods may be in advance or in arrears of delivery. This becomes very important when a currency is under pressure, since import payments will be accelerated and exporters will try to delay receipts as long as possible (leads and lags).

[13] For a discussion of other functions of the foreign-exchange market (credit provision and hedging) see Kindleberger, *International Economics*, Ch. 3.

[14] The effects of gold movements, exchange-rate stabilization and speculation will be discussed in Ch. 9.

CHAPTER 8

The Foreign Exchange Market

As WE saw in the previous chapter, the basic function of the foreign exchange market is the clearing of the demand for and supply of foreign exchange, thus effecting payments into and out of a country.[1]

Now, in order to develop a theory of foreign-exchange rates, let us assume, for the sake of simplicity a two-country model, where all partial foreign-exchange markets can be merged into a single market with one currency being bought and the other currency acting as "money." Like all prices determined by the market, exchange rates will tend to settle where the aggregate quantity of foreign exchange demanded equals the aggregate quantity supplied. It follows, therefore, that in our theory of exchange-rate determination, we must analyze the sources of supply and demand, and also the effects of changes in the parameters of the supply and demand functions. Initially, let us assume that the monetary authorities do not intervene to fix or alter artificially exchange rates (e.g. by buying or selling gold), and that the only factor affecting the supply or demand for foreign exchange is commodity trade. We therefore rule out, for the moment, foreign lending and borrowing, unilateral transfers, etc. (which we shall reintroduce at a later point), and study commodity trade in isolation.

The demand schedule for foreign exchange relates the various quantities of foreign exchange which will be demanded at different exchange rates (i.e. different prices), and since we are considering only commodity trade, we can say that the demand for foreign exchange is a derived demand, derived from the demand for imports.

(a) DISEQUILIBRIUM UNDER FLEXIBLE EXCHANGE RATES

As we saw in Chapter 7, a divergence between the autonomous demand for and supply of foreign exchange can be eliminated if the rate of exchange is permitted to fluctuate freely. Any excess demand for (supply of) foreign exchange will be eradicated by a rise (fall) in the exchange rate to some new equilibrium level at which autonomous receipts and payments balance. Thus, through a system of fluctuating rates, any payments inbalance which appears will only last for as long as it takes the exchange rate to find its new equilibrium level. Providing rates of exchange are allowed to find their own levels in accordance with market forces, disequilibria can only be temporary phenomena. Much more will be said about such a system in the next chapter.

(b) DISEQUILIBRIUM UNDER FIXED EXCHANGE RATES

In the following chapter we shall look at the functioning of the monetary system under fixed and flexible exchange rates; meanwhile it is sufficient to realize that the basic difference between a fixed exchange-rate system and a flexible one is that under the latter, market forces operating as a result of a payments imbalance are allowed to work themselves out via exchange rate changes, whereas under the former, foreign exchange rates are maintained fixed in relation to either gold or another currency (e.g. the U.S. dollar) so that other variables (e.g. national income, employment, prices, etc.) must adjust to restore payments balance. Bearing this in mind, suppose that a country is in deficit (i.e. autonomous payments exceed receipts) so that to bridge the gap an additional supply of foreign exchange must be forthcoming. This supply may arise through selling gold, using convertible currency reserves or through an inflow of accommodating short-term capital; but since all of these sources are not inexhaustible, the deficit cannot persist indefinitely. Gold and convertible currency reserves are obviously limited in amount and private short-term capital inflows induced by higher interest rates are clearly susceptible to quick turn-around. If the capital inflow consists of a build-up of officially held currency balances, then a limit is imposed by the willingness of foreigners to increase the proportion of their short-term liquid assets held in the form of one particular currency. As the deficit persists, this willingness will decline at a faster and faster rate as the risk of loss through depreciation of the currency increases. Capital inflows brought about by borrowing are also only a temporary expedient since eventually such borrowing must be repaid.

For these reasons, a deficit cannot persist indefinitely, and therefore, since surpluses are simply reflections of deficits, surpluses cannot persist either. Somehow or other, then, payments imbalances must be corrected and equilibrium restored. Basically, it is with such disequilibria, and the way in which balance is restored, that the adjustment process is concerned. As we shall see, balance of payments disequilibrium inevitably leads to some kind of change brought about through market forces or policy measures, and it is just such change which creates problems for the international monetary system.

Since the matter of payments balance is an important policy problem for most countries, it is necessary to analyze in some detail the process of adjustment which is possible in order to arrive at equilibrium. Johnson[2] has argued that, fundamentally, balance of payments problems are monetary problems. This is to some extent correct in that imbalance means that the monetary claims of a country created over a specified period do not match the monetary obligations incurred, but it should be realized that such monetary imbalance is only a symptom of an underlying state of affairs created by "real" factors such as national income and employment levels, relative prices, interest rates, etc. It is how the adjustment process reacts on such "real" factors that will concern us for the rest of this chapter.

Whatever the international monetary system in existence, there are really only three methods of adjusting to a payments imbalance, and one or a combination of these methods will generally be operative.

The first method of adjustment depends for its effectiveness on alterations in the structure of relative prices internationally either through the so-called price-specie-flow mechanism under the gold standard, or through changes in exchange rates. This method is conventionally called the *Price Adjustment Mechanism*.

The second method of adjustment is relatively modern and relies for its effectiveness on alterations in the level of national income and employment – the so-called *Income Adjustment Mechanism*. The third method of adjustment relies for its effectiveness on the direct control by the authorities of imports and exports either via quotas or some system of *Exchange Control* involving discrimination by currency and/or commodity. As we shall see, the Price Adjustment and Income Adjustment mechanisms work so as to alter the underlying factors (prices, income levels, etc.) which are causing the payments imbalance, whereas Trade and Exchange Controls do nothing to affect the underlying forces but simply treat the symptoms. However, whether this method is adopted or not depends mainly on the priorities and value judgments of the authorities. For instance, by allowing the Price and Income Adjustment mechanisms to work, unemployment may result in the case of a deficit country, or inflation may rear its ugly head in the case of a surplus country. If the policy objectives of the authorities are such that full employment and price stability are their major aims, then they may well adopt policies to dampen the working of the adjustment mechanisms and substitute direct control over the balance of payments.

Turning now to a more detailed examination of each mechanism, it is interesting to observe that in the past quarter century there has been a considerable shift in emphasis away from the classical formulations of mechanical adjustment working through the price mechanism, as expounded by Hume, Ricardo and Mill, towards more modern formulations of involuntary adjustment, working through national income levels. This change in emphasis is to a very large extent associated with the Keynesian revolution in economic theory and also with the post-depression reorientation of government policy objectives, placing full employment and price stability at the top of the list. It is also a shift away from an automatic mechanical-type adjustment mechanism where certainty of adjustment prevailed and long-run equilibrium was always possible, to an uncertain non-mechanical-type mechanism where disequilibrium in the balance of payments is a distinct possibility, even in the long-run.

(i) THE CLASSICAL PRICE ADJUSTMENT MECHANISM

Before the publication in 1936 of Keynes' *General Theory*, many economists held the view that balance of payments disequilibrium set forces in motion which tended to restore balance *automatically*. According to the Mercantilists, a favourable balance of payments would be eliminated by an inflow of specie (gold coin) from the deficit countries. They also held the idea that additions to the monetary stock arising from specie inflows would raise the level of economic activity and bring about a rise in prices. However, it was David Hume[3] with his price-specie-flow mechanism who suggested that a balance of payments disequilibrium would be *self*-equilibrating and so could not continue indefinitely. According to the *price-specie-flow* mechanism, if a country had a payments deficit, the balance was restored by a transfer of gold to the surplus country(ies). Since the domestic money supply was tied directly to a country's gold stock under the gold standard, an outflow of gold would cause a reduction in the quantity of money in the deficit country.

Similarly the money supply of the country(ies) acquiring gold would increase.[4] These gold flows (specie flows) would result via the change in the money supply, in an alteration in relative international prices such that the balance of payments was restored to equilibrium. Prices in the deficit country would fall as gold flowed out and, conversely, prices in the surplus country would rise as gold flowed in, leading to an increase in the exports of the deficit country and a reduction in its imports. In this way, gold would flow internationally until autonomous receipts and payments balanced once again. The mechanism outlined above relied explicitly on an acceptance of the quantity theory of money, according to which a reduction in the money supply would lead directly to a fall in aggregate demand and therefore in prices. Because productive factors were assumed to be mobile domestically and prices were assumed to be flexible upwards and downwards (including wages), the effects of changes in aggregate demand were solely on prices and costs, output and employment being left unaffected. I should also be noted that it was implied that the elasticities of demand for imports and exports were assumed to be such that the alteration in relative international prices brought about by the gold flows would lead to an improvement in the balance of trade.

This simple version of the price-specie-flow adjustment mechanism was subsequently refined to take account of newer institutional developments such as the use of interest rates to influence international short-term capital flows. It was gradually realized that gold flows did not produce automatic balance in a country's balance of payments; a great deal depended on what policy the central bank followed. Beach[5] suggests that central bank policies under the gold standard, by stimulating capital flows, helped produce what seemed to be "automatic" adjustment. Morgenstern and others who have studied the gold standard system, also fail to give much support to the automaticity of the classical adjustment mechanism, and partly as a result of these empirically raised doubts, the price-specie-flow mechanism came into disrepute. Also, with the rejection of the assumptions of fully flexible prices as expressed in the "quantity theory," it was realized that an important element in the adjustment process had been completely neglected – namely, the effect of payments disequilibrium on national income and employment levels.

Nevertheless, it is an interesting exercise to analyze the effect of gold movements on the balance of payments, using the technique developed in Chapter 7. We shall proceed to do so.

The basis of the gold standard system lies in the existence of institutions prepared to buy and sell gold at fixed prices, so maintaining the value of currencies in a fixed relationship to the value of gold. This means that at a certain rate of exchange, the supply of foreign exchange becomes infinitely elastic. (Note that the authorities themselves do not buy or sell the foreign exchange; they deal only in gold.) It is the gold "arbitrageurs" who deal in foreign exchange. Thus, at a certain rate of exchange, gold "arbitrageurs" will buy gold from the authorities and sell it abroad, supplying the foreign exchange so acquired to the foreign exchange market where the actual importers can buy it. Similarly, at some lower exchange rate, the gold "arbitrageurs" will buy foreign exchange and use it to buy gold abroad, which they will then sell to the authorities.

Suppose that, initially, the demand for and supply of foreign exchange are DD and SS, giving an equilibrium rate of exchange OR which is within the limits set by the cost of buying (selling) gold, insuring it, storing it, transporting it, etc.[6]

Imports equal exports and have a value of OQ in terms of foreign currency. Now, suppose that the demand for foreign exchange increases, for some reason or other, to D_1D_1 so creating a tendency for the exchange rate to rise towards OR_1. But given that the country

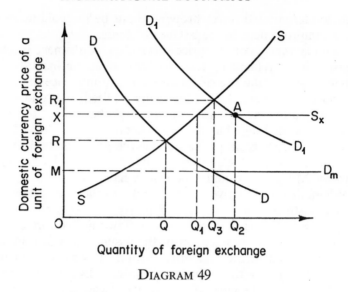

DIAGRAM 49

concerned is on the gold standard, the rate cannot rise above OX, the gold export point, since gold "arbitrageurs" will step in as explained above and supply foreign exchange. Thus, at a rate OX, the supply curve of foreign exchange becomes perfectly elastic (SSx). At A, the supply curve meets the new demand curve, OQ, foreign exchange being supplied by traders, and Q_1Q_2 foreign exchange being supplied by gold "arbitrageurs." Thus, in our new situation, autonomous receipts, OQ_1 fall short of autonomous payments OQ_2, by an amount Q_1Q_2 made up by gold exports, the balance of payments being written as follows:

Commodity exports (OQ_1) +gold exports (Q_1Q_2) = Commodity imports (OQ_2).

Had the exchange rate not been fixed, exports would be greater (OQ_3) and imports smaller (OQ_3), at a higher exchange rate OR_1. However, although the gold standard prevents the rate rising above OX, it does so by drawing on limited gold stocks, so that the picture in Diagram 49 is strictly temporary. However, the price-specie-flow advocates would claim that it was temporary, not because gold stocks were limited, but because the fall in the supply of money consequent upon the gold outflow would lead to a reduction in the price of exports and a fall in the demand for imports. Similarly, in the surplus country(ies) the price of their exports will rise, as will their demand for imports. Thus, D_1D_1 will shift to the left and SS will shift to the right until demand for and supply of foreign exchange are equated within the range OM–OX. When this happens, gold flows will cease. Under the gold standard, therefore, a "natural" distribution of gold would occur, this distribution depending upon the relative economic strengths of countries, and unalterable by monetary policy, without creating balance of payments disequilibria. Domestic economic policy was thus to a large degree dependent upon international forces and was assumed to follow the so-called "rules of the game," so that equilibrium was always regained.

(ii) THE PRICE ADJUSTMENT MECHANISM UNDER FLEXIBLE EXCHANGE RATES

According to the price-specie-flow mechanism outlined above, international equilibrium was achieved through an adjustment of prices caused by altering levels of aggregate demand, not directly by changes in the exchange rate. Thus it was the secondary effects operating via the money supply which led to relative price changes and ultimately to equilibrium. Full employment existed throughout, because it was assumed that the price adjustments led to a speedy redistribution of factors and that a high degree of competition prevailed so that demand curves were fairly elastic. Ignoring changes in income (due to the assumption of full employment), and with elastic demand and supply curves, the price system was able to return the economy to international equilibrium. Once we abandon the gold standard and rate-fixity, the price adjustment mechanism will still work, but in this case the relative price adjustments take place directly as the exchange rate fluctuates. Thus, in the example portrayed in Diagram 49, the exchange rate would be allowed to rise to OR_1, at which rate the demand for and supply of foreign exchange are equated. At this higher exchange rate, export prices in terms of foreign currency would have fallen, leading to a rise in exports, and import prices, in terms of domestic currency, would have risen, leading to a fall in imports. However, what is important in determining whether such price and volume changes eliminate the payments imbalance, is the relative movements in export *receipts* (i.e. Price × Volume) and import *payments* (i.e. Price × Volume). For the payments position to improve, import payments must fall relative to export receipts, and whether or not this will happen depends to a large extent on the *elasticities* of the demand and supply curves relating to imports and exports.

We must now consider the role of elasticities in the analysis of exchange market equilibrium to discover how these elasticities affect the process of adjustment.

Consider the demand curve for imports (DD_1) shown in Diagram 50. Since DD_1 is a straight line, the price elasticity of demand[7] for imports will vary from infinity at point D, through unity at the mid

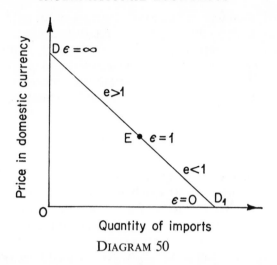

Quantity of imports

DIAGRAM 50

point E, to zero at point D_1. In terms of the amount spent on imports, this means that for price increases (decreases) (*a*) in the range ED_1, payment for imports will increase (decrease); (*b*) in the range DE, payment for imports will decrease (increase). At point E, where the elasticity of demand is unity, payment for imports will stay the same when price varies by a small amount around E. In the range ED, demand is said to be elastic; in the range ED_1, demand is said to be inelastic. When we translate the demand for imports into a demand for foreign exchange at varying rates of exchange, we saw in the previous chapter that the elasticity of demand for the actual imports was reflected in the elasticity of demand for foreign exchange. Thus, if at current import prices and rates of exchange, the demand for imports were elastic, then the demand for foreign currency at current rates of exchange would also be elastic.

However, a difficulty arises when we consider the demand for our exports. Suppose, again, that DD_1 below represents the demand curve for our exports (prices, of course, being expressed in foreign currency).

If the price of our exports is within the range DP, where demand is elastic, then a fall in export prices will lead to a rise in the quantity of foreign currency supplied, because Price × Quantity increases as we move down DE. Now, since export prices will fall if the rate of exchange depreciates, this means that the supply curve of foreign exchange corresponding to DE will be upward sloping from left to right. However, if the price of exports is within the range PO (where demand is inelastic), a fall in the price of exports will lead to a fall in the quantity of foreign currency supplied, because, Price × Quantity decreases as one moves down ED_1. This means that the supply curve of foreign

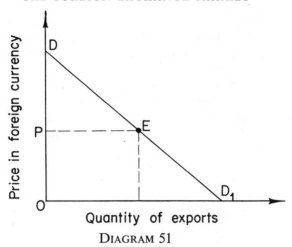

DIAGRAM 51

exchange corresponding to ED_1 will slope upwards from right to left, indicating that less foreign exchange is supplied as the exchange rate depreciates over a certain range. The complete supply curve of foreign exchange will therefore be backward-bending (i.e. negatively inclined) over a certain range, as shown below –

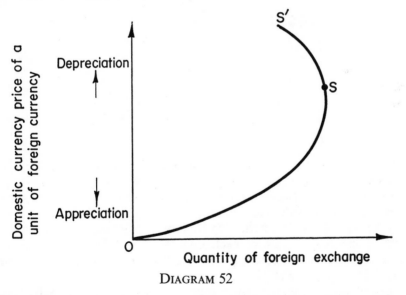

DIAGRAM 52

After a certain point S, the supply curve turns back on itself,[8] but note that the curve cannot rise backward more sharply than a certain amount since the slope of the negative inclination must at every point be steeper than the slope of the rectangular hyperbola passing through that point.

This is so because, as depreciation takes place, the price of our exports falls but only in terms of foreign currency, not in terms of domestic currency. Thus, even although the demand curve for our exports were of zero elasticity over the relevant range, the quantity of domestic currency demanded would not fall but would stay constant. Since the quantity of domestic currency demanded is given by the product of the quantity of foreign exchange supplied and the exchange rate (i.e. the area under the OS' curve), it follows that the backward bending part SS' has the above constraint applied to it.[8]

The possibility of such a supply curve is theoretically (if not practically) important because it creates problems so far as the ability of flexible exchange rates to restore balance of payments equilibrium is concerned. If the demand for and supply of foreign exchange are as shown in Diagram 53, then an unstable market will exist in which pay-

DIAGRAM 53

ments disequilibria may be aggravated by the movement of exchange rates in accordance with market forces. It is our task, therefore, to discover in what circumstances such instability might appear, using demand and supply curve diagrams for exports and imports.

Let us assume initially that the balance of payments is in balance, so that at the current rate of exchange, the demand for and supply of foreign exchange are equated. This is illustrated in Diagram 54, where $OQ_XEP_X = OQ_ME_PM$.

Let us also assume that the supply curves of exports and imports have infinite elasticity, so that changes in the demand for traded goods do not alter their prices but affect only the volume of trade. Suppose, now, that the rate of exchange is altered by the authorities. How will this affect the balance of payments?

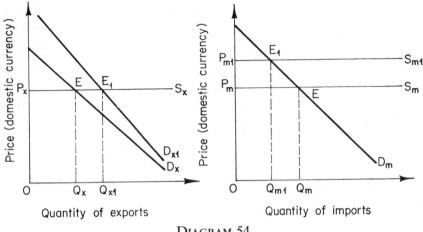

DIAGRAM 54

Clearly, the effect of a change in the exchange rate on the balance of payments depends on how the *value* of exports and imports change – that is, on whether the change in the value of exports is greater than, equal to, or smaller than the change in the value of imports, with respect to the rate of exchange. Let us suppose that the exchange rate is lowered, so that a unit of foreign currency exchanges for more units of domestic currency. Therefore, the demand curve for exports will shift out to the right and the supply curve of imports will rise, to Dx_1 and S_{M1} respectively. Clearly, the domestic currency value of exports will increase[9] (to OQx_1E_1Px) whilst the change in the value of imports (from OQ_MEP_M to $OQ_1E_{M1}P_{M1}$) will depend upon the elasticity of the demand for imports. If the demand for imports is inelastic, the value of imports will rise, if elastic, it will fall. Thus, if the demand for exports is completely inelastic and the demand for imports is also inelastic, then the value of exports will be unchanged whilst the value of imports will rise, so worsening the balance of payments. If the demand for exports has some elasticity so that the value of exports rises, then the outcome so far as the balance of payments is concerned will depend upon what happens to the value of imports (i.e. on the elasticity of demand for imports). It can be seen therefore that both the elasticity of the demand for exports and the elasticity of demand for imports are important in determining how a change in the exchange rate affects the balance of payments.

The so-called *Marshall-Lerner* condition states very neatly the relationship which must exist between these elasticities if a lowering of the exchange rate is to improve the balance of payments. According to the Marshall-Lerner condition, a lowering of the exchange rate will improve (worsen) the balance of payments if the sum of the elasticities of demand for exports and imports is greater than (less than) unity. If the sum of the elasticities is equal to one, then a change in the exchange rate will leave the balance of payments unaltered. However, the Marshall-Lerner condition is valid only if

(a) the balance of payments is initially in balance, and
(b) the elasticities of the *supply* of exports and imports are fairly high.

What happens when these conditions are not satisfied will be analyzed later. It should also be noted that the Marshall-Lerner condition refers to an improvement (deterioration) in the balance of payments expressed in *domestic currency*; it does not always follow that an improvement (deterioration) in the balance of payments in domestic currency is reflected in an improvement (deterioration) when expressed in foreign currency.[10] In order to demonstrate the derivation of the Marshall-Lerner conditions, consider the case where the rate of exchange is lowered by the authorities. As we saw earlier, the supply curve of imports drifts upwards, leading to a rise in the price of imports and a reduction in the quantity demanded.[11] Similarly, the demand curve for exports shifts out and the quantity sold increases, and price stays constant.

For balance of payments purposes, what is important is whether the change in the *value* of imports is greater than, less than, or equal to the change in the *value* of exports.

In other words, it all depends on the relationship between *the elasticity of the value of exports* (with respect to the rate of exchange) and *the elasticity of the value of imports* (with respect to the rate of exchange) –

$$\text{i.e. on whether } \eta X,r \gtreqless \eta M,r$$

where $\eta X,r$ is the elasticity of the value of exports with respect to the rate of exchange and $\eta M,r$ is the elasticity of the value of imports with respect to the rate of exchange.

Let the volume of exports be x and the volume of imports be m. Let the domestic currency price of exports be Pi and the foreign currency price of imports be Pf. Let one unit of foreign currency = r units of domestic currency. Then, the balance of payments, B, = the value of exports less the value of imports.

$$\text{i.e.} \quad B = X - M$$
$$\therefore \quad B = Pi.x - Pf.r.m$$

Now, assuming that the levels of national income at home and abroad are constant (so isolating price effects), then the volume of exports will be a function of relative prices at home and abroad. This is simply saying that, as the price of exports falls, relative to the price of foreign substitutes, then the overseas buyers will increase their purchases of imports (i.e. our exports) at the expense of overseas producers. Similarly, import volume will be a function of relative prices at home and abroad, so that as the price of imports falls relative to domestically produced substitutes, then the quantity of imports bought will rise at the expense of domestic production.

We can represent the demand for exports as

$$x = h\left(\frac{Pi}{Pf.r}\right)$$

Similarly, the demand for imports can be represented as

$$m = g\left(\frac{Pi}{Pf.r}\right)$$

Note that $\left(\frac{Pi}{Pf.r}\right)$ represents the *terms of trade* of the country concerned.

Given the above relations, the balance of payments is

$$B = Pi.x - Pf.r.m = Pi.h\left(\frac{Pi}{Pf.r}\right) - Pf.r.g\left(\frac{Pi}{Pf.r}\right)$$

Now, assuming that Pi and Pf do not change, consider the effect on the balance of payments of altering the rate of exchange. Suppose that the rate of exchange is increased so that one unit of foreign currency exchanges for more units of domestic currency.

Now, the total value of exports, $X, = Pi.h\left(\frac{Pi}{Pf.r}\right)$

$$\therefore \frac{dX}{dr} = Pi.\frac{d\left[h\left(\frac{Pi}{Pf.r}\right)\right]}{dr}$$

Multiply both sides by $\dfrac{r}{h.\left(\frac{Pi}{Pf.r}\right)}$.

That is

$$\frac{dX}{dr}.\frac{r}{h\left(\frac{Pi}{Pf.r}\right)} = Pi.\frac{d\left[h\left(\frac{Pi}{Pf.r}\right)\right]}{dr}.\frac{r}{h\left(\frac{Pi}{Pf.r}\right)}$$

or $\dfrac{dX}{X}.\dfrac{r}{dr} = \dfrac{dx}{x}.\dfrac{r}{dr}$ (dividing both sides by Pi).

In other words, the elasticity of the total value of exports equals the elasticity of the demand for exports, both with respect to the rate of exchange.

That is $\boxed{\eta X,r = \eta x,r}$

This is to be expected since a change in the rate of exchange affects only the volume of exports, not their price in domestic currency (see Diagram 54). Given that an increase in the exchange rate lowers the foreign currency price of exports, the volume of exports will most likely rise and so the elasticity of the total value of exports will be positive (or zero at the limit where the elasticity of demand for exports is zero).

On the import side, $\dfrac{dM}{dr} = Pf.r.\dfrac{d\left[g\left(\dfrac{Pi}{Pf.r}\right)\right]}{dr} + g\left(\dfrac{Pi}{Pf.r}\right).Pf$

$$\therefore \frac{dM}{dr} = Pf.g\left(\frac{Pi}{Pf.r}\right)\left[1 + \frac{r}{g\left(\dfrac{Pi}{Pf.r}\right)}\cdot\frac{d\left[g\left(\dfrac{Pi}{Pf.r}\right)\right]}{dr}\right]$$

$$= Pf.g\left(\frac{Pi}{Pf.r}\right)\left[1 + \frac{r}{dr}\cdot\frac{dm}{m}\right]$$

$$\therefore \frac{dM}{dr} = Pf.g\left(\frac{Pi}{Pf.r}\right)\left[1 + \eta m,r\right]$$

Multiplying both sides by $\dfrac{r}{M}$,

$$\frac{dM}{M}\cdot\frac{r}{dr} = \frac{r.Pf.g\left(\dfrac{Pi}{Pf.r}\right)\left[1 + \eta m,r\right]}{M}$$

Now, $M = Pf.r.g\left(\dfrac{Pi}{Pf.r}\right)$, so –

$$\boxed{\eta M,r = (1 + \eta m,r)}$$

Thus, the elasticity of the total value of imports with respect to the rate of exchange is greater by one than the elasticity of total imports with respect to the rate of exchange. Since the price of imports rises with a rise in the exchange rate, the import volume falls, so that $\eta m,r$ is usually negative. Thus the way in which the total value of imports varies in home currency depends upon whether the arithmetic size of $\eta m,r$ is greater than, less than, or equal to one.

If $|\eta m,r| > 1$, then $\eta M,r < 0$ and the total value of imports falls.
If $|\eta m,r| = 1$, then $\eta M,r = 0$ and the total value of imports is unchanged.

If $|\eta m,r| < 1$, then $\eta M,r > 0$ and the total value of imports rises.

It is now possible to give the connection between changes in the exchange rate, the elasticity of the value of imports and the elasticity of the value of exports, and the balance of payments.

Since $\eta X,r = \eta x,r$ and $\eta M,r = 1 + \eta m,r$, the effect of a change in the exchange rate on the balance of payments depends upon whether

$$\eta x,r \gtreqless 1 + \eta m,r \left(\text{or } \eta x,r - \eta m,r \gtreqless 1 \right)$$

Generally, $\eta x,r$ will be positive and $\eta m,r$ will be negative. Thus, if the sum of the elasticities of demand for exports and imports is greater than unity (less than unity) the balance of payments will improve (deteriorate) as the rate of exchange increases. Note that the Marshall-Lerner condition has been expressed in terms of the elasticities of demand for exports and imports *with respect to the rate of exchange*. If one calculates the requirements to be fulfilled in terms of the elasticities of demand *with respect to prices in the importing countries*[12] the Marshall-Lerner condition becomes

$$\eta m,p + \eta x,p \gtreqless -1$$

Since both $\eta m,p$ and $\eta x,p$ will normally be negative a devaluation will improve the balance of payments if $\eta m,p + \eta x,p < -1$
worsen it if $\eta m,p + \eta x,p > -1$
and leave it unchanged if $\eta m,p + \eta x,p = -1$.

A few illustrations may help clarify this. Assume, as before, infinite supply elasticities. In Diagram 55, the demand for exports D_X is completely inelastic whereas the demand curve for imports is elastic D_m.

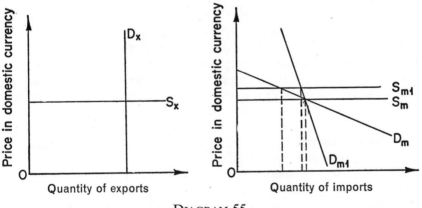

DIAGRAM 55

A rise in the exchange rate will leave the domestic currency value of exports unchanged, whilst the domestic currency value of imports falls.

In this case, $\eta x,p = 0$ and $\eta m,p < -1$ so that $\eta x,p + \eta m,p < -1$ and so a rise in the exchange rate improves the balance of payments. Had the elasticity of demand for imports been minus unity, then the value of imports would have remained unchanged and so the balance of payments would also be unchanged ($\eta x,p + \eta m,p = -1$). If the demand curve for imports were D_{m1} (i.e. inelastic), then the domestic currency value of imports would have risen and so worsened the balance of payments ($\eta x,p + \eta m,p > -1$). Thus, in the case where the elasticity of demand for exports is zero, the effect on the balance of payments of a change in the exchange rate depends solely on the elasticity of demand for imports.

Going to the other extreme, suppose that the demand for imports has zero elasticity whilst the demand for exports is elastic (D_x in Diagram 56).

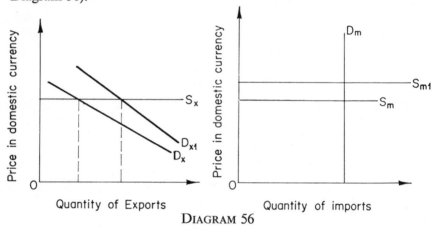

DIAGRAM 56

In this case, the domestic currency value of imports rises by the same amount as the variation in the exchange rate. However, since the elasticity of demand for imports is greater than one, the value of exports will rise by more than the value of imports. Correspondingly, had D_x been inelastic, the value of imports would have risen by more than the value of exports.

It is possible therefore, for a devaluation of a currency to worsen the balance of payments. This may happen if the quantity of imports is highly inelastic with respect to domestic currency prices.

We must now abandon the assumption that trade was always balanced and see what affect this has on the Marshall-Lerner condition. We already know that the balance of payments effect depends on how the *value* of exports changes in relation to the *value* of imports.

$$\text{i.e. on whether} \quad \frac{dX}{dr} \gtreqless \frac{dM}{dr}$$

Now, $\dfrac{dM}{dr} = \dfrac{dM}{M}\cdot\dfrac{r}{dr}\cdot\dfrac{M}{X}\cdot\dfrac{X}{r} = \eta M,r\cdot\dfrac{M}{X}\cdot\dfrac{X}{r}$

And, $\dfrac{dX}{dr} = \dfrac{dX}{X}\cdot\dfrac{r}{dr}\cdot\dfrac{X}{r} = \eta X,r\cdot\dfrac{X}{r}$

Thus, we can rewrite $\dfrac{dX}{dr} \gtreqless \dfrac{dM}{dr}$ as

$$\eta X,r\cdot\frac{X}{r} \gtreqless \eta M,r\cdot\frac{M}{X}\cdot\frac{X}{r}$$

$$\text{or}\quad \eta X,r \gtreqless \eta M,r\cdot\frac{M}{X}$$

$$\text{or}\quad \eta x,r \gtreqless \frac{M}{X}(1+\eta m,r)$$

$$\text{or}\quad \frac{X}{M}\eta x,r - \eta m,r \gtreqless 1$$

Thus, if one starts off with an export surplus (i.e. $X > M$) the elasticity of the demand for exports (with respect to the exchange rate) will be more heavily weighted than previously and so, even if $\eta m_1 r$ is fairly low; a devaluation may improve the balance of payments. A similar calculation for *price* elasticities would show that the balance of payments effect depends on whether:

$$\frac{X}{M}\eta x,p + \eta m,p \gtreqless -1$$

It is very interesting to compare the conditions as expressed in terms of elasticities of demand with reference to price and with reference to the exchange rate, especially since students may find the conditions so similar as to confuse them.

In terms of price elasticities, the Marshall-Lerner condition states that for devaluation to improve the balance of payments,

$$\frac{X}{M}\eta x,p + \eta m,p < -1$$

In terms of exchange rate elasticities, the condition becomes

$$\frac{X}{M}\eta x,r - \eta m,r > 1$$

These can be rewritten as

$$\frac{X}{M} > -\frac{(1+\eta m,p)}{\eta x,p}$$

$$\text{And}\quad \frac{X}{M} > \frac{(1+\eta m,r)}{\eta x,r}$$

To illustrate the effects of introducing the state of the balance of payments, suppose that the price elasticities of demand for exports and imports are both equal to a half, and that the balance of payments is balanced.

$$\text{Then } \frac{X}{M} = 1 = \frac{-(1-\frac{1}{2})}{-\frac{1}{2}} = -\frac{(1+\eta m,p)}{\eta x,p}$$

and therefore devaluation will not affect the balance of payments. However, if an export surplus exists, then $\frac{X}{M} > 1$ and is therefore greater than $\frac{-(+\eta m,p)}{\eta x,p}$ so that a devaluation would improve the balance of payments even although the sum of the demand elasticities were only unity. Correspondingly, starting from an initial deficit (i.e. $\frac{X}{M} < 1$), a devaluation may worsen the balance of payments even although the sum of the elasticities of demand is greater than unity. It is important to remember that the conditions given above refer to the balance of payments expressed in terms of *domestic* currency. If one works in terms of foreign currency, the conditions are somewhat modified.[13]

Suppose for example that Britain has exports of £1,000 and imports of £2,000 so that $\frac{X}{M} = \frac{1}{2}$. Assume that the rate of exchange is 1 dollar = £100, that a 1% devaluation takes place, and that the price elasticity of demand for her exports is 0·4 and the price elasticity of demand for imports is −0·8.

$$\text{Then, } \frac{X}{M} = \tfrac{1}{2} \text{ and } \frac{-(1-0\cdot8)}{-0\cdot4} = \tfrac{1}{2}, \text{ so that}$$

$$\frac{X}{M} = -\frac{(1+\eta m,p)}{\eta x,p}.$$

The devaluation should leave the balance of payments unchanged, even although $\eta x,p + \eta m,p < -1$. Assuming that the elasticities of supply are infinite, the devaluation will increase the value of exports to £1,004 whilst the value of imports will also increase, to £2,004, leaving the deficit unchanged.

However, in terms of foreign currency, exports will fall in value by approximately 0·6% (= $3/50) whilst the value of imports will fall by approximately 1% (= $10/50), so that the balance of payments improves, when expressed in terms of foreign currency. When dealing with the effects of exchange rate changes on the balance of payments, the student should make sure that he is using the relevant conditions for the currency in which he is working as it does not always follow that an improvement in one currency is always reflected in a corresponding improvement (deterioration) when expressed in another.[14]

We must now consider how the Marshall-Lerner condition is altered when we allow for the more realistic possibility that supply elasticities will be less than infinite. Without going into the derivation of the following definitions, it is possible to show that:

$$(a) \quad \eta M,r = \frac{1 + \eta m,p}{Em,p - \eta m,p} . Em,p$$

where Em,p is the elasticity of *supply* of imports with respect to their price in terms of foreign currency; the other notation being as before

$$\text{and } (b) \quad \eta X,r = -\frac{\eta x,p(1 + Ex,p)}{Ex,p - \eta x,p}$$

where Ex,p is the elasticity of *supply* of exports with respect to the price in the exporting country; the other notation being as before.

Where Ex,p and Em,p are both equal to infinity, (a) becomes

$$\eta M,r = 1 + \eta m,p$$

and (b) becomes $\eta X,r = -\eta x,p$
giving us the condition that an improvement in the balance of payments would only take place if

$$\frac{X}{M}\eta x,p + \eta m,p < -1.$$

When supply elasticities are not infinite, the balance of payment effect of a devaluation depends on whether or not

$$\frac{-\eta x,p(1 + Ex,p)}{Ex,p - \eta x,p} > \frac{M}{X} . \frac{Em,p(1 + \eta m,p)}{Em,p - \eta m,p}$$

If the balance of payments were initially in balance, and the elasticities of demand for exports and imports were both a half, the balance of payments would be unchanged by a devaluation, provided that the supply elasticities were infinite. However, if we substitute values for Ex,p and Em,p of 10, we get:

$$\frac{\frac{1}{2}(1 + 10)}{10 + \frac{1}{2}} = \frac{5.5}{10.5} \text{ for the left hand side,}$$

$$\text{and } \quad \frac{10 - (1 - \frac{1}{2})}{10 + \frac{1}{2}} = \frac{5}{10.5} \text{ for the right hand side.}[15]$$

The L.H.S. > R.H.S. and so a devaluation would improve the balance of payments. Had the values for Ex,p and Em,p been lower, say 5, then the L.H.S. would become $\dfrac{3}{5.5}$ and the R.H.S. $\dfrac{2.5}{5.5}$, again showing that devaluation would help the balance of payments. However, if the elasticities of supply were high (say 30) then the L.H.S. $\left(\dfrac{15.5}{30.5}\right)$ is still greater than the R.H.S. $\left(\dfrac{15}{30.5}\right)$ but the degree of divergence is much lower than when elasticities were low.

Thus, when supply elasticities are low, the Marshall-Lerner condition (that the sum of the elasticities of demand be greater than unity) is sufficient for a balance of payments improvement, but not necessary. It can be seen that when ηx,p is, say, a half and the elasticity of supply of exports is high (say 20) then

$$\eta X,r = \frac{\frac{1}{2}(21)}{20.5} = \frac{10.5}{20.5}$$

which is very slightly greater than a half. However, when the elasticity of supply of exports is low (say $\frac{1}{3}$) then

$$\eta X,r = \frac{\frac{1}{2}(1.33)}{5/6} = \frac{4}{5}, \text{ greatly}$$

increasing the size of ηX,r. Thus, the lower is Ex,p, the higher will ηX,r tend to be.

On the side of imports, it can be shown in similar fashion that the lower the supply of elasticity of imports, the lower will be the elasticity of import value with respect to the rate of exchange. Thus, the lower the elasticities of supply, the more below unity can the sum of the demand elasticities become and yet provide a situation where devaluation will improve the balance of payments. This must be qualified since if trade is not initially balanced, then an import surplus will make it more difficult for devaluation to work, whilst an export surplus will loosen even more the conditions which have to be met for improvement to take place.

In cases where devaluation (i.e. a rise in the exchange rate) brings about an improvement in the balance of payments (i.e. an increased surplus or reduced deficit), the balance of payments is said to react *normally*; if devaluation causes the balance of payments to worsen, the balance of payments is said to react *perversely*. These reactions can be analyzed not only by looking at the elasticity values, etc., but also by looking at the demand for and supply of foreign exchange in relation to exchange rates. Thus, suppose that DD and SS represent the demand for and supply of foreign exchange:

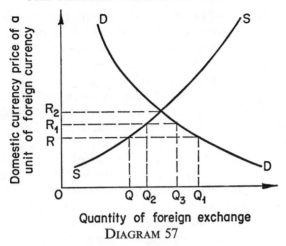

Quantity of foreign exchange

DIAGRAM 57

Now, at the current rate of exchange OR (which, let us suppose, is fixed by the authorities) the demand for foreign exchange exceeds the supply (i.e. an import surplus exists to the value of QQ_1 in foreign currency, or $QQ_1 \cdot OR$ in domestic currency). If the authorities now devalue the currency (i.e. raise the exchange rate to OR_1) then the excess demand will shrink (in terms of foreign exchange) to Q_2Q_3. Thus, in terms of foreign exchange at least, the import surplus has declined (but will only disappear if the rate is raised to OR_2) and so the balance of payments is reacting normally. However, if the demand for exports is price inelastic then, as we saw earlier (Diagram 53), the supply curve of foreign exchange will bend backwards over some range and, as a result, two possibilities exist as illustrated in Diagram 58 below. In case (a) the supply curve and demand curve intersect in such

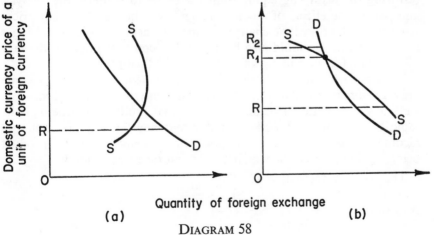

Quantity of foreign exchange

(a)   (b)

DIAGRAM 58

a way that a raising of the exchange rate will decrease the deficit and so the balance of payments reacts normally to the devaluation. In case (b) at rate OR an export surplus exists, and in this situation an appreciation of the currency (i.e. a lowering of the exchange rate) will worsen the surplus (i.e. make it even bigger). Similarly, at rate OR_2, an import surplus exists but a devaluation would make the deficit even bigger. Thus, in case (b) the balance of payments reacts perversely to exchange rate changes, with the result that the exchange market depicted in (b) would be unstable in the sense that a deviation of the exchange rate from OR_1 would create forces which lead to an even bigger deviation away from the equilibrium rate. We can see, therefore, that the price adjustment mechanism operating either via the gold standard or a system of fluctuating exchange rates need not necessarily eliminate balance of payments disequilibria. Both systems stressed the automaticity of adjustment by allowing the price mechanism to operate freely, so leaving income and employment levels free to fluctuate under international pressures. However, with the emphasis in the early 1940s on full employment and price stability, the old doctrines of the price adjustment mechanism gave way to the more modern theory of income adjustment. It should be remembered, nevertheless, that the adjustment process will operate through both the price mechanism and the income mechanism, the two being treated separately for convenience and simplicity of exposition. At the end of this chapter an attempt will be made to synthesize the two approaches.

(iii) THE INCOME ADJUSTMENT MECHANISM[16]

In the analysis of the income mechanism, we attempt to show how changes in income levels can affect the balance of payments by either restoring or disturbing equilibrium. In order to simplify the analysis and isolate the effects of income changes, we shall assume that prices remain constant so that changes in money income represent changes in real income. It should also be noted that constant prices in the face of changing incomes implies that less than full employment prevails.

To begin with, let us consider how the elements of national income are related *to* national income. Now, in an analysis of a *closed* economy, we know that national income and national product are one and the same thing, simply viewed from different angles; and that national income is made up of consumption and savings, national product being made up of consumption goods and investment goods.

That is,   Y (actual) = C + S

               O (actual) = C + I

And since $Y \equiv O$, C + S = C + I

               $\therefore$ S = I.

Thus, actual (or ex-post) savings always equal actual (or ex-post) investment in a closed economy. Also, in accordance with national income analysis, we can represent the functional relationships between the above variables in the following way:

(i) $C = C(Y)$ – the consumption function;
(ii) $S = S(Y)$ – the savings function;
(iii) $I = I(Y)$ – the investment function,

equilibrium national income existing when planned (or ex-ante) savings and planned (or ex-ante) investment are equal (i.e. where the savings and investment functions intersect). This is conventionally written as $S(Y) = I(Y)$.

Now, once we drop the assumption of a closed economy, we must modify our definitions of national income and national product. National income can either be consumed (C), saved (S), or spent on imports (M). National product now comprises the output of consumption goods consumed domestically, investment goods, and exports.

Thus,
$$Y = C + S + M$$
$$O = C + I + X.$$

And since
$$Y \equiv O,$$
$$S + M = I + X,$$

so that actual savings plus imports always equal actual investment plus exports. However, for equilibrium, planned savings plus planned imports must equal planned investment plus planned exports; so that if we represent the relationship between imports and income as $M = M(Y)$, and the relationship between exports and income as $X = X(Y)$, we have the equilibrium condition that

(A) . . . $$S(Y) + M(Y) = I(Y) + X(Y)$$

Since $S(Y) = Y - C(Y)$, substituting for $S(Y)$ we have,
$$Y - C(Y) + M(Y) = I(Y) + X(Y)$$
or $\quad Y = C(Y) + I(Y) + [X(Y) - M(Y)]$

In equilibrium, therefore,
$$Y = C(Y) + I(Y) + [\text{Balance of Trade}]$$

Equation (A) may also be expressed as –
(B) . . . $$S(Y) - I(Y) = X(Y) - M(Y)$$

showing that in equilibrium, the difference between planned savings and planned investment must exactly equal the balance of trade. This corresponds to the equilibrium condition for a closed economy because, since exports and imports are both zero, the balance of trade is zero and therefore planned savings must equal planned investment for equilibrium to exist. Note the important distinction between the ex-post equation which always holds,

$$S - I = X - M$$

and the ex-ante equation which expresses the equilibrium condition for income:

$$S(Y) - I(Y) = X(Y) - M(Y)$$

Now, we know that consumption and investment both depend upon many variables (habit, rates of interest, etc.), but let us assume, for the sake of simplicity, that the level of national income is the major determinant of both consumption and investment. To make things really simple, assume that the consumption function can be represented by a straight line (as therefore can be the savings function), and that the level of investment does not change with the level of income. Assume also, that the level of exports is constant irrespective of the level of income and that the imports function is also a straight line showing increasing imports as income rises. The purpose of such simplicity is to allow us to isolate the effect on income of, for example, a change in the level of exports. As we shall find, important concepts in the income adjustment analysis are the marginal propensity to import and the marginal propensity to save. Since consumption is a rising function of income, then so must be savings and we can define the marginal propensity to save (MPS) as the change in savings associated with a given unit change in income. Correspondingly, the marginal propensity to import (MPM) is the change in imports associated with a given unit change in income. In other words, the MPS (s) is the first derivative of the savings function and the MPM (m) is the first derivative of the import function.

Thus,

$$s = \frac{dS}{dY} \text{ and } m = \frac{dM}{dY}.^{[17]}$$

Since we have assumed that investment and exports are constant with respect to income, equation A (the equilibrium income condition) becomes

(C) . . . $$S(Y) + M(Y) = I + X.$$

This condition can be represented in a simple diagram as below where $(I + X)$ represents the sum of autonomous investment and exports, and $[M(Y) + S(Y)]$ represents the sum of the savings and import functions.

At E, the point of intersection of the $[M(Y) + S(Y)]$ and $(I + X)$ lines, the level of income is OY, which is the equilibrium level of income. At this level of income, a balance of trade deficit exists ($= AB$) equal to the difference between planned savings and investment. At any other

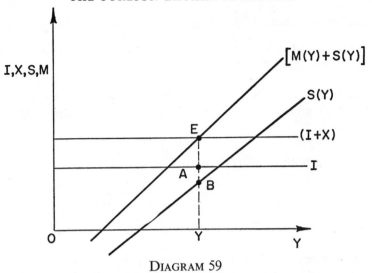

DIAGRAM 59

level of income, equation C is not satisfied and so such levels of income cannot be equilibrium levels.

Consider the effect of a shift upwards of the export function (due, for example, to a change of tastes abroad). The $(I+X)$ line will move upwards by an amount dX to $(I+X_1)$, where dX represents the increase in exports forthcoming at every level of income.

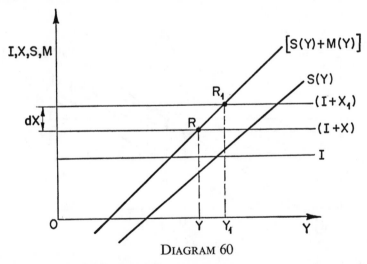

DIAGRAM 60

As can be seen, R_1 is the new equilibrium point giving a level of income of OY_1, showing that the increase in exports, dX, has caused an increase in income of YY_1. The ratio of the change in income to the change in exports $\left(\dfrac{dY}{dX}\right)$ is called the *export* (or foreign-trade) *multiplier with respect to income*; and its size is determined by (in our simple example) the marginal propensities to save and import, as is shown below.

In equilibrium, $I + X = S(Y) + M(Y)$, so that if exports rise by dX, then, for equilibrium to be restored, dX must equal (dS + dM). So, for equilibrium,

$$dX = dS + dM$$

and dividing both sides of the equation into dY, we get

$$\frac{dY}{dX} = \frac{dY}{dS + dM} = \frac{1}{dS/dY + dM/dY}$$

$$\therefore \frac{dY}{dX} = \frac{1}{s + m} = k \text{ (the export multiplier)}$$

The smaller are s and m (i.e. the less steep is the $S(Y) + M(Y)$ curve), the larger will be the multiplier and, therefore, the larger will be the change in income for a given change in exports. It can be observed that since both exports and investment are constant, the investment multiplier will be the same as the export multiplier.

Suppose we complicate the analysis slightly and allow investment to be a rising function of income. Then the $(I + X)$ line will slope upwards to the right as shown below – $(I_1 + X)$.

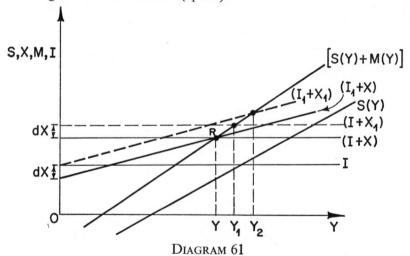

DIAGRAM 61

The diagram is drawn so that the upward sloping $(I_1 + X)$ function cuts the $[S(Y) + M(Y)]$ function at the same point, R, as the horizontal $(I + X)$ function. Now, suppose the export function shifts upwards by dX to $(I_1 + X_1)$ and $(I + X)$. As can be seen the new equilibrium level of income is larger, OY_2, when the $(I + X)$ function slopes upwards than when it is horizontal, OY_1, indicating that the export multiplier must be larger now than before.

This can be seen by considering the equilibrium income equation below

$$Y = C(Y) + I(Y) + X - M(Y)$$

Let $\quad C = a + bY$ and $I = i + gY$ and $M = 1 + mY$,

then $\quad Y = a + bY + i + gY + X - 1 - mY$

$$\therefore Y - bY - gY + mY = a + i + X - 1$$

$$\therefore Y(1 - b - g + m) = a + i + X - 1$$

$$\therefore Y = \frac{a + i + X - 1}{1 - b - g + m} = \frac{a + i - 1}{1 - b - g + m} + \frac{X}{1 - b - g + m}$$

Since $(1 - b) = s$, we have,

$$Y = \frac{a + i - 1}{s - g + m} + \frac{1}{s - g + m} \cdot X$$

and the change in income, dY, $= \dfrac{1}{s - g + m} \cdot dX$

$$\therefore \frac{dY}{dX} = \frac{1}{s - g + m} = k, \text{ the export multiplier}$$

Thus, for given values of s and m, the multiplier will be larger than before, how much larger depending on the size of g, the marginal propensity to invest. The larger is g (i.e. the steeper the $(I_1 + X)$ line), the larger will be the multiplier. Similarly, if exports are a rising function of income, the multiplier becomes

$$\frac{dY}{dX} = \frac{1}{s - g - x + m}$$

which is larger still.

It can be seen, then, that a rise in exports will have an expansionary effect on income, this effect being greater, the larger are g and x and the smaller are s and m since g and x represent injections into the system whereas s and m are leakages out of the system.

Having seen how changes in the level of exports are related to changes in the level of income via the multiplier, we must now attempt to relate this to the balance of payments.[18] As can be seen from any of the previous diagrams, the change in exports leads to a rise in income which leads to an increase in the level of imports. Thus, it is rising incomes, and not changing prices, which cause the increased level of imports, but whether imports change by an amount exactly equal to the change in exports is a different story.

To relate the balance of payments (B) to the income mechanism, let us return to our simple multiplier

$$k = \frac{1}{s+m}$$

Now, $B = X - M$ and $dB = dX - dM$. Also, for a given change in income, $dM = mdY$ and we know from our multiplier analysis that

$$dY = \frac{1}{s+m} \cdot dX$$

$$\therefore dM = \frac{m}{s+m} dX$$

$$\therefore dB = dX - \frac{m}{s+m} dX$$

$$= dX\left(1 - \frac{m}{s+m}\right)$$

$$\therefore dB = \frac{s}{s+m} dX$$

$\frac{m}{s+m}$ is called the export multiplier with respect to imports and $\frac{s}{s+m}$ is called the export multiplier with respect to the balance of payments, both multipliers always being less than one. The smaller is s and the larger is m the smaller (larger) will be the export multiplier with respect to the balance of payments (with respect to imports).

In this simple case, then, it can be seen that an increase in exports will lead to the creation of an export surplus (or a bigger export surplus or a smaller deficit) but that the change in the balance of payments is less than the change in exports. It is important to realize, therefore, that the balance of payments surplus which arises, or is increased as a result of the increased exports, is not completely eliminated, so that the balance of payments does not return to what it was originally. Suppose, for example, that the level of income is OY and the balance of payments is in equilibrium (i.e. $B = O$).

Now let exports rise by dX, giving a new equilibrium level of income OY_1, at which level exports are R_1A and imports R_1B, giving a balance of payments deficit of AB which is less than CD. The balance of payments will only remain unchanged if $s = O$ so that $dB = \frac{O}{m} \cdot dX = O$.

In general, therefore, the balance of payments does not return to its initial position. The effect of the increase in income is to partly correct

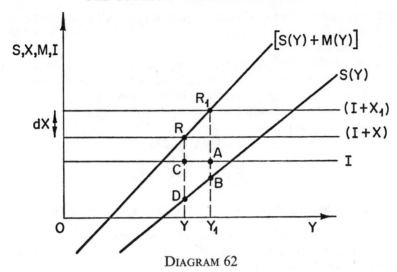

DIAGRAM 62

the balance of payments, the degree of correction depending upon s and m.

When we allow for a functional relationship between investment and the level of income, the export multiplier with respect to the balance of payments becomes

$$\frac{s-g}{s+m-g}.$$

The above analysis can, of course, be used to study the effects of a change in the level of imports. Thus, suppose the $[S(Y)+M(Y)]$ function shifts upwards to $[S(Y)+M_1(Y)]$ giving a new, lower, equilibrium level of income OY_1

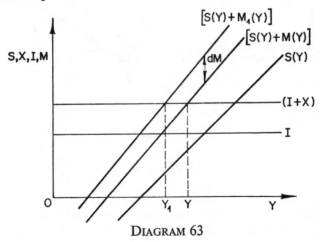

DIAGRAM 63

Since, in equilibrium $(I + X)$ must equal $S(Y) + M(Y)$, and since at the new level of income $(I + X)$ has not changed, it follows that $S(Y) + M(Y)$ cannot have changed either.

Therefore $(dS + dM)$ must equal zero, i.e. $dS = dM$. In other words, the increase in imports must be exactly offset by a decrease in savings. Now, given a consumption function of the form

$$C = a + bY, \quad dS = (1 - b)dY.$$

Therefore, in equilibrium

$$(1 - b)dY = dM$$

$$\therefore \frac{dY}{dM} = \frac{1}{(1 - b)} = \frac{1}{s}.$$

$\dfrac{dY}{dM}$ is the *import* multiplier with respect to income. The student is left to work out for himself the relationship between changes in imports and the level of income, balance of payments, etc., when the functions are more complex than above.

The student should also note that although, as mentioned earlier, the export multiplier and the investment multiplier with respect to income are the same, when the exports and investment functions are horizontal straight lines, the balance of payments multipliers are not the same. A rise in exports will lead to an export surplus (or at least a balance of payments improvement), whereas a rise in investment leads (via an inflow of imports) to a balance of payments deterioration.

This is illustrated in Diagram 64 below.

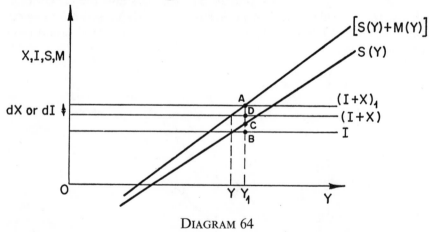

DIAGRAM 64

Initially, income is at equilibrium at a level OY with exports equal to imports. Now, suppose that the export function shifts upwards by dX giving a new level of income OY_1. At this level of income, exports are AB and imports AC, giving a balance of payments surplus of CB. Had the export function not shifted but the investment one had (by dI) the new level of income would still be OY, but at this level, exports would be DB, imports AC, giving a deficit of DB − AC. Now, since the investment and export multipliers (with respect to income) are the same in this example, we can write:

$$k = \frac{1}{s+m} dI.$$

Also,
$$dB = dX - dM$$

$$= dX - \frac{m}{s+m} dI$$

$$\therefore dB = -\frac{m}{s+m} dI$$

Again the balance of payments will be unaltered by a change in investment only if m is zero. In all other cases, the balance of payments deteriorates by an amount depending on the sizes of m and s. The smaller is m and the larger is s, the smaller will be the size of the balance of payments multiplier with respect to investment.

Up to this point it has been assumed implicitly that the effects on other countries of changes in the domestic level of income are non-existent or so small as to be negligible. Obviously, this need not be the case, and so we must now analyze the so-called *"foreign-repercussion effect"*[19] which is the effect of the change in exports (imports) in one country, on the level of income abroad, and the corresponding feed-back effects of this on domestic income and so on. The importance of the repercussion effect will depend oupn the economic size of the country so far as international trade is concerned. Thus a "small" country, by increasing its imports from a large country, will have little effect on the level of income of the large country. Also, if the income effect were important, the repercussion effect will still be small if the marginal propensity to import from the small country is low. In the case of a large country, the foreign-repercussion effect is likely to be significant, the final equilibrium depending on the marginal propensities to save and import. It should also be noted that it is possible to neutralize the foreign-repercussion effect by the use of fiscal or monetary policy. Thus, for example, if country A increases its exports to country B, the income of country B will decline (its import function has shifted upwards) and so its demand for A's exports will fall off, leading to a contraction in A's income and so on. A can, by the use of fiscal and monetary policy, neutralize this effect on her income. However, cases where the repercussion effect is not neutralized, or where it is too big to be neglected, must now be studied.

For the sake of simplicity we shall consider only two countries, A and B, operating as before with unused resources (i.e. less than full employment), and therefore constant prices, so enabling us to isolate the income effects of a change in exports.

When we allow for the existence of the repercussion effect we have a situation where the income of country A is related functionally to the income of country B, and similarly the income of country B is related functionally to the income of country A. That is,

$$Y_A = f_1(Y_B) \text{ and } Y_B = f_2(Y_A)$$

Also, since the exports of country A are identical to the imports of country B and *vice versa*, we can write

$$X_A \equiv M_B \text{ and } X_B \equiv M_A$$

which, in functional terms becomes

$$X_A(Y_B) \equiv M_B(Y_B)$$
$$\text{and } X_B(Y_A) \equiv M_A(Y_A)$$

The equilibrium income condition for the two countries can therefore be written as

$$Y_A = C_A(Y_A) + I_A + X_A(Y_B) - M_A(Y_A)$$
$$\text{and } Y_B = C_B(Y_B) + I_B + M_A(Y_A) - X_A(Y_B)$$

and assuming that the marginal propensities to consume and import are constant, the equilibrium income equations will be linear and can be represented diagrammatically as below, where Y_A and Y_B are the income equations for countries A and B respectively.

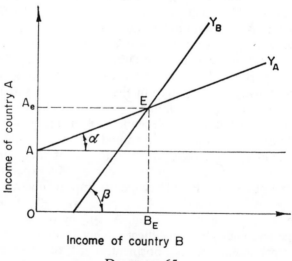

DIAGRAM 65

Y_A starts at A on the y-axis, since, even if B's income is zero, A will still have a positive income ($Y_A = C_A(Y_A) + I_A - M_A(Y_A)$). Correspondingly Y_B starts at B on the x-axis. At E, where the two curves intersect, we have a stable equilibrium with the level of income in A equal to OA$_E$ and that in B equal to OB$_E$. The student may be wondering if the Y_A and Y_B lines must always intersect to give a stable equilibrium. The answer is "yes" – it can be shown that Y_A is always less steep than Y_B.

Thus, if we take the income equation for A:

$$Y_A = C_A(Y_A) + I_A + X_A(Y_B) - M_A(Y_A)$$

i.e. $Y_A - C_A(Y_A) + M_A(Y_A) = I_A + X_A(Y_B)$

∴ $dY_A - C_A'(Y_A)dY_A + M_A'(Y_A)dY_A = X_A'(Y_B)dY_B$

Therefore,

$$\frac{dY_A}{dY_B} = \frac{X_A'(Y_B)}{1 - C_A'(Y_A) + M_A'(Y_A)}$$

$$= \frac{\Delta X_A(Y_B)}{\Delta S_A(Y_A) + \Delta M_A(Y_A)} = \frac{\Delta M_B(Y_B)}{\Delta S_A(Y_A) + \Delta M_A(Y_A)}$$

$$= \frac{MPM_B}{MPS_A + MPM_A}$$

∴ $\dfrac{dY_A}{dY_B} = \dfrac{m_B}{s_A + m_A}$

Similarly, using the equation for Y_B, it can be shown that

$$\frac{dY_A}{dY_B} = \frac{s_B + m_B}{m_A}$$

In other words, Y_B is always steeper than Y_A, so that a stable equilibrium exists. Note also, that although at E the incomes of the two countries are in equilibrium, the balance of payments need not be zero.

Let us now consider the effects of an upward shift in the export function of country A ($X_A = f_1(Y_B)$), and suppose that the level of exports of country A is given by the relation

$$X_A = a + bY_B$$

Then a shift of the function means that "a" has increased (say to a_1). The effect of this is to shift upwards the Y_A curve in Diagram 65. This can be seen by considering the equilibrium income equation for country A.

$$Y_A = C_A(Y_A) + I_A + X_A(Y_B) - M_A(Y_A)$$

Suppose the consumption function is of the form $C = cY_A$ and the import function is of the form $M = mY_A$. Then

$$Y_A = cY_A + I_A + a + bY_B - mY_A$$

An increase in "a" will mean therefore that for a given level of income in country B, there corresponds a bigger level of income in country A (i.e. the Y_A curve shifts upwards). However, the Y_B curve also shifts – *to the left*. Consider the equilibrium income equation for country B

$$Y_B = C_B(Y_B) + I_B + X_B(Y_A) - M_B(Y_B)$$

and suppose the consumption function is of the form $C = cY_B$ and the import function is of the form $M = mY_B$. Then

$$Y_B = cY_B + I_B + mY_A - mY_B - a$$

so that for a given level of income in country A, an increase in "a" means that a smaller income in country B is associated with it (i.e. the Y_B curve shifts to the left by "da"). We have therefore the following:

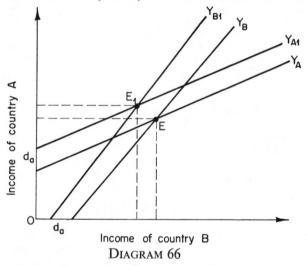

DIAGRAM 66

The shift of A's export function has the effect therefore of increasing A's income and lowering B's. This is shown by the movement from E to E_1. But what happens to the balance of payments? To discover the answer to this, consider the equilibrium income equations for the two countries:

$$Y_A = cY_A + I_A + a + bY_B - mY_A$$
$$\text{and} \quad Y_B = cY_B + I_B + mY_A - mY_B - a$$

Now, if "a" changes by "da", Y_A and Y_B change by dY_A and dY_B respectively as below:

$$dY_A = dC_A + da + dX_A - dM_A$$
$$\text{and} \quad dY_B = dC_B - da - dM_B + dM_A.$$
$$\text{But,} \quad dY_A = c_A dY_A + da + m_B dY_B - m_A dY_A$$
$$\text{and} \quad dY_B = c_B dY_B - da - m_B dY_B + m_A dY_A$$

Therefore $dY_A(1 - c_A) = da + m_B dY_B - m_A dY_A$
and $dY_B(1 - c_B) = -da - m_B dY_B + m_A dY_A$
That is, $s_A \cdot dY_A = da + m_B dY_B - m_A dY_A$
and $s_B \cdot dY_B = -da - m_B dY_B + m_A dY_A$

It is possible to solve these equations,[20] the solution giving:

$$dY_A = \frac{1}{m_A + s_A + \frac{s_A}{s_B} \cdot m_B} \cdot da = k_A \cdot da$$

and $$dY_B = \frac{1}{m_B + s_B + \frac{s_B}{s_A} \cdot m_A} \cdot -da = k_B \cdot -da$$

where k_A and k_B represent the export multipliers with respect to income for countries A and B respectively. As can be observed, an upward shift of A's export function causes a rise in A's income level and a fall in B's income level; the extent of the changes in incomes depending upon the sizes of m_A, m_B, s_A and s_B.

Having discovered how incomes will be affected by a change in the export function, we can go on to analyze the effects of these income changes on the *balance of payments*:

$$B = X - M$$
or $$B = a + m_B Y_B - m_A Y_A.$$
$$\therefore \quad dB = da + m_B dY_B - m_A dY_A$$

Substituting the values for dY_B and dY_A[21] into the above equation, we get

$$dB = \frac{1}{1 + \frac{m_A}{s_A} + \frac{m_B}{s_B}} \cdot da = k\beta \cdot da$$

where $k\beta$ is the export multiplier with respect to the balance of payments. It can be seen that $k\beta$ is always less than one and positive which again means that the balance of payments does not return to its original position but shows an improvement for the country whose export function has shifted.

Before leaving the income adjustment mechanism, a few words of warning may be in order. The student should always bear in mind the highly simplified nature of the models of the multiplier which we have used. These models, it will be recalled, were mostly built on simplifying assumptions concerning the nature of the savings and import functions (linear) and the investment functions (horizontal). These functions may well not be straight lines; other variables may have an important effect on consumption, etc. (e.g. past levels of consumption, the level of wealth of the individuals, price changes and so on). Also, investment may be a rising function of income, which will mean in the case of the foreign-repercussion effect that a shift of the export function, by changing income levels, will also cause investment to change, creating further income and balance of payments effects. Or, we can conceive of an acceleration-type mechanism working in foreign trade.[22] An increase in the level of exports may lead to increased investment in the export sector, leading to increased income, more investment and so on. As income rises, imports will be sucked in and we may end up in a position where an initial increase in exports leads to an import surplus. When considering the income adjustment mechanism as developed above, one should therefore bear these qualifications in mind.

All our analysis so far has been conveniently divided into studies of the income and price adjustment mechanisms in isolation. However, in real life, a shift of the export function will affect not only incomes, but also prices; similarly, a change in the exchange rate will affect not only prices, but also incomes. We must attempt therefore to bring together both adjustment mechanisms into a single model.[23]

Harberger's approach uses price elasticities as the chief explanation of balance of payment adjustment in contrast to Polak,[24] whose empirical studies suggest that it was mainly national income levels which altered to restore balance of payments equilibrium. However, the price elasticities approach conflicts seriously with the so-called "absorption" approach introduced by Alexander.[25] Basically the argument revolves round the problem that in analyzing the effect on the balance of payments of, say, a change in income, one cannot get a determinate solution unless one also takes account of what is happening to relative prices. Similarly, in analyzing the effect of a devaluation, one must take account of changing income levels. Let us study Alexander's approach in more detail.

As we have now come to realize, the balance of payments outcome with devaluation is described by the elasticities approach as depending upon the elasticities of demand for and supply of exports and imports. These elasticities, however, and with them the responses of importers and exporters to changing relative prices, were valid only if both incomes and the prices of other domestic commodities were held constant. However, in real life, devaluation will affect incomes and also other prices (e.g. via the effects of higher prices of raw material imports). This was realized by various writers[26] who attempted to refine the traditional elasticities approach by taking income effects into the analysis of devaluation. The results of such refinements were to demonstrate that income effects of devaluation tended to counteract the beneficial price effects so that the conditions for effective devaluation became more stringent. In view of the estimates made of elasticities, which suggested that elasticities in trade tended to be low, it seemed that devaluation could never seriously be contemplated as a measure to correct a trade deficit.

Some noted economists,[27] however, argued that the estimates were biased downwards and that the estimators had measured short-run elasticities, whereas it was the long-run elasticities which were relevant in the analysis of devaluation. In the long-run, when all adjustments have been made to the new exchange rate, elasticities (it was argued) will be higher. Once we try to allow for income effects, then, the analysis becomes more complex yet more realistic. Alexander, in his model, attempts to retain the realism of the traditional approach (as refined) whilst at the same time reducing the complexity of disentangling the income and price effects of devaluation. Alexander's model is built on the familiar Keynesian system for a closed economy by extending it to included exports and imports. In such an open system Alexander defines "*absorption*" as total domestic expenditure on goods and services produced domestically

$$\text{i.e.} \quad A \equiv C + I,$$

and using the accounting identity for national income in an open economy, we have:

$$Y = C + I + (X - M) = A + (X - M)$$
$$\text{or} \quad Y - A = X - M = B \text{ (the balance of trade).}$$

The effectiveness of devaluation will depend therefore on the extent to which an exchange rate alteration induces changes in domestic output (Y) relative to changes in absorption (A). If devaluation increases Y relative to A, then a balance of trade improvement will have taken place. The major problem tackled by Alexander is to explain how devaluation will affect output and absorption, absorption being treated as functionally related to income, although devaluation may cause absorption to change independently of the level of income. It will be recalled from the elasticity approach that for policy prescriptions a knowledge would be required of the magnitudes of the relevant elasticities. In the absorption approach, answers to the same sort of problems require a knowledge of the change in output due to an exchange rate alteration, the marginal propensity to absorb (i.e. to spend on domestic consumption and investment) and the *direct* effect on absorption itself.

Alexander's model is basically built up in two stages – firstly the effects of devaluation on the trade balance are looked at in terms of elasticities.[28] If devaluation improved the trade balance, then incomes would expand[29] and set in motion various forces which could reinforce or tend to reverse the initial improvement. These forces are analyzed in the second stage of Alexander's analysis – the absorption stage.

Now, we saw earlier that the trade balance will improve if ΔB (the change in the balance of trade) is greater than $\Delta Y - \Delta A$. If $\Delta B > (\Delta Y - \Delta A)$ then some "hoarding" (H) must have taken place, so we can rephrase the condition by saying that a trade improvement will occur if ΔH is positive. In the model, it is assumed that C and I are functionally related to real income (Y) so that if Y increases, then C and I will also increase (i.e. A increases). However, devaluation may also affect directly the level of A for any given level of Y.

These changes can be expressed in the absorption equation –

$$\Delta B = \Delta Y - a\Delta Y - \beta A = \Delta H$$
$$\therefore \Delta B = \Delta Y(1 - a) - \beta A$$

where a is the marginal propensity to absorb income $(1 - a)$ is M.P. to hoard and βA is the net of the direct effects of changes in Y on A. Now, assuming that devaluation raises Y (by raising X relative to M) then ΔY is positive and the balance of trade will improve if a is less than unity and βA is negative; or if βA is positive it is less than $(1 - a)\Delta Y$.[30] This can be represented diagrammatically.

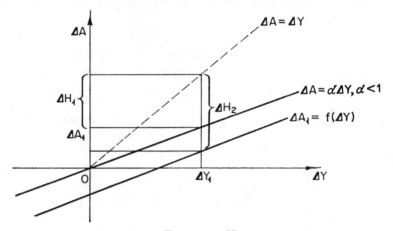

DIAGRAM 67

It is assumed above that βA is negative and that $a < 1$. Suppose initially that devaluation raises real income by ΔY_1, causing absorption to increase by ΔA_1 and creating an increase in hoarding (i.e. balance of trade improvement) of ΔH_1. However, due to the rise in income of ΔY_1, the absorption function shifts downwards to ΔA_1, giving a final increase in hoarding of ΔH_2. Had βA been positive, the absorption function would have shifted upwards, reducing or even reversing the income induced effects of devaluation. From this highly simplified account of Alexander's analysis, it can be seen that the major policy problem with devaluation will be to ensure that the change in income due to devaluation is larger than the total change in absorption. Despite the apparent simplicity of Alexander's approach, it has been severely criticized by Machlup[31] and Tsiang,[32] following which Alexander modified the analysis somewhat. The problems and issues involved are too complex to go into here, but their existence serves to show that as one tries to take account of more realism in models of devaluation the complexity increases at a fantastic rate and the difficulties of handling such models become immense. One of the most recent attempts to synthesize the income and price analyses has been made by Vanek[33] so let us for the rest of this chapter consider his approach.

He begins by noting that under the classical price-adjustment approach, Say's Law guaranteed full employment, and the gold standard disallowed any alteration in the rate of exchange. Thus, only the balance of payments was considered as a true variable in the system. Any imbalance in payments and receipts would automatically correct itself via the price-specie-flow mechanism. The rate of interest and elasticities were largely ignored and even at a later date, when the rate of interest was introduced into the analysis, it was treated as an element in the monetary adjustment rather than in the real adjustment. With the advent of the gold-exchange-standard, however, the neo-classicals introduced the rate of exchange as an element of the adjustment mechanism, conducting the analysis in terms of import and export elasticities and giving us the familiar Marshall-Lerner condition.

As Vanek points out, however, the neo-classical approach is imperfect because changes in the output of exports and imports will affect income and employment levels. Basically, what the Keynesian multiplier analysis does is to consider income and employment as variables in the system. Taking the simple Keynesian system where, in equilibrium, we have

$$s(Y) + M(Y) = I(Y) + X,$$

Vanek proceeds to develop a more realistic theory of the adjustment mechanism in which both income (Y) and relative prices are treated as adjustment variables. Not only this, but savings, investment and imports are treated as being related to the rate of interest as well as the level of income. This gives us one relation in two variables (Y and the rate of interest "i") which can be written as

$$\phi(Y_1 i) = 0.$$

With these two variables affecting the outcome, an infinite number of solutions are possible to this equation, the relation between income and the rate of interest being represented by AA in Diagram 68 below.

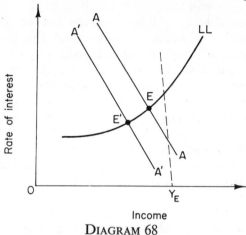

Income

DIAGRAM 68

AA shows the equilibrium possibilities for the goods markets (S − I) and also contains the foreign balance (X − M) when related to Y and "i". AA is similar to the Hicksian IS curve except that (i) real rather than money income is used, and (ii) it contains the foreign trade balance. LL represents the equilibrium possibilities between the demand for money and the price level, and resembles the Hicksian LM curve. The position of the LL curve will depend upon the price level and money supply, so that a reduction in the supply of money or in the price level will shift upward to the left the portions of the LL curve which are less than infinitely elastic. Also, an increase in domestic prices (foreign prices and imports assumed constant) will cause a reduction in expenditure on domestic goods and an increase in expenditure on imports. Thus, the effective demand for domestic goods falls and real income falls so that the AA curve shifts to the left (A'A'). The AA curve would also shift to the left if the domestic currency were appreciated (domestic prices constant). E indicates the initial equilibrium where, with given prices and money supply, domestic and foreign trade are compatible with liquidity preference (LL) and propensities to save. If YE represents full employment income, then E is a less than full employment equilibrium situation.

Thus, according to Vanek the classical price-adjustment mechanism and the Keynesian income-adjustment mechanism are partial equilibrium approaches and therefore special cases of the general theory. One of the important conclusions from Vanek's study is that the traditional Marshall-Lerner condition is considerably weakened if income is introduced as a variable of adjustment. For a "normal" balance of payments reaction to a devaluation, the sum of the elasticities of demand must be considerably higher than unity since the income effects will tend to offset the price effects.[34]

The complexity of the analysis once both income and price are treated as variables, and the effects on the conclusions of partial equilibrium analysis, bear out the warning that when discussing income changes prices should be borne in mind and, similarly, when discussing price changes, incomes should be borne in mind. A consideration of the complexity yet simplicity of the models used in this chapter will show that it is extremely difficult for a country experiencing balance of payments difficulties to make a policy decision, the outcome of which is known with any great degree of certainty. The purpose of the next chapter will be to look at possible policies of adjustment to balance of payments disequilibrium, and analyze closely the effects of one – namely flexible exchange rates.

[1] For a discussion of other functions of the foreign-exchange market (credit provision and hedging) see Kindleberger, *International Economics*, Ch. 3.

[2] H. G. Johnson, "The Balance of Payments," in *Money, Trade, and Economic Growth*, 1962.

[3] D. Hume, "Of the Balance of Payments," in *Political Discourses*, 1752.

[4] Under the gold standard, gold either is money (e.g. in the form of gold coins) or is held as backing for paper money. If the backing is 100%, then the money supply is reduced by the amount of the gold outflow; if less than 100%, the money supply will fall by more than the amount of the gold outflow. If in the face of a gold outflow the central bank raised its discount rate, then this would lead to a contraction in the money supply but, what is probably more important, it would induce a movement of short-term capital into the country which would not only affect the money supply contraction but also improve the balance of payments.

[5] W. E. Beach, *British International Gold Movements and Banking Policy* 1881–1913, (1935).

[6] See Kindleberger, *International Economics*, 3rd edition, Ch. 4.

[7] Price elasticity of demand is defined as the proportionate change in the quantity of a good demanded, divided by the proportionate change in its price $\left(\text{i.e.} \dfrac{dQ/Q}{dP/P} \right)$.

[8] See F. Machlup, "Theory of Foreign Exchanges," *Economica*, 1939; M. J. Wasserman, C. W. Hultman and Laszlo Zsoldos, *International Finance*, New York, 1963.

[9] At the limit, where the demand curve for exports is completely inelastic, the value of exports will remain unchanged.

[10] See E. Schneider, *Money, Income and Employment*, pp. 254–262, 1962.

[11] Unless the elasticity of demand is zero.

[12] See E. Schneider, *op. cit.*, pp. 249–254.

[13] See, for example, Kindleberger, *International Economics*, Appendix D.

[14] Schneider, *op. cit.*, gives a very interesting analysis of the conditions which determine whether the change in the balance of payments is in the same or opposite direction when looked at from the point of view of either domestic or foreign currency.

[15] Assuming $\dfrac{M}{X} = 1$.

[16] See F. Machlup, *International Trade and the National Income Multiplier*, 1943. L. A. Metzler, "Underemployment Equilibrium in International Trade," *Econometrica*, 1942; H. Giersh, "The Acceleration Principle and the Propensity to Import," *International Economic Papers*, 1954.

[17] Note that the MPM and MPS tell us nothing about the *average* propensities (APM and APS) defined as S/Y and M/Y. Thus, for example, the APM may be low whilst the MPM is high. Also, the MPS and MPM will differ for different sectors of the economy so that the concepts relate to the "average" MPM and the "average" MPS.

[18] The treatment of this section follows closely that of Schneider in *Money, Income and Employment*.

[19] See R. Robinson, "A Graphical Analysis of the Foreign-Trade Multiplier," *Economic Journal*, 1952.

[20] The solution is:

$$s \cdot dY_A = da + m_B dY_B - m_A dY_A$$

$$s \cdot dY_A + m_A dY_A = da + m_B dY_B$$

$$dY_A(s+m) = da + m_B dY_B$$

$$dY_A = \frac{da + m_B \, dY_B}{(s_A + m_A)} \qquad \ldots (1)$$

Similarly

$$dY_B = \frac{-da + m_A dY_A}{(s_B + m_B)}$$

Substituting in (1) for dY_B, we get:

$$dY_A = \frac{da + m_B \left(\dfrac{-da + m_A dY_A}{s_B + m_B} \right)}{s_A + m_A}$$

$$= \frac{\dfrac{da \cdot s_B + da \cdot m_B - da \cdot m_B + m_A m_B \cdot dY_A}{s_B + m_B}}{s_A + m_A}$$

$$= \frac{da \cdot s_B + m_A m_B dY_A}{(s_B + m_B)(s_A + m_A)}$$

$$\therefore \ dY_A(s_B + m_B)(s_A + m_A) = da \cdot s_B + m_A m_B dY_A$$

$$\therefore \ dY_A[(s_B + m_B)(s_A + m_A) - m_A m_B] = da \cdot s_B$$

$$\therefore \ dY_A = \frac{da s_B}{(s_B + m_B)(s_A + m_A) - m_A m_B}$$

$$= \frac{s_B}{s_A s_B + s_A m_B + s_B m_A + m_A m_B - m_A m_B} \cdot da$$

$$= \frac{s_B}{s_A s_B + s_A m_B + s_B m_A} \cdot da$$

$$\therefore \ dY_A = \frac{1}{s_A + \dfrac{s_A}{s_B} \cdot m_B + m_A} \cdot da$$

Similarly,

$$dY_B = \frac{1}{m_B + s_B + \dfrac{s_B}{s_A} \cdot ma} - \cdot da$$

[21] The solution is

$$dB = da + m_B dY_B - m_A dY_A$$

Substituting for dY_A and dY_B gives

$$dB = da + m_B \frac{1}{m_B + s_B + \frac{s_B}{s_A} \cdot m_A} \cdot -da - m_A \frac{1}{m_A + s_A + \frac{s_A}{s_B} \cdot m_B} \cdot da$$

$$= \frac{\dfrac{da m_B + da s_B + da s_B m_A - m_B da}{s_A}}{m_B + s_B + \frac{s_B}{s_A} m_A} - \frac{m_A da}{m_A + s_A + \frac{s_A}{s_B} \cdot m_B}$$

$$= \frac{+da s_B s_A + da s_B m_A}{m_B s_A + s_B s_A + s_B m_A} - \frac{m_A da}{m_A + s_A + \frac{s_A}{s_B} \cdot m_B}$$

$$= \frac{da \cdot s_B \cdot s_A}{m_A s_B + s_A s_B + s_A m_B} = \frac{1}{\dfrac{m_A s_B}{s_B s_A} + \dfrac{s_A s_B}{s_A s_B} + \dfrac{s_A m_B}{s_B s_A}} \cdot da$$

$$\therefore dB = \frac{1}{1 + \dfrac{m_A}{s_A} + \dfrac{m_B}{s_B}} \cdot da$$

[22] See H. Giersch, "The Acceleration Principle and the Propensity to Import," *International Economic Papers*, 1954.

[23] See, A. C. Harberger, "Currency Depreciation, Income, and the Balance of Trade," *Journal of Political Economy*, 1950.

[24] J. J. Polak, *An International Economic System*, 1954.

[25] S. S. Alexander, "Effect of Devaluation on a Trade Balance," I.M.F. Staff Papers, 1952; also, "Effects of a Devaluation: A Simplified Synthesis of Elasticities and Absorption Approaches," *American Economic Review*, 1959.

[26] Meade, *The Balance of Payments*, 1951, F. Machlup, "Relative Prices and Aggregate Spending in the Analysis of Devaluation," *American Economic Review*, 1955, Sohmen, "Demand Elasticities and the Foreign Exchange Market," *Journal of Political Economy*, 1957; also, "Effect of Devaluation on the Price Level," *Quarterly Journal of Economics*, 1958.

[27] Machlup, Harberger, etc.

[28] Note that Alexander pointed out that the elasticities involved were "total," that is, meaningless unless the economic system is specified.

[29] Even with full employment (see Machlup, *op. cit.*, and *The Terms of Trade Effects of Devaluation upon Real Income and the Balance of Trade*, Kyklos, 1956).

[30] Note that the analysis is considerably complicated by the possibility that a may exceed unity, and that real income may fall with a devaluation even although money income and real output expand. See Machlup on effects of devaluation on real income (Kyklos 1956).

[31] Machlup, *op. cit.*

[32] S. C. Tsiang, "The Role of Money in Trade Balance Stability," *American Economic Review*, 1961.

[33] J. Vanek, *The Balance of Payments, Level of Economic Activity and the Value of Currency*, 1962.

[34] Vanek, *op. cit.*, p. 36.

CHAPTER 9

Balance of Payments Adjustment –
Which Way?

IN THE preceding chapter, we looked at theoretical models of how a change in certain variables would affect the balance of payments and national income of a country, without much reference to the problem of discovering which variables a country in balance of payments difficulties will choose to act upon in order to equilibrate its external accounts. It is to this problem which we shall now turn our attention, examining the possible ways of adjusting to disequilibrium, with special reference to the controversy surrounding the "fixed versus flexible exchange rates" argument. A great deal of the content of this examination will be relevant to an understanding of the so-called problem of international liquidity which we shall be studying in the final chapter, and it is as well to bear this in mind while reading this chapter.

Generally speaking, there are four ways of dealing with a persistent imbalance in the balance of payments – deflation/inflation, flexible exchange rates, manipulation of direct controls over trade and capital movements, and devaluation/revaluation of the pegged exchange rate. Let us look briefly at each in turn:

(1) *Deflation/Inflation*. The use of domestic monetary and fiscal policy affects the level of aggregate expenditure and production which in turn affect the balance of payments. Suppose, for instance, that a country in deficit reduces the money supply, raises taxation, and in general attempts to lower the level of aggregate demand by operating on income and the incentive to invest (through interest-rate policy, investment grants, etc.). If incomes fall, domestic expenditure will fall, and with it, expenditure on imported goods and services. Imports may also fall, due to a fall in domestic prices relative to foreign prices, causing a switch of expenditure towards home produced goods. The outcome of these processes will be to improve the balance of payments, although such improvement will probably bring with it some unemployment of resources, the degree of such domestic disruption depending upon the severity of the deflationary measures, which in turn will be determined by the elasticities of demand for exports and imports and the propensities to spend at home and abroad.

176

(2) *Flexible Exchange Rates.* As we shall see later, many economists support this policy as being the best for equilibrating the balance of payments without at the same time having harmful side effects on the level of employment at home. Many proponents also feel that the adoption of a flexible rate system would considerably reduce the need for international liquidity and to that extent help to kill two birds with one stone. The fundamental principles of such a system have already been described in Chapter 8, where we saw that if the exchange rate is allowed to fluctuate freely and find its own market-determined level, then any excess demand for or supply of foreign exchange will be eliminated. Thus, through a system of fluctuating rates, any payments imbalance can only be a temporary phenomenon, the balance of payments automatically equilibrating itself. Of this, much more later.

(3) *Direct Controls.* If elasticities of demand are such that price adjustment (brought about either through rate changes or domestic policies of inflation/deflation) fail to correct the balance of payments, or if the adjustments are working too slowly, then direct controls over imports/exports may be resorted to. Due partly to the realization that to correct a balance of payments disequilibrium, any excess spending must be eliminated, the use of import controls *alone* has been greatly discredited. In conditions of full employment, import controls may distort expenditure and reduce savings with little impact on the balance of payments. Even if trade controls are successful, they can have detrimental effects on one's trading partners. Thus, if import controls are imposed to correct a deficit, they will directly affect the exports (and therefore incomes and employment levels) of other countries – this is exactly the reason why on economic welfare grounds any form of direct control over trade is frowned upon. For underdeveloped economies, with low levels of employment and trying to expand their export sectors, the problem is obviously of critical importance. Controls may quite easily lead to retaliation, a reduction in the level of world trade, and consequent adverse effects on world welfare.

Despite these objections and the recent trend towards freer trade (G.A.T.T., and Kennedy Round cuts of July 1968), many countries still insist on retaining the right to impose controls on trade as the current discussions in the United States indicate. Also, even where countries have removed barriers to trade they have still retained the use of controls over capital movements. Thus, countries in deficit may attempt to reduce the outflow of capital seeking investment overseas by, for example, taxing heavily the profits on overseas investments or by making it difficult to acquire the necessary foreign exchange.

Countries may also impose controls over the amount of money that can be taken abroad on vacation purposes and so influence directly the balance of payments. There is always the problem, of course, that by restricting overseas investment one may indirectly reduce the level of one's exports and also reduce the earnings being made from such investment (which appear in the invisibles account). Nevertheless, two advanced industrial nations (U.K. and U.S.A.) have recently imposed such forms of control over capital flows in order to help correct their deficits – (the U.S. Interest Equalization Tax was introduced in order to curb U.S. purchases of foreign investments by taxing such purchases). However, as Machlup[1] points out, direct controls are no solution to the problem – they are likely to break down, are wasteful in their effects on the allocation of resources, and often inequitable in their effects on the distribution of income. In any case, they only treat the symptoms and not the disease, the imbalance in the supply of and demand for foreign currency remaining, so that if the controls are removed the imbalance is likely to reappear. According to Machlup, the greatest objection to controls lies in their inconsistency – to resort to controls in order to maintain fixity of rates (which is supposed to reduce trading risks and therefore increase the level of world trade) is obviously inconsistent. Controls imposed for a short period of time to allow adjustment to take place are acceptable, provided that the level of world trade will be greater after their removal than before their imposition.

Controls are also inappropriate when used to try to correct imbalance due to uncompetitiveness, since they would have to be maintained permanently in order to offset it. Likewise, controls are inappropriate when the problem arises due to domestic inflationary pressures, since such controls would have to increase in severity as the inflation continued.

It can be seen, then, that very strong economic arguments can be used against the use of direct controls over trade and capital flows used solely to correct a balance of payments disequilibrium. The problem is, of course, that the decision as to whether or not to impose such controls is seldom (if ever) made on the basis of the economics of the situation.

(4) *Devaluation/Revaluation*. These policy measures differ from flexible exchange rates in that it is the authorities who decide (*a*) if an exchange rate adjustment will take place, (*b*) when the adjustment will take place, and (*c*) how much of an adjustment will take place. Since the rate movements are no longer determined by market forces, it follows that the decisions made may be wrong – adjustments may well be seriously delayed and of excessive amount, so creating other strains on the balance of payments. However, like flexible rates, adjustments of the peg have the immediate effect of altering import/export price

relationships, the effect of this on the balance of payments being a function of the demand and supply elasticities involved. As we saw in Chapter 8, devaluation/revaluation also has important effects on domestic (and foreign) income, employment and output, operating through multiplier mechanisms. The major problem, as we saw, is that of combining the income and price effects so as to produce a comprehensive system of analysis. Consider, for example, a country in deficit which, in order to correct the deficit, devalues its currency but, for a variety of reasons, devalues excessively, so creating an excess demand for domestic currency. One effect of this will be to inject money into the domestic money stream which will have an expansionary effect and so (along with falling income levels abroad) tend to counteract the beneficial effects of devaluation on the balance of payments.

Many economists also believe that, if devaluation is resorted to, it should be accompanied by deflationary monetary and fiscal policies, since domestic prices will rise as a result of the devaluation. These price rises may be followed by wage claims, cost increases, and further price increases, so tending to nullify the desired outcome. As we shall see, this criticism can also be made of flexible exchange rate adjustments.

It is apparent, therefore, that adjustments to balance of payments disequilibrium is by no means automatic – it requires a delicate combination of the appropriate instruments of policy both at a domestic and at an international level. To illustrate this, let us now proceed to a study of the present adjustment mechanism and proposals which have recently been made concerning a modification of the system.

The Present System of the Adjustable Peg

Under the old gold standard, countries had to subordinate their domestic policies to what was happening on external account. Gold flows (and later capital flows in response to interest-rate differentials) performed the adjustment function and so kept the balance of payments in equilibrium. However, external equilibrium might easily result in internal disequilibrium of employment and output in situations where prices and costs (e.g. wages) were inflexible downwards. During the 1930s this system led to the international transmission of depression and to competitive devaluations aimed at reflating domestic economies. The gold standard was therefore abandoned and replaced by a system of fluctuating exchange rates in an effort to insulate the domestic from the international economy. Rate fluctuations, however, proved too chaotic and this led, towards the end of the Second World War, to an agreement to set up a new system which would retain the advantages of the rigid gold standard *and* freely fluctuating rates, without suffering from the disadvantages of either.

The agreement set up a body (the I.M.F.), members of which would commit themselves to stabilizing their economies at full employment and maintaining within 1% the par value of their currencies. Since the United States was tied directly to gold and all member currencies were tied directly to the U.S. dollar, it follows that all currencies are tied indirectly to gold; hence the title "Gold-Exchange-Standard." Exchange rates became rigid, therefore, but if a country was suffering from persistent balance of payments imbalance ('fundamental disequilibrium") then the I.M.F. could permit (after discussion) such a country to adjust its exchange rate. By means of such a system, exchange rates were held rigid but not inflexible – a seemingly paradoxical state of affairs. The aim was to allow countries to employ domestic policies in order to achieve high, stable employment levels without inflation, whilst at the same time permitting basic balance of payments adjustments through infrequent exchange-rate adjustment. Temporary disequilibria will be eliminated by using up (or adding to) owned or borrowable reserves. Similarly, and tendency for the pegged rate to move outside the 1% limits will cause the monetary authorities to intervene in the foreign exchange market and stabilize the rate by buying or selling gold and/or foreign exchange. If the disequilibrium persists, then "appropriate" domestic policies will have to be adopted – deflationary monetary and fiscal policies for the deficit country, and inflationary measures for the surplus country. Only if these fail will an alteration of the peg be permitted.

However, the present pegged-rate system has been seen by many to have serious defects, the arguments against the current system being as often as not the arguments in favor of a system of flexible exchange rates. It is to these defects and the "fixed versus flexible exchange rates" controversy which we shall now turn.

Now, as Haberler[2] points out, the adjustment mechanism is more important than the liquidity problem since, if the adjustment mechanism does not work, then no amount of liquidity is enough. On the other hand, if the adjustment mechanism works well, then there is little need for liquidity. The problem of adjustment is to ensure that threatened lasting imbalances in foreign payments (i.e. a substantial worsening of the direct or indirect call which the monetary authorities can make upon other currencies; a worsening which will continue unless something special is done to stop it) are avoided by some appropriate structural change in the economy.[3] Such a change could be brought about by controls over trade and capital flows, but such methods are undesirable for various reasons. Trade controls are biased against the deficit countries and are harmful to the underdeveloped economies. Also, for maximum economic welfare, exports and imports should take place in accordance with relative costs, not in order to adjust to the overall balance of payments. Similarly, with capital movements, there is no reason to suppose that a surplus country (which *might* be an underdeveloped economy) should export capital in order to equilibrate its balance of payments – such flows of investment funds and aid should be determined by a country's real wealth, etc., and not by its balance of payments position. Similarly, a country's need for such funds is determined by its wealth position, not its balance of payments. In reality, the way the system has worked can be described as one of differential rates of inflation with the deficit countries trying their hardest to contain inflation at lower rates than the surplus countries. Theoretically, the balance of payments would equilibrate itself if deficit and surplus countries followed the appropriate domestic policies – that is, deficit countries should deflate (budget surpluses and high rates of interest), whilst surplus countries inflate, thus altering cost/price relationships and correcting the disequilibrium through the price (and income) adjustment mechanism. However, in practice it has proved impossible to adjust wages (and therefore costs and prices) downwards except by creating politically unacceptable levels of unemployment and economic stagnation. Attempts to reduce prices through deflationary measures have caused reductions in output, employment and real income with little impact on prices. Things are made worse by the fact that surplus countries have no great desire (for obvious reasons) to inflate deliberately their economies, so that almost the entire burden of adjustment falls on the deficit countries, who, in turn, are extremely unwilling to apply the corrective policies because of the cost in terms of unemployment and stagnation.

Another criticism of this mechanism is that the required policy measures are even more unacceptable where (*a*) the deficit country is already suffering from underemployment, or (*b*) the surplus country is fully employed. Also, since no real pressure is put on the surplus countries to inflate, the whole system is given a deflationary bias which is harmful to underdeveloped countries. Deflation may also lower the relative profitability of domestic investment and so cause an outflow (or smaller inflow) of foreign funds seeking investment opportunities, so tending to worsen the balance of payments.

In recent years, the relatively slow-working deflationary/inflationary measures have been augmented by attempts to directly decrease the rate of growth of money, wages and prices through some form of *incomes policy*. In effect, this means trying to adjust wage and price changes to the balance of payments situation, and has proved totally impracticable in many countries. Because of the serious possibility that the policies required for internal and external equilibrium may conflict, and since most countries give priority to the domestic objectives of high employment with price stability, the system of pegged rates provides no variable for adjustment in the short or medium run, when the imbalance will be financed by the use of reserves and/or borrowing. In the long run, the exchange rate will have to change to restore equilibrium. As Meade[4] says, the stress in the present adjustable peg system has come to be put on the fixity of the peg rather than its adjustment. Under this system the decision makers, when considering a change in the peg, are faced with the problems of deciding when to alter the rate and how much alteration is required. For example, suppose a deficit appears in the balance of payments. How *long* must it last before it is regarded as persistent; how *large* must it be before it is regarded as serious – in short, what are the criteria for determining when a disequilibrium is "fundamental"? Even if an alteration in the rate is decided upon, it tends to be postponed for as long as possible, which postponement permits the imbalance to worsen, increases the pressure on the currency and makes an even bigger alteration necessary in order to restore confidence in the currency. The likelihood of an excessive alteration is also increased since the I.M.F. agreement allows only infrequent adjustments of the rate, so that a country will want to make sure that the new rate is low/high enough to eliminate the imbalance and ensure that no further change will be required for a considerable time. Adjustments tend to be rare and, when they do occur, excessive, a major adjustment only taking place by a procedure that involves severe strains and may end up by exploding. Since they are rare, great reliance is placed on the use of reserves in the short and medium run, which does little to help solve the problem of international liquidity.

A further major criticism of the present system is that it leads to large-scale de-stabilizing speculation. Consider, for example, a country with a continuing deficit. Speculators, realizing that the currency may be devalued, have no doubts as to the direction of change of the rate, should a change occur, and will therefore transfer their funds out of the weak currency into stronger ones in order to avoid capital losses (e.g. U.K. 1964–65). The "speculators" are not really speculating under the present system, since there is no real threat that the weak currency will appreciate; the worst that can happen being the maintenance of the current rate with consequent insignificant losses to the "speculators" – interest foregone plus the cost of transfer of funds. This sort of one-way speculation serves no useful purpose and obviously brings with it the dangers of causing a country to devalue unnecessarily or take some other inappropriate action (e.g. deflation, import controls, etc.). These dangers are recognized in the Basle arrangements and swap agreements between central banks whereby countries suffering from de-stabilizing speculation can have access to fairly large supplies of foreign exchange.

However, the I.M.F. and key central banks will only offset such speculative movements if the debts thereby incurred are effectively gold guaranteed and if they are satisfied that the deficit countries are taking the appropriate remedial action (i.e. deflationary monetary and fiscal policies). Again this imposes a deflationary bias to the whole system.

Friedman[5] criticizes the present system as being the worst of two worlds – firstly it is not a system of permanently fixed rates and so may deter some long-term foreign investment or threaten international trade if countries impose direct controls in order to avoid devaluation; secondly it does not provide the sensitive, gradual adjustments of a floating rate, with consequent shocks to the economy when an exchange rate adjustment is made. Advocates of the present system do not deny that it has certain disadvantages, but argue in support of it that alternative systems which allow the exchange rate to vary are so much worse. Let us now consider possible flexible-rate systems, how they would work and the advantages/disadvantages associated with them.

FLEXIBLE EXCHANGE RATES

As Fellner[6] points out, reform of the international monetary system has focused on the temporary financing of imbalances through the provision of additional reserves and borrowing facilities. Little attention until recently, has been given to the use of some form of flexible rate system as a means of improving the adjustment mechanism, leaving the use of monetary and fiscal policy for domestic goals. Such a mechanism has many distinguished supporters,[7] who claim that the present mechanism must be replaced by one which gives more leeway for exchange rates to vary and so allow the simultaneous fulfilment of domestic goals and external balance. Flexible rate systems have a great appeal to economists (and others) who rely on economic laws to regulate the economic system and who lack confidence in the ability of governments to adjust the balance of payments without causing serious disturbances elsewhere.[8] But how much flexibility should be permitted – should rates be completely free to float in accordance with market forces, or should the monetary authorities continually be intervening to keep fluctuations within prescribed limits?

Very few economists would opt for a system of completely free rates[9] because of the inherent danger of de-stabilizing speculation in such a system. This danger arises because a change in the exchange rate will not immediately cause the required shift in commodity trade (in reaction to the changed price relationships) to take place, since flows of trade are likely to be insensitive to moderate changes in relative prices in the short run. Because of this, larger shifts in the rate will be needed and, as a result, speculators may behave perversely and so intensify these shifts. If this happens, the cost of living will be significantly affected (specially where imports form a high proportion of national product), and this will create a rash of wage claims, cost increases, etc., which in turn contribute to the adverse speculation and so further depreciate the rate.[10] However, one could argue in defense of free rates that speculators will realize that large short-run variations in the rate are "normal" (or "required") and will step in to support the currency, thus moderating the fluctuations which in fact take place. Most writers, nevertheless, would be extremely doubtful of relying on the expectations of speculators to stabilize the system in such circumstances. Friedman goes so far as to argue that even if speculation is de-stabilizing, government intervention in the exchange market to stabilize the rate should be ruled out, since speculators are likely to be better judges of what the exchange rate should be than government officials. Though there may be some truth in this, the dangers are too great to justify the risk. Since most proponents of flexible rates argue in favor of either a widening of the limits around parity within which rates can fluctuate (Band proposal) or some form of Shiftable Parity, we can concentrate our attention on these suggestions.

(A) *Band Proposal.* The chief advocates of this system are Haberler,[11] Halm, Hansen, Fellner, and Scammell, who argue that the present system should be replaced by a managed system of moderately flexible exchange rates whereby rates would be able to fluctuate within limits set by international agreement. The Joint Committee of the U.S. Congress has recently given a favorable airing to the proposal on the grounds that it offers a substitute for the adjustable peg, without giving up the concept of the peg. Fellner and Hansen suggest that the gold values of currencies should be allowed to vary by up to 4–5% on either side of parity, in contrast with the present system which only permits of a 1% variation. (Rolfe[12] suggests that the transition to this method could be gradual, with a 1% widening each year up to, say, 5%.) It is felt that most of the normal payments disequilibria could be taken care of by movements of the rate within a band of the suggested width – the maximum distance any two currencies could move relative to each other would be twice the permitted variation (i.e. 8–10%), whilst the maximum change in the relation between two currencies would be 16–20% (i.e. one currency at the upper band limit moving to the lower limit at the same time as the other currency moves from its lower to its upper limit). Thus, a 5% band could give a very reasonable scope for adjustment through rate changes, thus lessening the burden placed on domestic policy. With a relatively narrow band (say 5%) one could run the system without any official intervention for rate movements within the band. However, in order to increase credibility, the authorities would intervene if the rate threatened to move outside the limits of the band, thereby maintaining parity. This commitment would be necessary in order to counter de-stabilizing speculation. Thus, suppose that a disturbance to the rate is expected to be very short lived. Speculators, knowing that the authorities will intervene if necessary, will not all be of the same opinion as to the direction of change of the rate and so will buy the currency when cheap, thereby offsetting the disturbance. If a slower return to equilibrium is expected, then speculative capital movements will become stabilizing at a lower rate. If the effect is de-stabilizing (i.e. where the market overestimates the exchange rate movements that would take place in the absence of speculation), then intervention is required, but given that the speculators know this, they will in general tend to stabilize the rate. This brings us to one of the major criticisms made of any form of flexible rates – that speculation will be destabilizing.

The Role of Speculation. Critics of the flexible system argue that speculators will interpret a depreciation of a currency as a sign that it is going to depreciate even further and will therefore sell the depreciating currency, causing even greater depreciation. Eventually, some speculators will realize that the currency is excessively depreciated (i.e. excessive in relation to the "real" conditions) and will therefore start to buy the currency. Other speculators will follow and the result will be large fluctuations in the rate, going well beyond what could be considered the equilibrium rate. To support their case, the critics cite Nurkse's[13] data for the inter-war period, but Friedman replies by saying that the speculators were simply attacking overvalued currencies and therefore their actions were in fact stabilizing (i.e. bringing the rates to their proper level). Hansen and others go so far as to take up the reverse position and argue that speculation under the flexible system will be more stabilizing than under the present system; this is so because, as was mentioned earlier, speculation with current rates is extremely one-way whereas under the band proposal, expectations concerning future changes in the rate will not be uniform. However, as Hirsch[14] indicates, speculation could quite easily become de-stabilizing if parity changes were resorted to in order to restore equilibrium, or if faith was lost in the realism of the band limits. The band proposal should be accompanied, therefore, by a commitment that parity changes will be at least as rare as under the present system (which, of course, imposes undesirable rigidity in the system), and that the authorities will intervene to support the limits and take the appropriate domestic action should this also be required. Friedman[15] would consider that such safety precautions are unnecessary and that if one is going to have fluctuating rates they should be completely free to fluctuate. To support this view, he argues that if speculators actions had been de-stabilizing, they would probably on the whole have lost money. This is so, since if they had increased rate fluctuations, this would have been done by buying when the price was high and selling when it was low. Thus, the very fact that speculators continue to speculate implies that they gain overall and that speculation is consequently stabilizing. Convincing as this may sound, Friedman's case has been attacked by Baumol[16] and Kemp[17] who show that the propositions –

(a) that speculation which is de-stabilizing must be unprofitable, and
(b) that speculation which is stabilizing must be profitable – are untrue under certain conditions; conditions which in practice, however, are unlikely to be satisfied, as Kemp points out.

Speculator's profits (i.e. their sign) might then serve as a useful guide to the stabilizing or de-stabilizing effects of speculator's activities, although the issue can really be settled only by a careful study of particular foreign exchange markets. So far, however, empirical studies have not provided a satisfactory solution to the problem – as Haberler says, we have little experience of fluctuating rates except in times of high inflation. Rolfe[18] argues that speculation will probably be stabilizing (so long as a country's costs/prices do not get too far out of line with other countries' costs/prices), and claims that the large fluctuations of rates in the 1930s were not due to the system *per se* but to the depression, the rise of Hitler, uncertainty over the future of international trade and, finally, to exchange rate manipulation. The hot money flows which occurred were probably the cause of the abandoning of rate fixity rather than its effect. Most post-war studies regarding rate flexibility have necessarily been confined to the case of Canada,[19] 1953–61, where the evidence seems to suggest that short-term capital movements performed a stabilizing function (the maximum movement of the rate being in the region of only 5%), although this required a certain amount of coordination between the United States and Canada as regards monetary and fiscal policy. Scammell argues that in Canada's case, speculation was stabilizing, although Hirsch argues that Canada is a case where a flexible rate can prove embarrassingly immobile.

Since Canada provides us with one of the few post-war cases of the adoption of a flexible-rate system, it is desirable to spend a little time in examining her experience.

Beginning with the European devaluations of 1949, Canada found that she had to protect her currency in order to prevent its collapse. However, in September 1949, she devalued relative to the U.S. dollar by 9% and in 1950 finally adopted a floating rate. In doing so the authorities had confidence that the currency would not fluctuate widely and would, in fact, act as if it were fixed. It would give the authorities more independence in domestic monetary and fiscal policies and it was hoped that a new equilibrium rate would establish itself and allow Canada to readopt the pegged-rate (I.M.F.) system. The Canadian dollar appreciated, reached parity with the U.S. dollar in 1952 and achieved a premium of between 1% and 4% on the U.S. dollar until 1961.

The strength of the currency was due almost entirely in the first few years to the inflow of foreign capital (mainly U.S.) seeking profitable outlets. Later on, due to tight monetary policies at home, the capital inflow was mainly a result of Canadians being forced to borrow foreign capital.

Up to 1956, the Canadian authorities used monetary policy to restrain the upward pressure on prices resulting from the capital inflow, and this helped to maintain internal stability. Post 1956, however, the same policy was continued, even although unemployment was rising and growth slowing down, partly due to the slower growth of the United States and increased competition coming from Europe and Japan. The relatively high rates of interest attracted foreign capital and forced Canadians to borrow abroad. This increased inflow of short-term funds kept the currency at a premium even when the inflow of autonomous long-term capital had leveled off. The tight monetary policy kept the growth rate down and the overvalued currency meant that the current account tended to deteriorate, as shown below:

Current Balance – Canadian $, million

1955	1958	1960	1962	1964
−700	−1,130	−1,240	−870	−430

Fears of U.S. domination of industry, of inflation and of debt servicing grew, and in 1960 it was announced that rates of interest would be lowered, that import tariffs would be increased and that the Exchange Fund Account would take steps to bring the currency to a discount relative to the U.S. dollar. In 1961 the money supply was increased and interest rates lowered – as a result the rate dropped, reserves were lost and a speculative outflow of capital was followed by the rate being fixed at 92½ U.S. cents. Increasing uncertainty in the foreign exchange market led to an increased outflow of capital, and the authorities reacted by selling gold and currency reserves to prevent the rate falling below a 5% discount. It is arguable that, since unemployment was still high and the currency account in serious deficit, the exchange rate should have been allowed to fall further, which might have stopped some of the speculation and helped the current account get into balance. In 1962, a new par value of $92\frac{1}{2}$ U.S. cents was announced, but the devaluation and pegging of the rate only halted the fall in reserves briefly. In order to defend the new parity, the authorities announced a crash program involving higher rates of interest, import sur-charges and international support arrangements to the tune of 1,050 million U.S. dollars. Short-term capital began to flow back and long-term capital was attracted by the interest rate differential.

Looking back, it seems that the exchange crisis resulted more from a loss of cònfidence by the foreign investor than from any fundamental disequilibrium in Canada's balance of payments, the loss in confidence occurring largely because of inappropriate monetary and fiscal policies and a series of crises within the government. What the Canadian experience shows is that a flexible rate can be stable, but that inde-pendence of monetary and fiscal policy is often exaggerated and possible only if policies are appropriate to the circumstances – flexible rates are not a substitute for domestic monetary management. Specu-lation, then, may be stabilizing or de-stabilizing, depending upon the circumstances. In a recent approach to the problem, Kindleberger[20] suggests that the monetary and fiscal policies of countries are more important than the exchange system in determining the nature of speculation. If such policies are stable, then short-term capital move-ments will generally be stabilizing; if the policies are inappropriate, then de-stabilizing speculation is likely to occur.

A further criticism of flexible rates is that they will create a certain amount of *uncertainty* which will be harmful to international trade and capital flows. Even if speculation is not de-stabilizing, the critics argue that uncertainty about this future of the rate will increase the risks of investing overseas and of engaging in trade. Even although forward cover is available for trading purposes, this has a cost attached and so foreign trade will be discouraged. Fellner,[21] however, argues that most exporters/importers, debtors/creditors *already* cover themselves in the forward market and, so far as long-term investment is concerned, the effect is likely to be small since the present system does not ensure long-run stability of exchange rates, only temporary rigidity, so that a risk of rate alterations exists anyway. Rolfe[22] is of the same opinion, observing that the advantages of a 1% higher rate of return on a 20-year foreign investment can be offset only by a large shift of the exchange rate.

Scammell[23] also feels that the effect on investment (and trade) is likely to be small (borrowers and lenders are more sensitive to price level prospects in countries than to changes in the exchange rate) the constancy of the real *domestic* value of currencies being the true basis for international investments. Some writers[24] go so far as to argue that the present system may be a greater deterrent to trade and capital flows than a flexible system of the type proposed. Under the present system, indicators as to the amount and date of a change are uncertain, whereas it would not be too difficult to discern trends in flexible rates. Also, if flexible rates can prevent balance of payments crises from occurring, they will encourage trade and investment, unlike the pegged system where the risks of exchange restrictions, trade controls, etc., which may be imposed to protect the rate, are perhaps greater than the cost of hedging any risks involved in rate fluctuation.

Most writers feel, then, that the problems of uncertainty have been somewhat exaggerated; only when rate changes become large and unpredictable will they have a significant effect on trade and capital flows. Before considering other criticisms of the flexible system, let us look at another proposal, advocated chiefly by Meade,[25] Fellner[26] and Williamson,[27] – the so-called Shiftable Parity, or Sliding Parity, or Crawling Peg.

(B) *Shiftable Parity.* The basic arguments in favor of this system are as before – namely, that since countries under a pegged system are unwilling to deflate/inflate to preserve the rate, and therefore adopt trade controls and other measures, the only way of reconciling domestic objectives, external balance and free trade is by adopting some form of flexible rates.

Under the Shiftable Parity proposal, countries would use monetary and fiscal policy for domestic goals, but for long-run external equilibrium, exchange rate adjustment (combined with an incomes policy) should be used. Meade suggests that the I.M.F. rates should be revised to increase the difficulty of making large exchange rate alterations so that sudden, massive shifts in parities are more unlikely than under the pegged rate system. However, the interpretation of "fundamental disequilibrium" should be slackened so as to allow par value changes to take place up to a maximum of, say, 2% per annum (i.e. $\frac{1}{6}$% per month). Depreciation of currencies would take place if and only if persistent deficits were in existence (in order to prevent competitive depreciations), and even then only at a maximum rate of 2% per annum. Thus, the cost/price structure of the economy could be lowered by up to 2% per annum relative to other countries, a fairly slow process of adjustment which allows the economy to restructure itself gradually.

However, the slowness of the process raises problems in that a country in persistent deficit is going to find it difficult, unless it has large reserves, to stop the rate from depreciating at a faster speed than 2% per annum. Thus, ample reserves (owned or borrowable) are required to create general credibility in the stability of such a system, illustrating how the problems of adjustment and liquidity provision are closely associated.

Suppose we adopted a "crawling" peg with slow, continuous par adjustments available, and suppose that residents of country A expect their currency to appreciate at 2% per annum, whilst B's currency is expected to depreciate at the same rate (i.e. by 4% in terms of A's currency). Now, in order to prevent large-scale movements of short-term funds from B to A (which would greatly increase the difficulty of keeping the rates of change within the 2% limits, which, in turn would create even greater flows of capital, and so on, ultimately leading to the collapse of the system), the monetary authorities of the countries in question would have to cooperate by setting short-term rates of interest such that rates in B (the depreciating country) were at least 4% above those in A. As Hirsch[28] says, this is effectively an index bond in reverse, the loss of capital value through depreciation being offset, for so long as the depreciation continues, by an increase in the income flows from interest payments. Thus, short-term interest rates would have to be determined by the need to neutralize the incentive to transfer funds between countries, a greater reliance being placed on long-term rates of interest and budgetary policies for domestic expansion (increased tax concessions on investment, increases in investment allowance, subsidies to Building Societies to prevent the cost of house loans rising, etc.). Emminger[29] and Bernstien[29] have criticized such a system on the grounds that, although downward movements of rates would be helpful, upward movements would be greatly resisted by the exporting sector. Thus, after Germany's 5% revaluation in 1961, the exporters suffered such a shock that any further revaluation will be resisted to the utmost. Bernstein suggests that it would be better to maintain rate fixity but run the economy at higher levels of unemployment in order to get increased factor mobility and so transfer resources to the export sector.

For most countries this would seem to be a non-starter politically. Shiftable parities of the amount suggested could greatly increase the credibility of support commitments, since in the long-run larger rate shifts than allowed for in the band proposal may well be required in order to maintain equilibrium. Provided that an adequate interest-rate differential is set, no substantial movements of reserves would be required, even when a shift of the parity was expected. This is all very well, say the critics, but eventually such a system would break down because it has in it the seeds of *inflation*. Basically, the argument is that if a country has a payments deficit, the rate will depreciate and the cost of imports will rise, pushing up the cost of living and causing labour to push up wage rates, meaning higher prices, lower exports, further depreciation and so on. The inflationary forces will be augmented by the increased volume of exports, which will leave fewer goods and services available for domestic use. Triffin goes further and argues that speculators will anticipate the cumulative domestic inflation and move funds out of the weak currency, causing even more depreciation and inflation. In this way the speculation would justify itself. The whole argument rests on a requirement that imports have an important part to play in the cost-of-living index. Lutz,[30] however, argues that for most major trading nations this is not so, with the result that a rise in wage rates just sufficient to offset the higher cost of imports would never nullify the depreciation completely. For certain countries, of course, imports do form a high proportion of national income, so that falling exchange rates would have disruptive effects on trade and domestic price stability.

The advocates of flexible rates realize this, however, and admit that flexible rates may not be appropriate in such cases.[31] What one requires in such cases is a system of *Bloc Flexibility*, with fixed exchange rates between countries in a bloc, but flexible rates between blocs. Hirsch regards this as the ideal world system. A bloc would include countries with close trading, capital, and cultural ties (e.g. E.E.C., U.S.A./Canada) so that rate fixity would minimize any risks involved in trading or investing, and the nature of the bloc would ensure that the monetary and fiscal policies of the members are likely to be closely co-ordinated. The inter-bloc flexibility of rates would ensure, however, that basic differences in the economic development of the various blocs were not allowed to cause balance of payments problems. Such a system is appealing in that it parallels current political movements, and has in fact been advocated by the Brookings Committee, should the United States fail to solve its balance of payments problems. However, even without the bloc system, the fears of inflation are greatly reduced under a band and/or shiftable parity system since rate fluctuations would be limited by the width of the band and the permitted annual parity change.

In spite of these precautions, it can still be argued that for countries which are fully employed, a flexible rate could spark off an inflationary spiral which would result in continuous depreciation of the rate and instability of the whole system.[32] Are flexible rate and full employment with reasonable price stability inconsistent goals then? The answer is no, provided that a country with full employment and a payments deficit somehow or other reduces its real income in order to eliminate the deficit.

This problem, of course, is not unique to flexible rates, it applies equally to a devaluation under pegged rates or a system of deflation with fixed rates – real income must fall if the deficit is to be cured. Mundell[33] suggests that reductions in real income, brought about by changes in the prices of internationally traded goods, are more acceptable (money illusion?) than reductions brought about through deflationary measures (unemployment, etc.). This is a matter for empirical study, however, and cannot be decided upon by armchair reasoning.

Critics argue that flexible rates will be inflationary for another reason – since rate movements will maintain external balance, the authorities will be able to permit domestic inflation to continue more rapidly than abroad. In contrast, it is argued, under a pegged rate system, the authorities are severely constrained by the size of their reserves in relation to the deficit and by the loss of prestige should the rate have to be devalued. They must therefore take steps to deal with any excessive inflation. Fellner and Haberler, on the other hand, regard persistent depreciation of a currency brought about by a failure to deal with inflation, as incompatible with the proposed system which envisages a high degree of international cooperation and policy coordination. Also, there is no reason to believe that falling reserves are any more of a brake on inflation than a falling rate; it may well be the case that rate changes, by giving clearer signals of disequilibrium, will gradually increase rather than reduce effective pressures toward responsible behavior. This simply emphasizes that no international adjustment mechanism can eliminate the need for international coordination of economic policies.

Finally, let us consider Snider's concept of "optimum adjustment processes" and "currency areas."[34] According to Snider, optimum adjustment processes are ones which remove imbalances without:

(a) restricting the freedom of trade and capital flows, and/or
(b) interfering with domestic policies for full employment, and price stability.

The current international monetary system does not appear to fulfill either of the above conditions but, instead, is dominated by a downward inflexibility of costs and prices and a rigid exchange rate structure. These characteristics mean that the domestic goals and external equilibrium cannot be simultaneously fulfilled, as recent U.S./U.K. experiences indicate. Now, in order to solve this dilemma and at the same time satisfy the critics of the flexible rate system, Snider suggests that a *managed* flexible system should be combined with appropriate domestic monetary and fiscal policies.

Consider the possible combinations of external and internal imbalance:

(1) *Unemployment and balance of payments surplus*

Flexible exchange rates would cure the external imbalance but have adverse effects on employment by reducing the demand for exports and causing an increased supply of goods and services (via imports). It would be preferable, then, to expand the domestic economy whilst keeping exchange rates fixed – this would increase employment whilst at the same time eliminating the payments surplus.

(2) *Inflation and a balance of payments deficit*

Flexible rates would again cure the deficit but have possible adverse effects on the pace of inflation. Therefore, keep rates fixed and contract the economy by means of monetary/fiscal policy; this will ease inflationary forces and restore equilibrium externally.

(3) *Unemployment and a balance of payments deficit*

Expansion of the economy to cure the unemployment would worsen the deficit, so it would be better to let the exchange rate depreciate, so causing external equilibrium whilst at the same time increasing the level of employment (increased demand for exports and reduced supply of imports).

(4) *Inflation and a balance of payments surplus*

Here, we should let the rate fluctuate and restore external and internal equilibrium.

Using this system it is possible, of course, for internal (external) equilibrium to be achieved before external (internal) equilibrium has been reached. In such cases, a *combination* of exchange-rate changes and appropriate domestic policies should be used in order to have both internal and external equilibrium. One should not rely *solely* on either flexible rates or domestic economic policies – one requires a delicate combination of the two to achieve an optimum adjustment as defined above.

Optimum currency areas (areas with a common monetary unit) are ones *within* which optimum adjustment occurs with exchange rate *fixity*, whilst *between* which variable rates apply. This is similar to the previously discussed bloc system.

In conclusion, a fairly strong case can be made for adopting some form of managed rate flexibility, perhaps combining the band proposal with a form of sliding parity. The criticism that elasticities are too low to permit easy adjustment through rate changes is no longer so convincing[35] – elasticity pessimism is no longer fashionable. The major problem, both at the theoretical and empirical level, is concerning the nature of speculation – would it be stabilizing or not? Nevertheless, the proposed system, combined with the use of appropriate domestic policies (interest rate differentials, etc.), should help a great deal in easing fears concerning speculation and inflationary dangers. The important thing to note is that flexible rates are no panacea – they require close cooperation at an international level, a willingness to adopt the required monetary and fiscal policies and, lastly, an ample supply of international liquidity to allow the adjustment process to take place smoothly and gradually.

[1] F. Machlup, "In Search of Guides for Policy," in *Maintaining and Restoring Balance in International Payments*, Princeton University Press, 1966.

[2] G. Haberler, in Ch. 5 of *Gold and World Monetary Problems*, National Industrial Conference Board, 1965.

[3] See J. E. Meade, "The International Monetary Mechanism," *Three Banks Review*, 1964.

[4] J. E. Meade, "Exchange Rate Flexibility," *Three Banks Review*, 1966.

[5] M. Friedman, "The Case for Flexible Rates," in his *Essays in Positive Economics*, 1953.

[6] W. Fellner in Ch. 5 of *Maintaining and Restoring Balance in International Payments*, Princeton University Press, 1966.

[7] Among them, R. Caves, W. Fellner, M. Friedman, G. Haberler, G. Halm, A. Harberger, H. Johnson, F. Lutz, F. Machlup, J. E. Meade, L. Metzler, T. Scitovsky, J. Vanek, etc.

[8] See Wasserman and Ware, *The Balance of Payments*, 1965.

[9] The chief advocate of completely free rates is Friedman.

[10] See J. E. Meade, "Exchange-Rate Flexibility," *Three Banks Review*, 1966.

[11] G. Haberler, *Currency Convertibility*, No. 541 in the Series National Economic Problems, American Enterprise Association, Washington, 1954.

[12] S. E. Rolfe, *Gold and World Power*, Macmillan, 1966.

[13] R. Nurkse, *International Currency Experience: Lessons of the Inter-War Period*, 1944.

[14] F. Hirsch, *Money International*, Penguin Press, 1967.

[15] M. Friedman, *op. cit.*; see also L. G. Telser, "A Theory of Speculation Relating Profitability and Stability," *Review of Economic Statistics*, 1959.

[16] W. Baumol, "Speculation, Profitability and Stability," *Review of Economic Statistics*, 1957.

[17] M. C. Kemp, *The Pure Theory of International Trade*, 1964.

[18] S. E. Rolfe, *op. cit.*

[19] See, for example, T. L. Powrie, "Short-Term Capital Movements and the Flexible Canadian Exchange Rate, 1953–1961," *Canadian Journal of Economics and Political Science*, 1964; also H. H. Pinhammer, *Canada's Foreign Exchange Problems: a Review*, Kyklos, 1964.

[20] C. P. Kindleberger, "Flexible Exchange Rates," in *Monetary Management*, prepared for the Commission on Money and Credit (1963).

[21] W. Fellner, *op. cit.*

[22] S. E. Rolfe, *op. cit.*

[23] W. M. Scammell, *International Monetary Policy*, Second Edition, 1961.

[24] F. Machlup, "Plans for the Reform of the International Monetary System," Special Paper in *International Economics*, No. 3, Princeton University, 1962.

[25] J. E. Meade, "Exchange Rate Flexibility," *Three Banks Review*, 1966.

[26] W. Fellner, *op. cit.*

[27] J. H. Williamson, "The Crawling Peg," Essays in *International Finance*, No. 50, Princeton University, 1965.

[28] F. Hirsch, *op. cit.*, p. 312–315.

[29] See Ch. 5 of *Gold and World Monetary Problems*, National Industrial Conference Board, 1966.

[30] F. Lutz, "The Case for Flexible Exchange Rates," *Banca Nazionale del Lavoro Quarterly Review*, 1954.

[31] See Rolfe, *op. cit.*; Mundell, "A Theory of Optimum Currency Areas," *American Economic Review*, 1955; and D. Snider, "Optimum Adjustment Processes and Currency Areas," *Essays in International Finance*, No. 62, Princeton University, 1967.

[32] H. Henderson, "The Function of Exchange Rates," Oxford Economic Papers (New Series), Vol. 1, No. 1.

[33] R. A. Mundell, "The Monetary Dynamics of International Adjustment under Fixed and Flexible Exchange Rates," *Quarterly Journal of Economics*, 1960.

[34] D. Snider, *op. cit.*

[35] Estimates of the price elasticity of demand for exports and imports indicate an upward trend:

1949 (U.K. and U.S.) both < 1 (Change).

1957 (U.K. and U.S.) U.K. > 1.35, U.S. ≥ 1.65 (Harberger).

1958 U.K. $= 3$ (Zelder).

1962 U.S.A. $= 4$ (Polak and Rhomberg).

CHAPTER 10

Balance of Payments Equilibrium
and the Dollar Problem

DISEQUILIBRIUM in the balance of payments is perhaps the biggest problem facing international economies today. This alone is sufficient reason to devote some time to a study of payments disequilibrium, how it can arise and how it may be cured. Accordingly, for the first part of this chapter we shall concern ourselves with the concepts of equilibrium and disequilibrium and how one may move from positions of disequilibrium to ones of equilibrium. Following on from this, we shall then analyze the U.S. balance of payments position over a fairly long time period and give some explanation of attempts made by various economists to explain the existence of such long-run disequilibrium situations.

To begin with, we must clarify what we mean by equilibrium in international trade theory. To do this, consider what one normally envisages as existing in situations which we would describe as "equilibria" – a balancing of forces such that if nothing were to happen, then everything would go on as it is. Embodied in this concept are usually the ideas of disturbance and adjustment, of stability and instability, these latter two often being confused with equilibrium and disequilibrium.

Suppose, for example, that a pair of scales are set up with equal weights on either side so that the scales balance – we would think of this as an equilibrium situation, each side of the scales exerting an equal but opposite turning force around the fulcrum. Provided that one side of the scales did not increase (or decrease) its weight, then the scales would stay in balance or equilibrium; that is, everything would go on as it is. It is also a stable equilibrium, because if I lift one side up and let it go, the scales will eventually come to rest in their former position. However, if I add an extra weight to one side, the scales will no longer balance (i.e. they are in disequilibrium, with one side exerting a greater turning force about the fulcrum than the other), and they can only be made to balance (i.e. equilibrium restored) if I add an equal weight to the other pan. The initial disturbance to equilibrium is removed only when the appropriate adjustment is made. Similar simple examples could be given to illustrate unstable equilibria, but the important thing to observe is that they would all have in common:

(*a*) a starting point of equilibrium where the relevant forces are in balance and everything could go on as it is,

(*b*) the consideration of some disturbance to equilibrium, and

(*c*) the adjustments which the variables consequently make to this disturbance.

Whether or not a new equilibrium is reached cannot be determined until the specific relationships between the variables in a particular model have been stipulated. This is easily seen in the Cobweb model, where the convergence of prices towards, or divergence away, from a new equilibrium is determined by the relative slopes of the demand and supply curves (i.e. the specific relationships within the model). If a new equilibrium exists, then all the adjustments will have been made and no further change will take place as a result of the initial disturbance – in other words, everything will again go on as it is.

One can, of course, envisage situations which one would describe as equilibrium even if the values of the variables were still changing. Thus, suppose that the price of a commodity fluctuated over time as shown below –

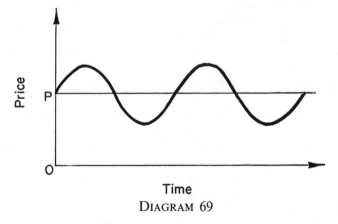

Time
DIAGRAM 69

One could then say that OP was in some sense an equilibrium price, provided that the fluctuations about it were of constant periodicity and amplitude. Normally, however, the use of "equilibrium" is confined to situations in which all the relevant variables are adjusted to each other in a final way, so that following Machlup,[1] we may define equilibrium in economic analysis as "a constellation of selected inter-related variables so adjusted to one another that no inherent tendency to change prevails in the model which they constitute." "Selected" here means that the model builder picks out from amongst the enormously large number of possible variables only those which he considers to be significant for the purpose for which the model is to be constructed. "Inherent" means that none of the variables so selected must, in equilibrium, still be trying to adjust to the initial disturbance. Whether or not a variable *outside* the model is liable to change is irrelevant – the variables in the model would still be in equilibrium. To illustrate this, suppose one builds a Keynesian-type model of employment-(income-) determination, selecting as one's relevant variables the level of income, the consumption function and the investment function.

One can then envisage values of income (employment), consumption, and investment which are compatible with one another (in the sense that none of them wishes to adjust away from its present value), yet result in less than full employment (i.e. a typical Keynesian underemployment equilibrium). This is an equilibrium situation and everything "can go on as it is." To say that the authorities will not allow less than full employment to exist, and will therefore instigate policies which result in the values of the selected variables changing, is not a valid reason for saying that the situation described as equilibrium is, in fact, a disequilibrium situation. One could only do this if one had, in the first place, built into the model a constraint that less than full employment is unacceptable, irrespective of the values of the other variables. All equilibria, therefore, are *relative* equilibria, relative only to the variables in the models concerned, and if one adds more variables to one's model, then situations previously described as equilibria may well become disequilibria.

When we move on to a consideration of the concept of disequilibrium in international payments, one comes up against the problem of distinguishing between a fair number of types of disequilibrium – short-term (or cyclical), long-term (or secular, or persistent), price-based disequilibria and income-based disequilibria – so that some sort of analysis of these various types is called for.

Consider, as an illustrative case, a situation which we have already come across in a previous chapter and which is represented diagrammatically in Diagram 70.

At the level of income OY_{FE} the $[S(Y) + M(Y)]$ function cuts the $(I + S)$ function giving us an equilibrium situation. At this level of income, imports equal exports and the economy is fully employed, but suppose now that the quantity of exports demanded falls so that $(I + X_1)$ represents the new function. Income will adjust downwards to OY_1, at which level imports exceed exports by an amount AB.

The balance of payments is therefore in deficit, and the problem we are faced with is that of deciding whether or not this new situation is

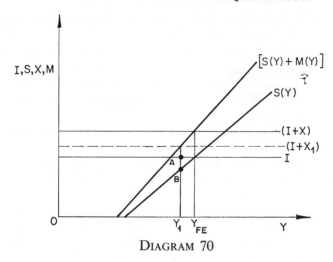

DIAGRAM 70

or is not an equilibrium one. Depending upon the constraints we have included in our model, it may or may not be equilibrium. Thus, if unemployment is acceptable and if a deficit in the balance of payments is also acceptable, then we can describe both the initial and the new situations as equilibrium ones – all adjustments (of income, imports and exports) have been made to the initial disturbance (the fall in demand) and the new situation could go on as it is for ever.

However, if a deficit is not acceptable (or is so only for a short length of time), then steps will be taken to *either* raise the export function to (or above) its old level, or lower the import function until imports equal exports. In other words, the situation depicted is not an equilibrium one unless exports equal or exceed imports. However, even with a new situation, where the balance of payments balances, one may still have less than full employment, and if one stipulates in the model that anything below full employment cannot be accepted, then further changes will take place until OY_{FE} is, again, that level of income corresponding to the intersection of the $(I+X)$ and $[S(Y)+M(Y)]$ functions. This need not be the old situation, since the measures taken to restore equilibrium may have shifted the functions away from their original positions. It can be seen, then, that the same situation and values of variables can be described as equilibrium or disequilibrium, depending upon the constraints of the model (i.e. all equilibria are relative). But suppose that equilibria involving payments deficits are acceptable as is less than full employment (though one may wish to restrain the permitted magnitude of unemployment), but that persistent (i.e. long-run) deficits cannot be maintained. In Diagram 70, then, OY_1 may represent an equilibrium in the short-run but a disequilibrium in the long-run, since if the deficit continues, then the authorities will initiate policies to eliminate this deficit.

There are equilibria and equilibria, therefore, depending upon the time period chosen: what is equilibrium in one time period becomes disequilibrium in another. On the basis of one's selected variables and relationships one can determine whether a particular situation (theoretically observed) is one of equilibrium or disequilibrium, whether it is short- or long-run, but to go further and determine the form a disequilibrium takes requires an analysis of the possible *causes* of disequilibrium. So far we have only discussed the common characteristics of disequilibria, but let us now look briefly at the factors which may lie behind such situations.

Disequilibria in the balance of payments may be caused by a great variety of factors but, for convenience of exposition, it is useful to break them down into two categories – disequilibria of price and of income, both of which may be short- or long-term. Thus, if a country's prices (or level of income) change in relation to prices (or levels of income) abroad, then this can lead to a payments disequilibrium of the price (income) type. Of course, a disequilibrium in real life will most likely be due to a combination of price changes, income changes, alterations in the distribution of income, etc., but this does not invalidate our procedure of isolating the various forces at work and giving them labels.

To see how alterations in relative income levels will affect the balance of payments, consider the following cases:

Case (a). Suppose we have two countries X and Y, whose income levels are growing at the same rate over time, and another two countries, A and B, whose income levels fluctuate cyclically over time around a constant level. These situations can be illustrated as shown in Diagram 71.

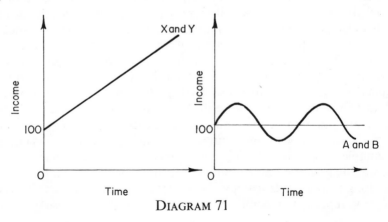

DIAGRAM 71

Now, if we assume that the income elasticities of demand for imports in each pair of countries are the same, then balance of payments equilibrium will not be disturbed by the growth or fluctuations of income so long as the initial levels of income are the same. If, initially, income levels in X and Y are 1,000 and 500 respectively, and imports and exports balance at a level of 300, then the growth of income in X will lead to a deficit appearing in its balance of payments. (Income elasticity of demand for imports assumed to be $\frac{1}{2}$.)

TABLE 1

	Income	Imports	Δ Income	Δ Imports	Δ Balance of Payments
X	1,000	300	$100 = \frac{1}{10}$	50	-25
Y	500	300	$50 = \frac{1}{10}$	25	$+25$

Similarly, unless income levels are identical for A and B, then deficits and surpluses can arise for the same reason. In the following discussion, we shall assume that, initially, income levels are identical, so that the above source of imbalance is ruled out. Under the stipulated conditions, then, disequilibrium may arise if:

(a) the countries X and Y grow at different rates or
(b) the countries A and B have different patterns of cycle.

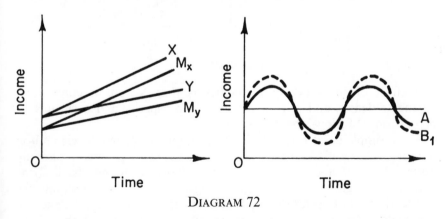

DIAGRAM 72

If X is growing at a faster rate than Y, then she will tend to develop import surpluses; similarly, if B's income fluctuates with greater amplitude, she will tend to run deficits in prosperity and surpluses in depression (B_1).

If her income fluctuates so that she has bigger booms than A but shallower depressions, then she may permanently run deficits, since, although her imports fall in depression, they do not fall as fast as her exports (i.e. A's imports). The student is left to consider what happens if the fluctuations in income are:

(*a*) of different periodicity but same amplitude and
(*b*) of different periodicity and different amplitude.

It can be seen, then, how differing rates of growth of income or differing cyclical patterns can lead to payments disequilibria.

Case (*b*). Consider now a situation where we have the same two pairs of countries with X and Y growing at the same rate, and A and B experiencing identical income cycles. However, drop our assumption that each pair of countries has the same income elasticity of demand for imports, and assume instead that X has a higher elasticity than Y, and A a higher elasticity than B.

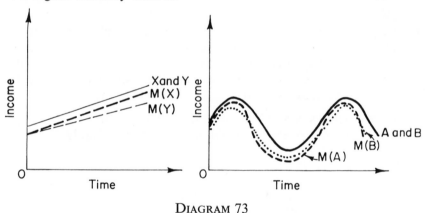

DIAGRAM 73

The effect of the differing elasticities is that X runs a continuous payments deficit, and A runs a deficit in prosperity and a surplus in depression. B follows the reverse course.

These simple cases illustrate how variations in income levels and/or differing income elasticities of demand can lead to payments disequilibria, either of a cyclical or persistent type. Although the cyclical pattern of Diagram 73 might seem to suggest that cyclical disequilibria will tend to offset each other so that over the long-term the balance of payments balances, this is not necessarily so. The student should be able to construct models which, although giving alternative surplus and deficits, result in a long-run cumulative imbalance. Similarly, if income elasticities change overtime, or are a function of the level of income, then seemingly persistent imbalances of the income-growth type may reverse themselves as time goes on and higher income levels are reached.

How does one deal with cyclical disequilibria? If one uses monetary and fiscal policy to deflate or inflate the economy, then the payments fluctuations may be smoothed, but at the expense of income fluctuations. For example, it is possible for a country to experience balance of payments disequilibria of the cyclical type, even although its own level of income is not fluctuating. This will happen in the income of its trading partner fluctuates cyclically as shown in Diagram 74.

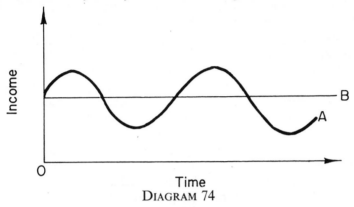

DIAGRAM 74

Now, if country B uses monetary/fiscal policy to eliminate the payments imbalances, then it will create an income cycle similar to A's (the cycle may or may not be more severe than A's, depending on the income elasticities of demand for imports). The cure may be just as bad as the disease. To avoid such problems, one could use controls over imports, foreign exchange, etc., in order to eliminate the imbalances. Such a method, however, would cause frequent disturbances to export and import markets, costly shifts of resources, etc., all of which would increase traders' uncertainty and decrease the willingness to trade. It is much simpler to use up or add to one's international reserves and absorb the disequilibria in this way. Just as inventories allow a firm to absorb fluctuations in sales, so reserves allow a country to absorb payments fluctuations. Reserves, therefore, perform an extremely useful function by allowing a country to maintain its imports level in prosperity by using up these reserves, acquired in depression. (This function could be especially important for underdeveloped economies.) Essentially the I.M.F. was constructed on the principle that disequilibria would be cyclical and so a pool of currencies, subscribed by members, could be used as a revolving fund to allow countries to ride out temporary difficulties in the balance of payments field. In practice, the trouble has been that certain countries have been running persistent deficits and as a result continually borrowing from the fund. It is this problem of long-run disequilibrium which will concern us for the second part of this chapter. Before doing so, let us consider another cause of short-run disequilibrium – namely, *prices*, which are incompatible with the other variables in the system.

Prices may get out of line in basically two ways:

(*a*) differing rates of relative inflation, or

(*b*) changing demand or supply conditions.

(*a*) *Relative Rates of Inflation.* If one country is inflating at a faster rate than its trading partners, then, assuming a pegged rate system, imports will become relatively cheaper and so increase in volume, whereas exports will become (to foreigners) relatively expensive and so decrease in volume. Depending upon the price elasticities of demand and supply, it is possible, therefore, that payments deficits will tend to appear and continue for as long as the country inflates relative to others. Many, in fact, regard relative inflation as the cause of the majority of payments problems and accordingly argue that they can be cured only by the appropriate measures – that is, deflation or, more correctly, disinflation, perhaps combined with exchange-rate changes. The economic arguments for and against exchange-rate alterations and domestic deflation or inflation were presented in the preceding chapter, so there is no need to go into them here.

(*b*) *Changing Demand or Supply Conditions.* Suppose that foreign demand for some of a country's exports falls off for some reason or other. Export value will fall, and if the country concerned had previously been in payments equilibrium, a deficit will appear in its balance of payments. To eliminate the imbalance, resources must shift into other export lines or import substitute production. Similarly, if a country experiences a fall in supply (due, for example, to a general strike as in France, 1968), then exports will tend to fall and imports rise, and the cure for this situation is either to increase production and/ or reduce expenditure by an amount depending upon the income elasticity of demand for imports and the size of the disequilibrium.

If the required resource shifts do not take place, then the payments disequilibrium will persist. To help the price system bring about equilibrium, alterations in the exchange rate could be used making it more profitable to enter exports or import substitute lines. If one tries to get the resource shifts to take place by altering relative factor rewards (e.g. by increasing wages in the export/import substitute fields), then inflationary forces may be unleashed which will require treatment by the monetary authorities. To cure disequilibrium caused by changing demand or supply conditions, one should therefore use exchange-rate variations combined with adequately controlled inducements to effect resource shifts. We have seen, then, how cyclical and commodity price disequilibria are normally regarded as being short-term problems solvable by the use of reserves, exchange-rate alterations and monetary/fiscal policy.

Long-run disequilibria may arise if the cyclical disturbances do not cancel each other out, so leading to cumulative imbalance: if growth rates or rates of inflation are persistently out of line internationally; if technological progress is concentrated in a country or group of countries; if factor prices are inconsistent with factor endowments; or if capital flows have an existence independent of trade flows. But we are talking here of balance of *trade* disequilibria, not balance of *payments* disequilibria, and we know that trade imbalances may be offset by capital account imbalances in the opposite direction. Now, if a trading surplus (deficit) is automatically offset by a capital deficit (surplus), then no long-run disequilibria can ever occur. But, of course, capital flows do have an existence independent of trade flows, so that trading imbalances may be only partly offset by capital flows. If these autonomous capital movements (net) fail to offset completely the trading imbalances, then cumulative payments disequilibria will result and the country will be forced to adjust its trading accounts and/or use official lending/borrowing to adjust the capital accounts.[2] We can say then that long-run disequilibria occur if the trading balance (service income included) is not completely offset by long-run autonomous capital movements *and this failure is systematically in one direction or the other*.

There can be little doubt that the problem of long-run disequilibrium has troubled the world since the early 1940s and continues to do so today. It is fitting, therefore, that the causes of long-run disequilibrium be studied in relation to the U.S. experience where it will be found that a multitude of hypotheses have been advanced to explain her persistent payments imbalance.

Long-run Disequilibrium – the U.S. Experience

To begin with, a brief survey of U.S. balance of payments history is called for before we can proceed to an analysis of the so-called "Dollar Problem."

Following World War II, Western Europe had been so devastated by war that she found it impossible to "pay-her-way" internationally – she simply could not earn sufficient dollars to pay for the goods and services purchased from the United States. The result was that the United States continuous large surpluses on trade account, which were offset by large-scale U.S. investment overseas and by a flow of gold from Western Europe to the United States, part of the gold flow being an offset to a capital flight from Europe caused by the gloomy international situation and the outbreak of war.

TABLE 2   U.S. BALANCE OF PAYMENTS ($ BILLION) 1953–67

Item	1953	1954	1955	1956	1957	1958	1959	1960	1961	1962	1963	1964	1965	1966	1967
(1) Trade balance	1·3	2·4	2·8	4·6	6·1	3·3	1·0	4·8	5·4	4·4	5·1	6·7	4·8	3·7	3·5
(2) Government grants, military expenditures – sales	−4·3	−4·1	−4·6	−4·5	−4·5	−4·8	−4·4	−4·4	−4·4	−4·4	−4·2	−4·0	−3·9	−4·6	−4·8
(3) U.S. Government long- and short-term capital	−0·2	0·1	−0·3	−0·6	−1·0	−1·0	−0·4	−1·1	−0·9	−1·1	−1·6	−1·7	−1·6	−1·6	−2·4
(4) Other services	1·5	1·8	2·0	2·2	2·5	2·0	1·9	2·0	2·6	3·1	3·1	3·9	4·2	4·1	4·4
(5) Direct Investment	−0·6	−0·5	−0·6	−1·7	−2·3	−1·1	−1·1	−1·5	−1·5	−1·5	−2·0	−2·4	−3·4	−3·5	−2·9
(6) Other private long-term investment	+0·3	−0·2	0·0	−0·2	−0·6	−1·5	−0·5	−0·6	−0·7	−1·1	−1·4	−1·8	−1·2	1·0	—
(7) Private short-term investment	0·2	−0·6	−0·2	−0·5	−0·3	−0·3	−0·1	−1·4	−1·6	−0·5	−0·8	−2·1	+0·8	−0·4	−1·2
(8) Private remittances	−0·6	−0·6	−0·6	−0·7	−0·7	−0·7	−0·7	−0·7	−0·7	−0·8	−0·9	−0·9	−1·0	−1·0	−1·3
(9) Errors and Omissions	0·4	0·2	0·5	0·6	1·2	0·5	0·4	−0·9	−0·9	−1·1	−0·3	−0·9	−0·4	−0·3	−0·6
(10) Balance (1)–(9)	−2·0	−1·5	−1·0	−0·8	0·4	−3·6	−3·9	−3·8	−2·7	−3·0	−3·0	−3·2	−1·7	−2·6	−5·3
(11) Balance financed by official reserve changes (increase−):															
Gold	1·2	0·3	0·0	−0·3	−0·8	2·3	1·1	1·7	0·9	0·9	0·5	0·1	1·4	0·8	1·2
Foreign exchange	—	—	—	—	—	—	—	—	−0·1	—	−0·1	−0·2	−0·3	−0·5	−1·0
Liabilities to foreign official holders	0·9	1·1	0·9	1·0	−0·3	0·5	1·3	1·3	0·7	1·2	1·7	1·4	0·1	−0·8	3·3
(12) Balance financed by foreign commercial banks and other foreign short-term holders	—	—	0·1	0·8	1·0	0·7	1·6	0·7	1·3	0·3	1·0	1·8	0·4	2·7	1·8

Source: International Financial Statistics.

In 1934, the U.S. gold stocks were 4 billion dollars, in 1948 they had risen to their peak of 25 billion dollars – the European countries were simply being forced to transfer gold to the United States due to their shortage of dollars. However, although some economists took a long time to recognize the transition from "dollar shortage" to "dollar glut,"[3] one can safely argue that by 1950 the tables had turned so that with U.S. help (Marshall Aid, etc.) and Europe's own perseverence, the dollar shortage had virtually been eliminated. Beginning with 1950, the United States has become a deficit country and has covered these deficits by paying out gold and/or dollars to the surplus countries of Western Europe who, in turn, have been building up the level of their reserves at a rate fast enough to allow them in 1958 to allow limited convertibility of their currencies. This is illustrated in Tables 3 and 4 below.[4]

By 1958 the European nations were in a stronger competitive position with the productive capacity to win markets from the United States both in Europe and in third countries. Also, with European reserves at a new high level, additional increments of dollar-claims began to appear less attractive. So it was, that from 1950 onwards, we see a redistribution of reserves to a more normal pattern taking place, so reversing the post-war U.S. acquisition of gold.

In fact, this redistribution, although it entailed deficits for the United States was encouraged by the United States as being both a necessary and desirable development. As Bernstein[5] says, a deficit in the U.S. balance of payments is entirely consistent with external equilibrium in a situation where the dollar is in demand as an international reserve asset and where it reflects a recovery of war-devastated economies.

TABLE 3

GOLD STOCKS OF U.S.A. AND W. EUROPE ($M.)

Country	1953	1958	1960	1962	1964	1966	June 1968
U.S.A.	22,091	20,582	17,804	16,057	15,471	13,235	10,681
U.K.	2,263	2,807	2,801	2,581	2,136	1,940	—
W. Germany	325	2,639	2,971	3,679	4,248	4,292	4,312
France	617	750	1,641	2,587	3,729	5,238	4,739
Italy	346	1,086	2,203	2,243	2,107	2,414	2,673
Netherlands	747	1,050	1,451	1,581	1,688	1,731	1,697

Source: I.F.S.

TABLE 4

FOREIGN EXCHANGE HOLDINGS OF U.S.A. AND W. EUROPE ($M.)

Country	1953	1958	1960	1962	1964	1966	June 1968
U.S.A.	—	—	—	99	432	1,321	2,479
U.K.	283	298	430	225	179	1,159	—
W. Germany	1,411	3,093	3,752	2,760	2,721	2,479	2,971
France	212	300	430	1,023	1,376	507	778
Italy	422	1,053	980	1,622	1,571	1,612	1,504
Netherlands	426	420	291	162	396	305	225

Source: I.F.S.

However, in 1958 a new phase started. Following a small surplus in 1957, the deficits resumed but on quite a different scale from earlier ones, as can be seen from Table 2. The years from 1958 onwards saw the emergence of deficits of a size and nature which was neither approved officially (as had been earlier deficits) nor necessary for the repletion of European reserves. As a result, concern over the future of the U.S. payments position grew[6] and it was intensified by the behavior of U.S. imports and exports relative to G.N.P., since during the 1950s the ratio of exports to G.N.P. fell at the same time as the imports to G.N.P. ratio increased (by more). This seemed to point to a lack of "competitiveness" on the part of the United States and, as a result, great attention was paid to the trade account, especially to export performance, because since 1955 widespread relaxation of discrimination abroad against U.S. goods and services had taken place, so that the reduction of the exports to G.N.P. ratio probably understates the real deterioration in export competitiveness. The signs of genuine payments disequilibrium had appeared. Also, the United States was suffering from lagging domestic growth and relatively high unemployment levels (6% after the 1957/58 recession). How could the United States solve *both* problems? By 1960, the view was widespread in Europe that devaluation of the dollar was a distinct possibility, and so various countries began to exercise their option of converting surplus dollar claims into gold. This led to a gold drain from the United States to Europe, a drain which reached major proportions in 1960 and led ultimately to the setting up to Gold Pool, the primary purpose of which was to try to relieve some of the strain being put on the dollar by its conversion into gold. The impact of the Gold Pool has been to act as a temporary cushion on the U.S. gold stock, but by 1968 the pool could no longer stand the speculative pressure against the dollar, with the result that the pool was closed and the present "two-tier" gold-price system was adopted, whereby the official market for gold is separated from the private market, central banks agreeing for the meantime to buy and sell gold only from each other. Some Western European nations (e.g. W. Germany) have also agreed temporarily not to convert any more of their dollar holdings into gold. It remains to be seen just how long the present set-up can last.

Having seen the record of U.S. deficits and how they have reflected themselves in European surpluses and a redistribution of international reserves, we must now analyze the data a bit farther to see if we can isolate the weak spots in the balance of payments and the basic causes of this persistent disequilibrium.

Changes in the U.S. Balance of Payments. Diagram 75 below is derived from Table 2 and shows the trend over the last 15 years in the subsections of the balance of payments –

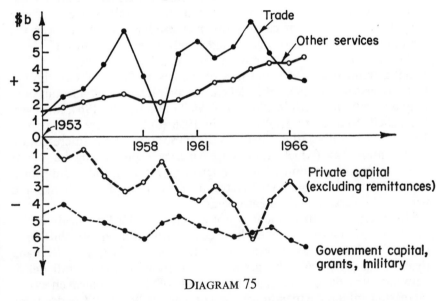

DIAGRAM 75

The major changes have taken place in merchandise trade (1957–60, and 1964–67), government expenditure (1965–67), and private capital.

With reference to *merchandise trade*, U.S. imports grew more rapidly than exports during 1958–59 (in fact, between 1958–59, exports actually fell in value and volume), so that the trade balance declined from 6.1 billion dollars in 1957 to 1.0 billion dollars in 1959. In 1960, however, exports showed a sharp increase, due mainly to the application of tying provisions to U.S. aid in 1959 and to the effects of a deliberate export drive.

Export value (and volume) rose relative to import value (and volume) up to about 1964, when the situation reversed and imports grew at a much faster rate than exports. (Between 1964–67, exports grew from $25.8 billion to $31 billion whilst imports grew from $18.7 billion to $26.9 billion.) It is interesting to note that from 1963–67, export prices rose by 10% whilst import prices only rose by 2%. Thus, a deteriorating balance of trade has been a major contributor to U.S. payments difficulties.

Net income from *"Other Services"* did not show any significant changes throughout the period, but exhibited a rather steady increase from $1.5 billion in 1953 to $4.4 billion in 1967.

Government expenditure overseas did not vary up to 1965 by very much, after which date it showed a fairly sharp increase, mainly due to the fact that the deficit on long- and short-term capital rose from $1.6 billion in 1965 to $2.4 billion in 1967, whilst the deficit on grants and military expenditures rose from $3.9 billion to $4.8 billion over the same period. The main factor causing this increase has, of course, been the increasing involvement of the United States in the Vietnam war.

So far as *Private Capital* movements are concerned, they showed a striking trend from 1953 onwards of increasing flows of U.S. investment overseas. In 1953 the deficit on private capital account was only $0.1 billion, whilst in 1964 it was $6.2 billion. After 1964, however, the deficit declined to $2.9 billion in 1966 (only to increase again in 1967 to $4.1 billion), due chiefly to the imposition of the Interest-Rate Equalization Tax (which applies to Americans purchasing long-term securities of foreign countries or foreign corporations), and to Johnson's 1965 program of "voluntary" restraint on the part of U.S. banks and firms with overseas investment operations.

However, *direct* investment is not affected by the Equalization Tax and in addition its effectiveness has been greatly reduced by a shifting of capital away from taxed transactions to other types (especially bank loans). Thus, in 1967, the gradual elimination of the overall deficit between 1964–66 was reversed as a result of the combined effects of increasing military expenditure, private capital flows and a declining favorable balance of trade.

So much for payments anatomy – we must now consider payments pathology and see if we can discover the reasons for the declining trade balance and increasingly unfavorable capital account balance since these two items are by far the most important symptoms of the U.S. payments disequilibrium. Before doing so, however, a word on the *transfer problem*. Now, we have seen that the overall deficits on the balance of payments were offset through gold sales and the accumulation of foreign liquid dollar claims. The question now is – "Why did the Current Account fail to develop a surplus sufficiently large to finance the deficit on government expenditure, private capital, etc. ?" – a question which relates to the "transfer" mechanism which is the process whereby *monetary* transfers are converted into *real* transfers (goods and services). To see how the transfer mechanism might work, consider the effects of a large outflow of capital from one country to the rest of the world. A part of this outflow may lead directly to an outflow of real goods and services, but in many cases there is no direct feedback effect on the Current Account. However, the effect on the capital receiving countries will be to increase their money supplies and raise incomes which may lead to increased imports and decreased exports, all of which will help the Current Account of the capital-exporting country. A similar income adjustment (and possibly price adjustment) mechanism will take place in the capital-exporting country, leading to relatively lower export prices and a tendency therefore for the capital receiving countries to concentrate their increased imports on the capital-exporting country.

However, the transfer mechanism may fail to work completely, so that the transfer is either over- or under-effected,[7] this failure of the adjustment mechanism being a consequence of a variety of factors. For instance, the capital exporting and receiving countries may be unwilling to allow the income adjustments to take place (especially if the exporting country is underemployed and the receiving countries are fully employed). Also, as in the U.S. case, the presence of a large volume of non-market transfers (military expenditures, etc.) may put sufficient strain on the mechanism to prevent its efficient working. For the United States, then, a large part of its problem is the outcome of an under-effected capital transfer. This, of course, only tells one half of the story; we must go further and discover the *reasons* for the growing private capital outflow and the declining trade balance.

(1) MERCHANDISE TRADE ACCOUNT

As can be seen from Table 5 and Diagram 76 below, imports and exports have been growing at similar rates from 1958 to 1963 (exports rose by 37%, imports by 35%), and U.S. export prices have risen over the same period by 2%, compared with a 1% increase in the export prices of its industrial competitors in Europe and Japan. However, from 1963–67, export prices in the United States rose by 10% compared with a 5% increase in its rivals' export prices. Part of this relative increase may be due to the fact that from 1963–67, U.S. import prices rose by a slightly larger amount than its rivals' import prices, although it is doubtful if much importance can be attached to this. It seems, therefore, that from 1958–63, the United States was not pricing itself out of world markets, but that from 1964 it has progressively failed to compete price-wise with its industrial rivals.

TABLE 5

EXPORT AND IMPORT GROWTH OF UNITED STATES 1958–67 $M.		EXPORT PRICES OF UNITED STATES AND INDUSTRIAL EUROPE (PLUS JAPAN) 1958 = 100		
	Exports	Imports	Export Prices (U.S.A.)	Industrial Europe	Import Prices
1958	16·4	13·4	100	100	100
59	16·4	15·7	100	—	99
1960	19·6	15·0	101	99	100
61	20·2	14·8	103	100	98
62	21·0	16·5	102	100	96
63	22·5	17·2	102	101	97
64	25·8	18·8	103	103	100
65	26·8	21·4	106	104	100
66	29·5	25·6	110	106	102
67	31·0	26·9	112	106	102

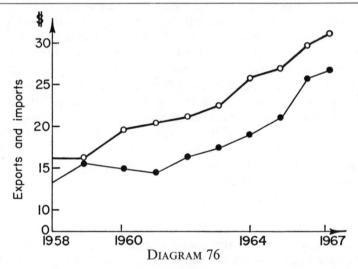

DIAGRAM 76

This is reflected in the decline in the trade balance from 1964–67. It is interesting to note that between 1954 and 1961[8] over $1 billion worth of exports was lost in the fields of motor vehicles, iron and steel and industrial machinery, which together constitute a large part of total industrial manufactures. Within this period of export loss (1955–57), prices of producers' equipment rose by 22%, metals and metal products by 18% and machinery and motor products by 17%. Although European steel product prices also rose during 1955–57, they fell afterwards while U.S. prices remained high. However, it would be a mistake to assume that price disparities are the whole explanation of the U.S. balance of trade behavior. It can reasonably be argued that a contributing factor in the decline in the U.S. share of manufactured exports was the slower growth rates in its principal export markets – especially Canada and Latin America. Thus, whilst the share of its merchandise exports in world trade remained constant from 1953–62, its share of manufactured exports fell from 26% to 20%.[9] Also, between 1955 and 1960, no growth took place in U.S. exports of automobiles, whilst imports of automobiles grew tenfold. The favorable balance of trade in automobiles was $1.2 billion in 1955 and only $0.3 billion in 1959, picking up after this to $0.9 billion in 1963. The major cause of this deterioration up to 1959 was the failure of U.S. car manufacturers to gauge accurately the changed tastes of the U.S. public towards the small car. Of course, manufacturers eventually cottoned on and began to produce the "compact" car, which did much to stem the inflow of European cars.

Part of the explanation for the deterioration post-1957 in the U.S. trade balance may well be the fact that up till the mid '50s it had been operating in a seller's market, so that when Western Europe and Japan had recovered their economic strength, the United States was faced with formidable competition for export markets, competition which the United States failed to meet. It may well be, however, that price competition is less important than marketing competition.[10]

Indeed, some writers[11] claim that the dollar glut is due not to any underlying structural disequilibrium, but to a series of events, the consequence of which was to maintain the U.S. balance of payments in deficit (e.g. increase in demand for small cars, Suez crisis, 1959 steel strike in the United States, changes in U.S. cotton pricing policies, etc.). On top of this, it is suggested[12] that Western Europe and Japan have only recently begun to exploit the great exporting opportunities in the United States. Since 1955, barriers to exporting to the United States have been progressively lowered, making a whole new range of products available to the U.S. buyer. The result has been a deficit, but a deficit, it is claimed, which will be temporary, disappearing after the novelty has worn off and the increased incomes of Europe and Japan begin to suck in greater imports from the United States.

However, such short-term explanations of the dollar problem do not loom large in the literature on the subject. Most of the controversy over the cause of the deficits (and surpluses) has been mainly concerned with secular factors affecting relative competitive trade positions.

However, although many of these theories sound reasonable, they seem to ignore the data relevant to the period. For instance, Hinshaw,[13] Triffin[14] and Schlesinger,[15] hypothesize that the changeover from dollar shortage to dollar glut was mainly due to a combination of overvalued European currencies and rising productive capacity in Europe and

Japan. It is argued that after the War, the European currencies were overvalued (this creating deficits in these countries) and that, when this was finally realized, the devaluations decided upon in 1949 were made excessively large in order to reduce speculation and ensure confidence in the new rates. European and Japanese products now became price competitive with U.S. ones, but the U.S. demand for these products could not be satisfied because of capacity shortages in Europe and Japan. Eventually, capacity expanded and allowed European exports to expand with adverse effects for the U.S. balance of payments. This sounds very reasonable until one looks at the statistics and observes that from 1953–57 (the period in which it is claimed productive capacity in Europe was expanding) the U.S. balance of trade was improving rapidly. No doubt, part of the upsurge in U.S. imports in 1958–59 can be accounted for by the French devaluations of that period, which would also tend to reduce U.S. exports.

A possible explanation of the dollar shortage was propounded by Hicks in 1953,[16] when he analyzed the effects of *biased productivity changes*. Now, suppose we have two countries A and B in initial trade balance and a uniform increase in productivity takes place in A (i.e. productivity in exports and import-substitutes increases). A's income will rise, and with it its demand for imports from B, which will improve B's terms of trade. On the other hand, with prices in A lowered, there will be a gold flow from B to A until prices and incomes in A have risen sufficiently and fallen sufficiently in B. However, if A is unwilling to inflate and B to deflate, then B's trade balance will probably become and stay adverse. If A represents the United States and B Europe, then a dollar shortage may or may not develop from a uniform increase in U.S. productivity. Assume now that A's productivity increase is confined to her export sector (i.e. an export-biased technological change in A). If A's prices fall, then B's terms of trade improve and a trade surplus (or deficit) for A will occur, depending upon B's price elasticity of demand for imports. If A's income is allowed to rise, then its tendency towards deficit will increase as its imports rise and exports expand less than previously. Thus the balance of trade effects of uniform and export-biased productivity change depend upon the relevant income and price elasticities of demand, although Hicks assumed these to be such as to create a dollar shortage when the change was uniform, and balanced trade when it was export biased. Export-biased productivity change, however, in one country, would seem to be preferable (so far as other countries are concerned) to uniform productivity change. However, if the productivity increase in A is import biased, then, according to Hicks, A's demand for B's exports will fall[17] and so lead to a trade surplus for A. Of course, it is possible, making various assumptions about income movements, price and income elasticities, etc., to reach a situation where B is not harmed by an import-biased technological change.

Hicks argued, however, that in the United States productivity had been rapidly advancing during the twentieth century relative to other countries and that, since a dollar shortage had arisen the rapid changes must have been heavily import-biased. Machlup[18] is extremely critical of Hicks and, as Johnson[19] points out, with alternative assumptions about elasticities and growth rates, the Hicksian argument can be used to support either dollar shortage or dollar glut. Nevertheless, this may be a virtue of the theory in that marginal changes in elasticities, etc., may, under certain circumstances, cause a switch over from shortage to surfeit. Thus the disparate productivity change theory can explain the problems of dollar shortage and dollar glut interchangeably. So far, however, the theory has been built on the assumption that only one country experiences a productivity change. If productivity in B rises as well, then, as Machlup[20] and others show, a dollar problem caused by productivity changes is not so likely. If the model is made even more realistic[21] by including more countries and commodities, then the hypothesis loses much of its force as an explanation of the dollar problem. One has to distinguish between the specific effects and the general effects of a productivity increase; the specific effects being those concerned with particular industries, countries, import supplies, etc., whereas the general effects refer to the trade balance changes as a result of income changes.

There is no way of telling *a priori* in which direction the trade balance will move as a result of productivity changes – according to the theory, a deficit country may be in deficit because its productivity growth lags behind its partners; on the other hand, it may be in deficit because its productivity growth runs ahead of its partners ! As the saying goes, "You pays your money and you takes your choice."[22]

Nevertheless, part of the explanation for the recent poor U.S. export performance may be that Western Europe and Japan have rapidly been automating and, in general, catching up with U.S. production techniques, so that the U.S.' comparative advantage position has been deteriorating. This is evidenced by the concentration of its poor export performance in a relatively small group of commodities – vehicles, metals and machinery. This, in conjunction with so-called "*demonstration effects*" (attempts by groups of people to copy the living standards and production techniques of others) could account for some part of the U.S. declining trade balance. It is by no means implausible to suppose that U.S. citizens are trying to imitate the high living standards of the higher levels of European life, and, as Vanek points out, a relatively small shift of U.S. expenditures from domestic to foreign goods could easily result, given the low ratio of imports to G.N.P., in a significantly adverse shift in her balance of trade.

Which of these theories should one choose as *the* explanation of the U.S. payments problems? The answer is that one should *not* choose but rather accept that a variety of factors have been responsible for her trading behavior – price changes, productivity shifts, demonstration effects have all played their part. On the other hand it would be reasonable to argue that many of these theoretical studies, concentrating as they do on the trading account, have been seriously misplaced in that the U.S. payments troubles stem not so much (if at all) from its trade account as from its capital and government accounts. After all, from 1953–60 its trade surpluses averaged $3 billion, while from 1960–67 they averaged almost $5 billion. Over the same periods, however, government expenditure deficits averaged $5 billion and $6 billion respectively, and deficits on private capital movements averaged $2.6 billion and $5.3 billion. Let us turn now, therefore, to a consideration of the government expenditure and private capital accounts.

(2) GOVERNMENT EXPENDITURE

So far as governmental transactions are concerned, there is little or no question of relative prices, productivity disparities, etc., influencing the situation (except in so far as they prevent the transfer mechanism from working). Government grants, loans, military expenditure, etc., represent a transfer problem based largely on political considerations, and imbalances resulting from such transfers are not the consequence of uncompetitiveness, although a highly competitive economy will be more able to transform the money transfer into a real transfer and so adjust to the imbalance. Table 6 below summarizes the data for governmental transactions along with that relating to private capital transfers and the goods and services account. This table illustrates how the overall surplus on goods and services was more than sufficient to cover the private capital outflows, but persistently large government transfers brought the overall balances into deficit.

TABLE 6

U.S. BALANCE OF PAYMENTS 1953–67 ($ BILLION)

	1953	1954	1955	1956	1957	1958	1959	1960
Goods and Services	2·8	4·2	4·8	6·8	8·6	5·3	2·9	6·8
Private Capital (including remittances)	−0·7	−1·9	−1·4	−3·4	−3·9	−3·6	−2·4	−4·2
Government transfers	−4·5	−4·0	−4·9	−5·1	−5·5	−5·8	−4·8	−5·6

	1961	1962	1963	1964	1965	1966	1967
Goods and Services	8·0	7·5	8·2	10·6	9·0	7·8	7·9
Private Capital (including remittances)	−4·5	−3·9	−5·1	−7·2	−6·4	−3·9	−5·4
Government transfers	−5·3	−5·5	−5·8	−5·7	−5·5	−6·2	−7·2

This, of course, is a gross oversimplification since the government transfers will have a certain amount of beneficial feedback effect on the trade account (e.g. loans to Canada, Japan, etc., quickly show up in the trade balance; about 80% of U.S. aid is tied). However, even "tying" is never completely effective, since recipients may spend the aid on goods they would have bought anyway and simply divert their cash orders to other countries (this is the so-called "aid-switching").[23] Also, the export orders through aid may frustrate other export orders and so reduce the effect of tying the aid. So far as military expenditures are concerned, the feedback effect is much less obvious – there is no direct link between money received by foreigners, as a result of spending by U.S. forces overseas, and U.S. exports. Although the United States' largest item on military expenditures (forces in Germany) is in theory fully offset by German purchases of U.S. military equipment, these purchases might have taken place anyway. As recently as 1966, the United States found it necessary to offer their forces rates of interest on personal savings as high as 10% in order to try to reduce the extent of the problem. Since then, of course, increased expenditure in Vietnam has offset these beneficial factors. Unlike private capital flows and the trading account, little can be said of the economic motives behind governmental transactions; one must simply accept that they exist and try to adjust the other items of the balance of payments to their existence since, once the decision has been made to grant $x billion of economic aid, or to spend $y billion on military outgoings, no other path of adjustment is available. The trouble recently (1956 onwards) has been that, although government expenditure was covered by trade balances, the enormous increase since 1953 in private capital outflows has more than used up any leeway given by the trade account.

Although from 1965–67 capital outflows were somewhat lower than the 1964 peak, the declining trade balance and rising government expenditure combined to keep the overall balance in deficit. Let us now look a bit more closely at the private capital account.

(3) Private Capital Outflows

In 1953, net capital outflows were $0.7 billion, by 1964 they were $7.2 billion, a 1,000% increase! Prior to 1955 the great bulk of funds flowing abroad consisted of government grants and loans. After 1955 the outflow of private capital grew tremendously. Why was this? The short answer is that private capital flows (with the exception of remittances) are directed by the profit motive and so opportunities for making profits must have been better in Western Europe and Japan than in the United States. Hansen[24] attributes the increase in long-term capital flow to a world-wide climate buoyant with profitable expectations, the easing of exchange restrictions, and the eventual return to convertibility of most European currencies. Expectations of an appreciation of European currencies against the dollar also had some influence, especially on the short-term capital movements. The 1963 Brookings report listed as possible causes – (a) the convertibility of European currencies, (b) the relatively rapid growth of European economies, (c) the formation of the Common Market, and (d) the increased military security of overseas investments. Of these, the major influences are probably the growth of Europe, making rates of return on investment there higher than corresponding rates at home, and the formation of the Common Market making it more necessary for U.S. companies to "get under" the tariff "umbrella" in order to be able to compete with European producers on a more even footing.

Another important influence is that European states and corporations with good credit ratings can (due to the relative superiority of the New York Capital Market), float bonds easily in New York at lower rates of interest than can be got in Europe, but at higher rates than U.S. investors can expect from corresponding U.S. securities. Also, the relatively slow growing and semi-depressed state of the U.S. economy meant that European funds were unlikely to be channeled to the United States; instead they would be invested at home or overseas in places like Japan. However, the relatively rapid growth of U.S. investment in Europe is a fairly recent phenomenon.[25] From 1958 to 1965, U.S. private investment in Europe increased by some $13 billion to a total of $20 billion yet European investment in the United States stood in 1965 at $33 billion, an increase of $25 billion since 1946. Thus, European investment in the United States in 1946 was higher than U.S. investment in Europe in 1958. Since the early 1950s, however, U.S. investment in Europe has grown at a much faster rate than European investments in the United States – hence the growing deficits on private capital accounts.

So far as the feedback effects on U.S. exports are concerned, we can say that the consequences of private portfolio investment will depend upon the income effects, marginal propensities to import from the United States, etc., of the receiving countries. But, given that the major share of U.S. private investment is *direct* investment in capital plant and equipment of foreign subsidiaries, it is reasonable to concentrate our attention on this particular outflow. If this type of investment means the building of new production capacity, then the U.S. subsidiaries concerned will probably buy a considerable proportion of their equipment from U.S. suppliers and therefore favorably affect the trade account. However, once the foreign subsidiaries begin to extend production, they may take over part of U.S. export markets in the recipient countries (after all, this is the aim of getting under the Common Market's tariff umbrella), and this will adversely affect U.S. exports. Finally, of course, the investments will return interest and dividends to the United States and in this way increase future foreign exchange receipts on "invisibles."

One argument, on a general level, against foreign investment, is that although the private benefits of such investment may be greater than the corresponding benefits from investing at home, the social benefits are lower. This is so because the foreign investment only brings in profits, whereas domestic investment creates profits *and also* jobs, income and economic growth. However, this argument, although applicable in times of less than full employment, loses much of its force when full employment is reached. In fact, one can reverse the connections and argue that with full employment, more investment will be inflationary and therefore, by allowing overseas investment to take place, one can to some extent lessen domestic inflationary pressures. To counter this, one could argue that if private capital outflows are such as to force the authorities to resort to import controls and/or deflationary measures, then the social costs of foreign investment are higher than the private costs involved. Whether one ascribes to this view or not depends upon, ultimately, the attitude one has towards government control of economic resources. Thus, if one agrees with government policies as regards the levels of economic aid, military expenditures, etc., then one will argue that the other items of the balance of payments (e.g. private investment abroad) must adjust to the given levels of government outlays.

On the other hand, one may argue that profit-motivated autonomous transactions should be allowed to take place at market determined levels and the level of government outlays adjusted to them.

Obviously, the connection between direct investment and increased exports is very flexible. In 1965, Dunning and Rowan[26] estimated that the British share of orders for capital equipment purchased by European subsidiaries of British firms might be as low as 5–6%. More recent studies[27] estimate that the "initial effects" on exports of an increase in overseas investment might on average be 9% (depending upon the industry, this varied from 1% to 19%), whilst the "continuing effects" on exports might, on average, be $1\frac{1}{2}$% per annum. However, the

H

"continuing effects" on the balance of payments invisibles account would, on average, be much higher at 8% per annum.

In conclusion, what we can say is that the U.S. payments' problem is fundamentally a transfer problem. As Machlup[28] says, ". . . even if there cannot be an empirical proof, the attribution of the long-lasting payments deficits to the enormous transfer obligations of the United States is highly plausible." This does not, of course, mean that adjustments cannot be made (trade will respond to established transfer flows, the invisibles account will benefit from the progressive rise of investment income, etc.), but what it does mean is that the adjustments will require time in which to work themselves out. However, if European capital markets are not improved, if a more equitable sharing of the aid burden cannot be achieved, if military expenditure continues to rise and if the export competitiveness of the United States continues to decline, then the day when investment outflows are more than offset by the return flows of income and export orders may never arrive – the United States will run even bigger deficits. The means which the United States has been using to reduce its deficits are, however, short-run controls – controls (voluntary or mandatory) over private investment, and bank loans, and export drives. Export drives help but they tend to create a once-and-for-all increase in exports; controls are unsatisfactory in the long run because they inhibit the operation of market forces in allocating resources efficiently, have undesirable effects on the development of integrated international capital markets, and reduce the future flows of foreign exchange in the form of interest and dividends. Given the level of government expenditure overseas, the only ways in which the deficits can be reduced and eliminated consist of increasing the trade surplus (by constraining wage increases, increasing productivity, etc.) and reducing the deficit on private capital account (by making domestic investment more attractive to both home and foreign investors). However, an attractive climate for investment normally requires a buoyant and growing home market entailing full employment which, in turn, may do little to help (and will possibly harm) the trade balance. On the other hand, an increased trade surplus brought about by deflationary domestic measures will drive U.S. investors to seek profitable outlets for their funds abroad. These difficulties demonstrate that there is no simple answer to such a complex problem as the U.S. balance of payments. That this is so will become even more apparent in our final chapter which follows.

[1] F. Machlup, "Equilibrium and Disequilibrium," in his *International Monetary Economics*.

[2] J. E. Meade, *The Balance of Payments*, 1951, defines disequilibrium as follows:

". . . an 'actual' balance-of-payments deficit (can be defined) as the actual amount of accommodating finance used in any period of time."

[3] As late as 1958, charts were being produced for *Lloyd's Bank Review* under the title "The Dollar Gap."

[4] Based on I.M.F. Analytical presentation of balance of payments statistics.

[5] E. M. Bernstein, "American Productivity and the Dollar Payments Problem," *Review of Economic Statistics*, 1955.

[6] As is evidenced by the report of the U.S. Congress, Joint Economic Committee on "Factors Affecting the U.S. Balance of Payments"; and by W. Salant, *et al.*, "The U.S. Balance of Payments in 1968," *Brookings Report*, 1963.

[7] See H. Johnson, "The Transfer Problem and Exchange Stability," *Journal of Political Economy*, 1956.

[8] See *Brookings Report*, p. 68.

[9] „   „   „ p. 65.

[10] According to T. Balogh, "Availability, knowledge, delivery periods, credit, servicing, and above all, quality, the embodiment of technical knowledge, therefore, and not merely price, are the determinants of competitive supremacy," statement on the Brookings Institute Study, 1963. See also, H. Junz and R. Rhomberg, "Prices and Export Performance of Industrial Countries, 1953–63," *I.M.F. Staff Papers*, 1965.

[11] Lary, "Disturbances and Adjustments in Recent U.S. Balance of Payments Experience," *American Economic Review*, 1961.

[12] G. D. A. MacDougall, "The World Dollar Problem: A Reappraisal," Essays in *International Finance*, No. 35, Princeton University.

[13] R. Hinshaw, "Implications of the Shift in the U.S. Balance of Payments," *American Economic Review*, 1959.

[14] R. Triffin, "The International Monetary Position of the United States," in *The Dollar Crisis*, S. E. Harris (Ed.), 1961.

[15] E. R. Schlesinger, "Discussion of International Trade and Payments in an Era of Co-existence," *American Economic Review*, 1959.

[16] J. R. Hicks, "An Inaugural Lecture," *Oxford Economic Papers*, 1953.

[17] ". . . an improvement in A-productivity, that is import-biased must make B worse off."

[18] F. Machlup, "Dollar Shortage and Disparities in the Growth of Productivity," in his *International Monetary Economics*, 1964.

[19] H. Johnson, "Increasing Productivity, Income-Price Trends and the Trade Balance," in his *International Trade and Economic Growth*, 1958.

[20] F. Machlup, *op. cit.*

[21] See T. Balogh, "The Dollar Crisis Revisited," *Oxford Economic Papers*, 1954; and "The Dollar Shortage once More: a Reply," *Scottish Journal of Political Economy*, 1955; also, E. M. Bernstein, "American Productivity and the Dollar Payments Problem," *Review of Economic Statistics*, 1955.

[22] See J. Vanek, "Long Run Factors in the United States Payments Disequilibrium," in *The Dollar Crisis*, 1961; also, G. D. A. MacDougall, *The World Dollar Problem*, 1957.

[23] "Feedback ratios," published by the Brookings study, show that on the basis of past experience, one dollar of U.S. aid will result in a net increase of U.S. exports of between 5 and 50 cents, depending on the recipient country.

[24] A. Hansen, *The Dollar and the International Monetary System*, p. 26, 1965.

[25] See A. Brimmer, U.S. Assistant Secretary of Commerce of Economics Affairs, his speech to the American Club in Paris, July 1965.

[26] J. Dunning and D. C. Rowan, "British Direct Investment in Western Europe," *Banca Nazionale del Lavoro Quarterly Review*, 1965.

[27] See the Reddaway Report on Overseas Investment.

[28] F. Machlup, "Involuntary Foreign Lending," being the 1965 Wicksell Lectures.

CHAPTER 11

Current International Monetary Problems

In this, our final chapter, we shall be concerned with the weaknesses of the present international monetary system, the strains put on it since the late 1950s by the U.S. payments deficits, and proposals which have been made for its reformation.

The present international monetary system is basically the same as that existing before World War II except that the structure of the I.M.F. has been added. The foundation on which the system rests is that member countries of the I.M.F. strive to maintain the values of their currencies relative to gold or a gold-based currency (i.e. the U.S. dollar and the pound sterling) which serves as a substitute for gold. Currencies should also be free from exchange controls, at least so far as current account transactions are concerned, and neither seriously over- or under-valued. In a world of fixed exchange rates and freedom from exchange controls, it follows that if countries are to be able to fulfil their commitments under the I.M.F.'s articles, they must be ready and able to operate freely in the foreign exchange market, selling or buying gold and/or foreign exchange as required. This means, then, that countries must hold international monetary reserves in the form of gold and key currencies, and in amounts adequate to withstand possible balance of payments deficits.

International reserves, then, perform a vital function in allowing countries to incur temporary deficits whilst keeping their exchange rates stable – in effect, they permit countries to maintain their policy objectives of full employment, price stability, growth, etc., whereas under the rules of the gold standard, deficits (and surpluses) would force governments to follow adjustment paths which left the domestic economy at the mercy of the external accounts. Under the gold-exchange standard, external economic events are not permitted to automatically force the authorities to abandon their domestic goals, but rather, international reserves are allowed to fluctuate and thereby absorb external "shocks." So long as these "shocks" are short-lived and non-cumulative, then holdings of monetary reserves act as a buffer and temporarily insulate the domestic economy from external happenings. When the disequilibrium is regarded as fundamental, reserves can also be used to "buy time" in which to bring about alterations to the economy; and when the disequilibrium is due to speculative or arbitrage-based capital movements, reserves can be used to accommodate such movements. Now, if it is assumed that payments imbalances will continue to occur in the future, and if governments continue to pursue the domestic goals of price stability, full employment, etc., independently of each other and of the state of the external balance, and if exchange rates are to be maintained in a fixed relationship to each other, then a necessity for the simultaneous fulfilment of these conditions is an adequate supply of international reserves; adequate in the sense that if the required level is not forthcoming, then one or more of the following consequences will ensue:

(*a*) exchange rates will be changed;
(*b*) domestic policy goals will be abandoned;
(*c*) direct controls over trade and capital flows will be introduced in order to restore balance of payments equilibrium.

It follows that if the supply of reserves if inadequate and if great prestige is attached to the maintenance of a country's exchange rate, then a deflationary bias will be imparted to the world economy. Deficit countries will have to adopt deflationary domestic policies and/or impose trade and exchange controls, both of which will harm the surplus countries as well as the deficit countries. Retaliation could take place and, in any case, the foreign repercussion effects will ensure an all round decline in incomes, employment and living standards, with attendant effects on world economic welfare.

It is also possible that if reserve supplies are excessive, then this could lead to increasingly liberal credit expansion policies which could, especially if economies are fully employed, give an inflationary bias to the world economy. Thus, the question of the adequacy or otherwise of international reserves is an exceedingly important one, which no doubt accounts for the vast volume of literature to be found on the subject since about 1955.

Before considering whether or not the present level of reserves is adequate, and attempting to ascertain the likelihood of a future inadequacy, it is first of all necessary to examine more closely the concepts involved in the term international liquidity.

A certain amount of confusion arises initially in that one tends to find the terms "international reserves" and "international liquidity" used interchangeably as if they were two aspects of the same thing. However, strictly speaking, "*liquidity*" in the international sense refers to the attributes or qualities of an asset which enable it to be instantly (or virtually so) transformed into a generally accepted means of settling international transactions. Machlup[1] regards "liquidity" as the "capacity to pay promptly," this capacity being determined only when it has been decided what sources of funds are available and to what uses they will be put. Thus, just as one can talk of the liquidity of a firm or of an individual, so one can talk of the liquidity (international) of a country, or group of countries. *Reserves*, on the other hand, are these assets which possess the attributes or qualities embodied in the concept of liquidity. In order to determine what constitutes a country's reserves, therefore, one must include only those assets which possess the ability to be transformed immediately into an internationally acceptable currency or currencies. However, the range of assets which satisfy this condition tends to increase over time, so that a historical review of a country's reserve positions would have to take this into account. Thus, before World War I, the only asset which was regarded as a reserve asset was gold, and countries held all their reserves in this form. After the war, gold production was falling and, in order to get round the problem, the monetary authorities recommended that countries hold foreign exchange balances as reserve assets, in addition to gold.

Following this recommendation, central bank holdings of dollars, sterling and short-term dollar and sterling assets grew, until by 1928 they represented approximately 40% of total reserve holdings. Although this system collapsed in the 1930s,[2] it was resurrected after World War II and, as a result, foreign exchange holdings of central banks have become a very important part of total international reserves. The growth of exchange holdings relative to gold can be seen in the following table, which shows the composition of reserves from 1950–67 for Europe, the United States, Canada and Japan.

TABLE 1

INTERNATIONAL RESERVE HOLDINGS 1950 AND 1967 ($M.)

	Total		Gold		Foreign Exchange		Exchange: Total		Imports		Total: Imports	
	1950	1967	1950	1967	1950	1967	1950 %	1957 %	1950	1967	1950 %	1967 %
U.S.A.	22,820	14,830	22,820	12,065	—	2,345	0	16	9,601	31,294	204	47
U.K.	3,668	2,695	2,900	1,291	768	1,404	21	52	7,305	17,778	50	15
Canada	1,770	2,709	580	1,015	1,190	1,260	68	47	3,128	11,260	57	24
Japan*	979	2,030	16	338	963	1,454	99	72	2,044	12,500	48	16
Austria	91	1,484	50	701	41	667	45	45	477	2,470	19	60
Belgium	793	2,590	587	1,480	206	782	26	30	1,942	7,928	41	33
France	791	6,994	672	5,234	119	874	15	12	3,030	13,077	21	54
Germany	274	8,752	—	4,228	274	2,872	100	35	2,697	19,069	10	43
Italy	602	5,463	256	2,400	347	2,221	60	40	1,488	10,347	40	53
Netherlands	606	2,619	311	1,711	295	556	49	21	2,056	8,782	30	30
Switzerland	1,580	3,555	1,470	3,089	109	466	7	13	1,056	4,186	150	85

* 1952.

Source: I.M.F. International Financial Statistics.

It can be seen from the above table that foreign exchange holdings have become increasingly important as a reserve asset. In 1950, foreign exchange holdings amounted to approximately 25% of total reserves for the whole world, but by 1967 they had increased to approximately 38% of total reserves. Thus, after World War II and throughout the 1950s and early '60s, the dollar (and to a lesser extent the pound sterling) came to be regarded as being "as good as gold" and perhaps even better, since reserve holdings in the form of gold earned nothing for the holder, whereas short-term dollar assets provided a return in the form of interest payments. This acceptance of the dollar and pound sterling was based on the economic strength of the United States and Great Britain, and on their importance in world trade – no one expected that the U.S. dollar could ever be devalued. During the 1950s, then, more than half of the increase in world reserves was due to the acceptance of short-term dollar balances created as a result of the continuous U.S. payments deficits, Western gold production accounting for less than a third of the expansion of world reserves.

Under the current international monetary system, then, international reserves are composed essentially of gold, dollars and pounds sterling. It follows, therefore, that any additions to the total of monetary reserves must come through increased gold production finding its way into official reserves, and/or increases in foreign-held dollar and sterling balances. (It might also be possible to increase world reserves if another asset, existing or newly created, were to become acceptable in the liquidity sense; and we shall examine these two possibilities later.)

We can see, then, that the present gold-exchange standard increases the growth potential of reserves by augmenting gold production with increases in the supply of other assets. Nevertheless, the present system is in some respects less stable than a pure gold standard in that, when more than one reserve center exists, it is possible for speculation on exchange-rate movements to take place by converting one reserve currency into another without suffering a loss thereby. Thus speculative activity will tend to take place if one of the reserve currencies shows any sign of weakness, and, of course, the speculation will intensify the weakness and lead to further speculation, etc. This is not too important for the system as a whole, so long as the speculators move into the currency of the other reserve center and so long as the weak center can satisfactorily absorb the increased supply of its own currency; all that happens is that the composition of exchange holdings alters but the total of reserves does not. However, if speculators move out of the weak currency and into non-reserve currencies or gold, then total reserves will decline by a corresponding amount. Also, if the weak currency country cannot meet its mobilized short-term liabilities, then it will be forced to devalue or abandon convertibility, either of which causes would tend to create the feeling amongst reserve currency holders that paper reserves were not as good as gold after all. The result might be that the other stronger, reserve currency comes under suspicion and consequently holders begin to transform their exchange holdings into gold, thereby reducing total international reserves and returning to a gold standard system. A means of avoiding such a breakdown of the system might be found if some method could be devised for supporting a reserve currency when it comes under pressure. In fact, in the second half of 1960, large-scale short-term capital movements occurred as a result of a lack of confidence in the dollar and pound sterling, and it was feared that the resources of the I.M.F. might be inadequate to protect the currencies of the United States and Britain. As a result, the Fund undertook negotiations with ten countries (the Group of Ten, or Paris Club), which resulted in the *General Arrangements to Borrow* (G.A.B.) which came into effect in 1962. Basically, the arrangement is that a country whose currency is under pressure can borrow from the Fund the currencies required to combat the speculation. The Fund, in turn, borrows these currencies from the relevant members of the agreement and, therefore, acts solely as an intermediary in the borrowing-lending process. Borrowings made under the Arrangement have to be repaid to the Fund within five years, at a fairly low rate of interest. The first, major use of the G.A.B. was in December 1964, when 405 million dollars was granted to the U.K., a further 525 million dollars being granted in 1965, these borrowings being part of loans of 1,000 million dollars and 1,400 million dollars extended to Britain in 1964 and 1965 respectively, in order to combat the heavy speculative pressure which had built up against the pound sterling following the very large deficits run by Britain in these years. Another arrangement to offset speculative movements is the so-called *Stand-by Arrangements*, whereby the Fund undertakes to supply currency, upon request, up to an agreed amount and within a certain (renewable) period. Such an arrangement is useful when the problem is not so much one of immediate assistance but rather one of having certain amounts of currency available. In 1961, speculative movements, based on the unfavorable competitive position of Britain, necessitated recourse to the Fund for 1,500 million dollars aid.

In 1964, the 1,000 million dollars referred to above was drawn under Stand-by Agreement, and in 1965, 1,400 million dollars was drawn. Following persistent speculative pressure as a result of the 1967 devaluation of sterling, a further 1,400 million dollars was required in 1968 for support operations, 476 million dollars of this coming from the G.A.B.

Two other recent innovations in this field are the so-called *Basle Agreements* of 1961 which allow each member of the Bank for International Settlements[3] to call upon the other members for grants of short-term credits. So far, the only requests have been made by Britain, in 1961, 1964 and 1966. The other mechanism for avoiding currency crises is the *Swap Arrangements*, drawn up in 1962 when the U.S.A. concluded such arrangements with the Group of Ten countries plus Austria and Switzerland. These arrangements are bilateral and consist of a combination of a spot purchase (or sale) of a currency and a forward sale (or purchase) of the same currency, at a fixed exchange rate. Finally, the Fund can increase its resources by raising members' quotas or by purchasing members' currencies with gold. In 1959 quotas were increased by 50% and by a further 25% in 1966.

By means of various *ad hoc* measures and increasing central bank coordination and cooperation, de-stabilizing speculation has to a large extent been contained by making short- and medium-term liquidity available to central banks whose currencies are under pressure.

Nevertheless, it is still claimed by many that the gold exchange standard system suffers from a most serious failing in the way in which it provides for increases in total international reserves. As we saw earlier, increases in total reserves can come about only if central banks can acquire more gold (which depends ultimately on the size of the output of new gold), or if the reserve currency centers are prepared to run deficits to allow other countries to acquire increased foreign-exchange holdings. Thus, when the supply of new gold is insufficient to meet growing demands for liquidity, then the reserve centers, by supplying the required liquidity supplement, will experience a deterioration in their net reserve positions (i.e. their short-term liabilities increase while their gold and foreign exchange holdings stay constant or decrease). One can expect that, as this process continues, a loss of confidence in one or both of the reserve currencies will ultimately appear and lead to increased possibilities of de-stabilizing speculation. As Kaldor[4] says, the paradox is that the system only provides liquidity when the reserve currencies are weak, whereas the basis of the whole system is that the currencies which serve as international reserves should be strong! This leads to a dilemma, according to Triffin,[5] in that if the reserve currency countries continue to run deficits and thereby pump liquidity into the system, then, due to decreasing confidence in their convertibility, runs on these currencies could force devaluation, exchange restrictions or other crisis measures. However, if the deficits of the reserve centers are eliminated, then a shortage of world liquidity could soon develop which would retard trade and investment and might result in competitive depreciations and other undesirable measures being used to equilibrate the balance of payments. It seems that no matter what the reserve countries do, the entire system is in danger of collapsing. This is due, ultimately, to the fact that although foreign exchange reserves have been accepted as being as good as gold, this belief weakens when the gold reserves of the reserve currency countries drop. It follows that when a loss of gold can shake confidence in a reserve currency, then the role of gold is still central to the continued existence of the international monetary system. Because of this reliance on the domestic currencies of Britain and the United States as international reserve assets, creating as it does problems of continued confidence in the system and the threat of inadequate supplies of reserves, several plans have been put forward concerning the reformation of the international monetary system. Before examining such proposals, we must consider more closely the fundamental criticism of the present system – namely, that it fails to provide for an adequate and planned increase in the total of international reserves.

Essentially, the problem revolves round the concept of reserve *adequacy*. Are the present levels of reserves adequate in some sense or other? Will the growth of reserves in the future be adequate? These questions, however, beg the more fundamental question of whether or not the criterion of adequacy is the relationship between world reserves and the need for them or an individual country's reserves and its need for them. Does it make sense to talk about a shortage of global reserves? It does, but only in the context of individual countries' adequacy. Global adequacy is definable only in relation to individual countries and their national policies (free trade, growth, fixed exchange rates, etc.).

Thus, if one country finds its reserves inadequate in the sense that it has to resort to import restrictions, exchange controls, etc., then global reserves are also inadequate; similarly, if all countries find their reserves to be adequate (i.e. impose no undesirable restrictions on trade or domestic goals), then global reserves are also adequate. This was recognized in the 1961 Report of the U.S. Congress Joint Economic Committee, when it was argued that if a deficiency of reserves exists in any one country, then an overall deficiency exists. Thus, the problem of global adequacy is solved if, and only if, the reserve problems of all individual countries have been solved. Now, although underdeveloped countries will normally experience a permanent insufficiency of reserves, this does not concern us here, since we have limited ourselves to a use of reserves for *temporary* payments deficits. Thus, we need only concern ourselves with the liquidity of the advanced industrial nations.

Adequacy determination involves a consideration of a country's international reserves against the functional needs or requirements which they are intended to serve. In a study of reserve adequacy undertaken in 1964 by Weir Brown,[6] a definition of international liquidity was used which stated that it consisted "of such resources as are readily available to a country's monetary authorities for the purpose of financing temporary deficits in its balance of payments and defending the stability of its exchange rate." This is an excellent definition[7] in that it embodies the essential characteristics of reserve assets and relates them functionally to given aims. However, we must state precisely what is meant by "readily available," since this will determine which assets we include in our reserve total.

Since monetary authorities regard resources which they can borrow (e.g. under the previously discussed I.M.F. arrangements) as being conditional (i.e. available *if* the country concerned agrees to follow certain conditions relating to domestic policy formation), then it can be argued that such assets are not *readily* available.[8] The resources which are regarded as international reserves cover only those assets which are *owned* by the country – that is, gold and foreign exchange holdings and the automatic drawing rights (Gold Tranche),[9] at the I.M.F. Machlup uses this same definition of reserves in his analyses of adequacy.[10] Now, having obtained a means of measuring a country's liquidity, how are we to judge whether or not it is adequate? In other words, what are the criteria of adequacy?

Triffin[11] uses as his criterion the relationship between the size of a country's reserves and its imports, expressed as a ratio which tells us how long a country could, by liquidating its reserves, maintain its imports if its foreign exchange receipts were to drop to zero. However, it is extremely unlikely that receipts would ever become zero. But, and more important, this ratio, associating as it does the size of probable imbalances with the volume of imports, is extremely suspect as a measure of adequacy, since it relies on two basic assumptions which are supported neither by appeals to theory nor to statistics. These assumptions are:

(*a*) that changes in the demand for foreign exchange depend solely on imports and not on capital exports or unilateral transfers; and

(*b*) that the size of probable deficits varies directly with the total value of imports. Although it is true that the level of imports for a country will tend to rise as time goes on, the influence of this on current reserve levels or future requirements is by no means direct; a rise in imports does not *per se* increase a country's liquidity requirements.

As Machlup[12] says, "If there is [any significance to be attached to this ratio], I do not know of any theory that would show and explain it." What is more relevant to adequacy is the relation between reserves and a country's external balance (in an "above the line" sense), since such imbalances will use up (or add to) a country's international reserves and affect *directly* the relationship between reserves and requirements.

This measure (i.e., liquidity : imbalances) is theoretically appealing since it shows *why* an increase in reserves may be needed (i.e. when imbalances increase) and also what the consequences would be if a required increase in reserves was not forthcoming; namely, an inability to finance payments deficits, leading to trade and/or exchange controls, domestic deflation, etc.

Over the period 1953–62, Brown[13] found that for the Group of 10 countries, plus Switzerland, there was a substantial and sustained growth in the liquidity available, although large differences did exist between countries. Imports were rising but, over the period studied, the countries showed a level of reserves generally well above the 35% of imports which Triffin considered to be a safe minimum. About half of the countries ended the period with virtually the same ratio as at the beginning of the other half; Italy, France and Germany experienced an increase in the ratio, whilst Sweden, Switzerland and the United States suffered a decline. Turning to the other measure of adequacy (i.e. ratio of liquidity to external balance), Brown found that in a large proportion of the cases the ratio was in the range of 4–10 for the period involved. The behavior of this ratio was not at all uniform, however, since for 7 out of 10 cases it rose or stayed the same, while for the United States it declined steadily, due mainly to continuous gold loss over the period. In a somewhat more refined study,[14] Machlup demonstrated that over the period 1949–65, many of the 14 industrial countries studied held reserves 4–14 times the size of their largest cumulative reserve loss during the period, although the United States and Britain were relatively ill-equipped to meet future deficits.

So far as the behavior of the imbalances themselves are concerned, the majority of the countries studied showed a stable or declining trend in the size of absolute imbalances and therefore a falling proportion of a country's total international transactions. This is the opposite of what Triffin and Salant[15] expected to happen, in that they argued that a progressive shortage of liquidity would arise due to inadequate gold production, a drying up of the supply of dollars and an increase in the size of payments deficits as a result of growing imports. What seems to have been overlooked is the fact that if the United States eliminates its deficit, then the surpluses of other countries will be reduced and liquidity requirements fall for the system as a whole. Brown feels, finally, that his interpretation of liquidity is probably a minimum interpretation, in that some other sources of reserves could be included (e.g. credit facilities at the I.M.F. beyond the Tranches, bilateral swaps, etc.), especially since we are living in "*an age of heightened central bank co-operation*" so that international credits extended between central banks are becoming increasingly available as an additional source of liquidity. On the basis of Brown's analysis and statistical evidence, it does not seem that Triffin and Salant's hypothesis concerning a progressive deterioration in the adequacy of liquidity finds much support.

Another study by Rhomberg[16] uses a similar definition of liquidity and argues that the levels of liquidity held will be related to the expected size of future deficits, and that the desired level of reserves will increase chiefly as a result of an increase in the size of expected payments imbalances.

Rhomberg criticized Brown on the grounds that his sample of countries was too small and that random events could cause peaks and depressions to appear in the historical data on imbalances, thereby giving the false impression of a rising or falling trend, or even of no trend at all. However, Brown's eleven countries account for over 70% of liquidity resources, dominate policy with respect to international monetary affairs, and cover 70% of world trade.

Also, since the underdeveloped countries (which account for approximately 60% of Rhomberg's sample) will tend inevitably (almost by definition) to experience continuous deficits (and perhaps rising ones due to the increasing burden of debt servicing and repaying), it would be preferable to examine only the deficit positions and histories of the advanced countries. In addition, Brown recognized that imbalances vary considerably from year to year and therefore he ignores extreme values for imbalances and operates with model values. Machlup, on the other hand, operates on the largest reserve losses experienced by countries over the period 1949–65, and compares these with reserves held by countries in 1965; the argument being that countries may wish to be able to cover the largest reserve loss experienced in the past. These ratios of liquidity to reserve loss varied from 142% for Britain to 1441% for Austria, with 6 of his 14 countries holding reserves between 417% and 506% of their largest past deficits. With such excessive safety margins, it seems likely that some other motive(s) for reserve holding are required in order to justify such holdings.

Returning to Rhomberg's analysis, he concluded that over the period 1952–64, the growth of annual imbalances was 3.5% (excluding U.S.A.), whilst the annual growth of trade was 6–7%, reserves growing by 6% per annum (excluding the United States); that is, at least as fast as imports and faster than imbalances. The influence of U.S. imbalances can be seen in that if the United States is included, then imbalances grew by $6\frac{1}{2}$% per annum, whilst total reserves only grew by 2.5% per annum. It would seem reasonable to infer from this that a liquidity problem has not arisen for most countries, and is not likely to provided that past trends hold good in the future. This, of course, is not to say that the United States (and Britain) do not face severe liquidity problems;

what it does mean is that the solution to their problems does not lie in a universal expansion in international reserves. On a universal level, then, is there no liquidity problem? According to Machlup, an annual increase in total reserves is required, but his basis for this argument does not depend upon the expected size of imbalances or the rising level of world trade. In his analysis, he shows that some countries hold large reserves no matter how the relative size is measured (reserves in relation to imports, past deficits, the money supply central bank liabilities, etc.), whilst other countries hold low reserves. In some cases the situation is confused, a country holding large reserves in one sense, but low reserves in another. Machlup argues that the absolute size of reserves held by a country is not a major target of economic policy except where reserves are so low that a false step would eliminate them entirely, or where, though reasonably high, they are showing signs of declining.

However, even though a country's reserves are adequate in whatever functional sense one uses the word, its central bank will always prefer to have more, just as one's wife prefers to have more dresses no matter how many she already has.[17] Thus, although total reserves are adequate, annual additions to that level (no matter what it may be) are always called for, and diminutions in a country's reserve level (though it may still be adequate) would call for policies to reverse the process. This does not, however, explain why some countries hold *relatively* high levels of reserves. The explanation, according to Machlup, is that the alternatives to accumulating reserves are disliked by the authorities, so that it is deemed better to let reserves accumulate than to revalue, inflate, relax import controls, etc. Thus, emphasis on the absolute size of reserves is mistaken, whereas emphasis on *additions to* reserves is perfectly justified since, if such additions are not forthcoming, countries may resort to trade and exchange restrictions, inappropriate domestic policies, and so on. The amount and form of such additions will be the subject of our discussion on plans for international monetary reform. What we can note for the moment is that the distribution of such additional reserves could make central banks more willing to relax domestic restraints on credit, growth, etc., and although this might be inflationary, there is no reason why the authorities could not control it. Clearly, the factors underlying the inclination of central bankers to accumulate reserves are extremely subjective and difficult to include in any formal estimate of the need for reserves, although Kenen[18] and Fleming[19] have attempted to provide a model which takes the preferences of the authorities into account.

If Machlup's conclusions are valid, then a strong case can be made for increasing total world liquidity annually at a rate sufficient to allow countries to avoid unnecessary restrictive policies as regards trade and the domestic economy. If all that central bankers are worried about, so far as their reserve position is concerned, is to ensure that their reserves do not fall but rather increase, then the annual growth of liquidity can be extremely small. Such a system, like any other international monetary system, would not allow countries to run continuous deficits – in such cases it is not the monetary system which is at fault in failing to provide sufficient liquidity, rather it is a structural alteration in the economies themselves that is required, or a change in the adjustment mechanism.

Recently, Clower and Lipsey have provided us with a very comprehensive and concise account of the current state of international liquidity theory.[20] In this article they deal at length with the problem of determining reserve adequacy and very soon come to the conclusion that "the adequacy of reserves to meet some contingencies cannot be assessed in terms of reasoned criteria." (As in Machlup's "Wardrobe Theory.") However, perhaps there are other reasons for holding reserves (i.e. apart from fears of speculation or the ambitions of central bankers) which are amenable to economic analysis – namely, reserves held to accommodate systematic and random fluctuations in current receipts and payments, and those held to allow for temporary non-speculative variations in capital account items. The authors then go on to analyze each of these two reasons in turn, examining the probablistic approaches of Haller,[21] Clark and others. The general outcome of such analyses is that one should be sceptical of the "common belief that the level of reserves should expand more or less in line with increases in the volume of trade." Numerous theoretical and statistical difficulties remain to be overcome before much faith can be placed in the practicability of such approaches. Once we try to take account of non-speculative and temporary capital transfers the problems become even more difficult. In addition, reserves are also held to meet speculative crises and buy time for domestic adjustment, and as the authors point out, if we are ever to be able to judge the overall adequacy of reserves, the system itself will have to be changed by working out techniques which allow governments to demoralize speculators at any desired point in time. Or it might even be preferable to move over to a flexible exchange-rate system with gold removed as a reserve currency. "The world might then go about its proper business of providing for the adequacy of more important things than international liquidity and related national status symbols."

Let us turn now to an examination of various plans which have been put forward for the reformation of the international monetary system, plans designed to avoid the dangers thought to be in the present system.

To recap, three major charges have been made against the present system – firstly, it is asserted that the growth of reserves will be inadequate for world needs. We have examined this criticism in some detail, noting the divergence of opinion between people like Harrod[22] and Triffin,[23] who claim that reserves are, or are likely to become, inadequate, and others such as Holtrop and Jacobsson, who argue that reserves have been excessive, leading to inflationary pressures. Secondly, the present system, relying as it does in an inefficient adjustment mechanism, allows countries to postpone necessary policies or allows danger signals to be ignored. Changes in exchange rates are seldom used, and when they are they tend to be postponed until a crisis arises. The system, it is alleged, allows the key-currency countries to run persistent deficits and in effect forces the surplus countries to accumulate unwanted holdings of foreign exchange.[24] For other deficit countries, the system is too harsh in that it places no obligation on the part of the surplus countries to adjust their imbalances. Also, due to the large foreign holdings of exchange, speculation becomes very dangerous for the system as a whole, so that a strengthening of the current arrangements for dealing with hot-money flows is required. Thirdly, the present system, by allowing countries to build up large short-term claims against the key-currency countries, leads to the dilemma that, if the United States fails to eliminate its deficits, then fears of devaluation will accumulate and speculators will move out of dollars and into gold. On the other hand, if the United States does balance its payments, then a vital source of international liquidity will dry up with undesirable consequences. If the system did collapse, then the dollar and pound sterling would cease to be reserve currencies and world liquidity would fall drastically. It is therefore in everyone's interests to protect the key-currencies and avoid such a collapse until some better system can be devised to overcome the above difficulties.

The proposals are of basically two types, one of which aims at improving the deficient adjustment mechanism, the other leaves the adjustment mechanism unaltered but, by increasing reserves, hopes to allow more time in which countries can adjust to payments disequilibria. Plans of the first type are:

(*a*) A return to the gold standard (with possibly an increase in the price of gold), and

(*b*) the adoption of a flexible exchange rate system.

Plans of the second type are:

(*a*) the extension of the gold exchange standard through the establishment of a "composite" or multiple reserve unit,

(*b*) an increase in the degree of mutual assistance between central banks, and

(c) the centralization of reserves and deliberate creation of new reserves through an international agency like the I.M.F.

ADJUSTMENT MECHANISM PLANS

(a) *Gold Standard.* The chief advocates of a return to the old gold standard are Rueff and Hirsch.[25] All international imbalances would be settled by gold transfers, and exchange holdings would be eliminated by having the U.S. and U.K. pay off their liabilities over an agreed period of time. The fundamental argument in favor of this system is that a system (as at present) which allows the reserve countries to continually increase the ratio of their liquid liabilities to gold holdings is inevitably bound to collapse. If gold were the sole international reserve asset, then this could not take place since adjustment to imbalances by following the rules of the game could not be avoided. A flexible rate system is unacceptable because it would allow countries to inflate without constraint and thus impart an inflationary bias to the world economy. Any system which permits the use of national currencies as international reserves is of no use, since it is subject to the same criticisms as the present system. The only trouble with a gold standard system is that it makes domestic policy dependent on the external position to an unacceptable degree – the very reason why it was abandoned. It is extremely unlikely that in this day and age when full employment and price stability are major aims of domestic policy, that governments would allow gold transfers to force them to abandon these policies. But what of an increase in the price of gold?

The main criticisms of such an increase are that it would affect the supply of reserves in an arbitrary fashion that it would favour the gold producing countries (Russia and South Africa), and that it would penalise most those who have done most to help the current system work whilst it benefited those who had done least. Nevertheless, if other ways of reforming the system could not be agreed upon, then a straightforward increase in the gold price could still be worth while. In Rueff's view a doubling of the price would be required in order to convince speculators and hoarders that a further increase was unlikely in the medium-term future. Two effects would follow such an increase – firstly the dollar value of gold stocks would be doubled thereby increasing liquidity (but by less than twice since currency holdings would no longer count as reserve assets) and secondly the annual value of the flow of new gold would be doubled, thereby increasing the rate at which new liquidity became available. The effect of all this would be to allow the key currency countries to repay their short-term debts to foreign central banks and yet maintain some gold in their vaults. Thus, at the end of 1965, dollar holdings of central banks were 14.8 billion dollars, while the doubled value of their gold holdings would have been 28 billion dollars. A higher gold price would also stimulate gold production and private dishoarding, and so do a great deal to allay fears of a liquidity shortage. However, if accumulations of foreign exchange and a deficiency of liquidity are to be avoided, then the gold price may have to be readjusted every so often, a practice which requires international monetary management, something which the suggested system is supposed to avoid.[26] A price increase would appear then to be only a short-term solution, if all other alternatives fail.

On the subject of the gold price, Machlup[27] makes the novel suggestion that it would be better to reduce the price of gold by, say, 4% per annum, although the price might be sometimes allowed to rise in order to prevent one-way speculation. The chief objective would be to make it perfectly clear to speculators that capital losses were just as likely as capital gains. Machlup expects that the result would be that private dishoarding would occur, although he recognizes that his plan is only an "expedient makeshift," useful in a situation where reformers fail to agree, or another dollar crisis appears.

On the role of gold in the system, some economists[28] argue that reliance on gold is, as Keynes put it, a "barbarous relic" based on the primitive idea that the precious metals are better than paper currencies, since, for one thing, their supply is not in the hands of the monetary authorities. They advocate plans which cut the dollar–gold link by either withdrawing the obligation of the United States to *buy* gold at 35 dollars per ounce or by doing away with both the buying and selling obligation (i.e. complete demonetization of gold). By removing the buying obligation, the United States would still set the maximum market price for gold but would not operate to prevent the price falling below this. Thus, speculators could have their fingers burned and this might lead to dishoarding and a dampening down of speculation against the key currencies. Lerner argues that the United States should go a step further and actually force the gold price down by selling off its entire gold stocks. Whether foreign governments would tie their currencies to the dollar or to gold is not known and therefore the future status of gold would depend upon the U.S. payments position and on the reaction of other governments to the low gold price. If both the selling and buying obligation was removed, then dollars would no longer be convertible into gold, so that other countries would have to decide whether to tie their currencies to gold or the dollar. If they chose the dollar, then gold would vanish as an international currency and dollar holdings would be the sole reserve asset. If they chose gold, then the United States would be on a flexible rate system whilst the rest of the world was on a fixed rate system. In the circumstances it is likely that most countries would prefer to maintain the dollar tie, given the size of the United States as a world trader.

(*b*) *Flexible Exchange Rates*. As a means of improving the adjustment mechanism, these have been discussed fully in Chapter 9. It need only be repeated here that flexible rates are no panacea for solving the world's payments problems, although they would lessen the need for international reserves and give a greater degree of independence to domestic policies. However, they do require cooperation between central banks and coordination of economic policies, but their attractiveness lies in the lesser *degree* of coordination required.

LIQUIDITY EXPANSION PLANS

(*a*) *The Extension of the Gold Exchange Standard*

The essential aim of this type of proposal is to put the monetary system on a broader basis and thereby ease the burdens imposed on the two key currencies. The idea is that other currencies (for instance, the franc and mark) would be used to supplement the dollar and pound sterling as reserve currencies. Such a Multiple Currency Reserve System was proposed by Zolotas in 1961,[29] and also by Lutz[30] in 1962, who argued that the surplus countries would be required to acquire the currencies (i.e. short-term liabilities) of the deficit countries as at least a part settlement of their deficits, and regard these holdings as reserves. Thus, new reserves and liquidity would be created in exactly the same way as the United States has created liquidity – by having the surplus countries, in effect, lend to the deficit countries. Such a system should help to avoid crises of confidence arising against the two present key currencies, especially if, as suggested, the reserve holdings have a gold guarantee to protect against devaluation, and also, if a rate of interest is paid to holders and taxation preferences given to countries holding a large share of their reserves in the form of foreign exchange. Roosa[31] has also proposed such a system, and in 1962 the United States implemented it by holding foreign currencies as part of its reserves (chiefly sterling and francs). It was also expected that should the United States run a surplus in its balance of payments, then it would accept foreign currencies rather than dollars so that total reserves could increase whether the United States was in deficit or surplus. The Roosa plan would seem, then, to be a means of economizing on gold holdings and multilateralizing a part of the role performed by the two key currencies at present. It should be noted, however, that Stand-By credits are not really of the same nature as Roosa's plan or Swaps since under these arrangements, actual *holdings* of currencies takes place, while with Stand-By credits, nothing happens until the credit is used.

The fundamental element in the Multi-Currency Reserve Plan is that it enables total world liquidity to increase by having the surplus countries extend their credit facilities to countries other than the United States and Britain, and at the same time lessen the somewhat unique problem of the pound and the dollar. A prerequisite of such a plan is that the United States (and Britain to a lesser extent) eliminate its deficit, or that other countries run deficits which the surplus countries are willing to finance. Only in this way could other currencies come into use as international reserves and therefore increase liquidity. If the United States does not eliminate its deficit, then the present system, with its inherent danger of collapse, will persist. Williamson[32] suggests that reserves composition should be such that gold constitutes 60% of holdings and foreign exchange 40%. This, it is claimed, would go far to reduce the fear of a shortage of international liquidity and decrease the dangers of speculative capital flights. Also, Posthuma[33] suggested that deficits should be financed by transfers of gold, foreign exchange and domestic currency in the ratio $3/7:2/7:2/7$, thereby treating all countries alike and increasing world reserves. Critics of these plans assert that, like the present system, they cannot cope with a chronic deficit country. However, this is rather unfair criticism, since persistent deficits cannot be coped with by any international monetary system, since any such system is based on the premise that deficits will only be temporary phenomena – if they are not, then no system can deal with the situation. Nevertheless, the plan is a most useful method of avoiding a liquidity crisis should the United States balance its payments, and also a means of increasing faith in the current fixed exchange-rate system.

In 1963, Bernstein[34] proposed the establishment of a Composite Reserve Unit (C.R.U.) in a plan which requires each member of the Group of Ten to place specified amounts of their currencies with the I.M.F., which in turn would create C.R.U.s (each equal in value to one U.S. dollar but representing fixed percentages of the currencies paid in). Subscriptions would be based on the importance of a country in trade and investment, or on its gold holdings relative to the total gold holdings of the group, and countries would be credited with a C.R.U. deposit equal to the value of their subscription.[35] Also, currency subscriptions would be gold guaranteed in the event of a devaluation.

It is suggested that C.R.U.s be created at the rate of 1–1.5 billion dollars per annum and that ultimately members would hold C.R.U.s equal to 50% of their reserves and settle deficits by using gold, foreign exchange, and C.R.U.s in fixed proportions. In this way, C.R.U.s would become a new international medium of exchange and would be subject to planned growth according to the needs of the world economy. C.R.U.s, however, have been objected to on various grounds – firstly, their rate of growth is arbitrary; secondly, their use is limited to the

Group of Ten (and Switzerland), and therefore excludes the under-developed countries; thirdly, they could increase the present rigidity of exchange rates by making countries even more unwilling to devalue; and finally, C.R.U.s are only a supplement to the holding of foreign currencies, and so the problems associated with such holdings will remain.

Now, for any of the above plans to work satisfactorily, confidence is required in the currencies held, which in effect means that confidence must exist in the credit and fiscal policies being pursued by the reserve-currency countries. To a large extent, therefore, an increase in the degree of mutual assistance among central banks is a prerequisite for these plans to work, although it is interesting to note that plans to increase liquidity by extending mutual assistance usually envisage a maintenance of the current two-currency reserve system.

(b) Increasing Mutual Assistance

Such plans have already been discussed in that mutual assistance will normally take the form of the surplus countries lending to the deficit countries by providing the required currencies in exchange for the currencies of the deficit countries. Thus, Stand-By Credits, the G.A.B., Basle Arrangements, etc., would all come under this type of plan. Credit may also be extended by persuading the surplus countries to accept medium- or long-term obligations of the deficit countries. The so-called U.S. Roosa Bonds[36] (of normally 2 years' duration) have been used by the United States for this purpose. Since these bonds are denominated in foreign currencies, any loss through a devaluation of the dollar is avoided; also the sale of these bonds has no effect on the U.S. balance of payments, since it only exchanges one type of liability (sight) for another (medium term). Thus, they are only a means of buying time, since the bond must be repaid in foreign currency. Although all of these *ad hoc* measures have been of great help in combating crises and increasing the availability of short-term liquidity, they do nothing to improve the basic imbalance on external accounts. However, in all fairness one must point out that they are not designed to do this. They are purely a short-run expedient which is most useful until some better system can be devised for the operation of the international monetary mechanism.

(c) Plans to Centralize and Create Reserves

Perhaps the best-known plans of this type are those of Keynes[37] and Triffin.[38] Under Keynes' proposal, the liabilities of the International Clearing Union would be expressed in terms of a new international currency unit called Bancor, which would have a fixed gold equivalent.

At the beginning members would receive a quota of Bancor based on past exports and imports, and these Bancor balances would be regarded as reserve assets and used, along with gold, in the settlement of international imbalances; surplus countries accumulating Bancor balances whilst deficit countries would lose their balances and possibly even have negative balances. Bancor deposits could be created by the sale of gold by members to the Fund or by allowing deficit countries the use of overdraft facilities at the Fund (i.e. the *creation* of international reserves). Rates of interest would be charged by the Fund on *all* Bancor balances, thereby penalizing both surplus and deficit countries and giving an incentive to adjust to payments imbalances. However, the surplus countries could lend their excess Bancor deposits to deficit countries and charge them a rate of interest, in this way avoiding the interest penalization. This would be most desirable, since it would lead to the establishment of an international market in reserves which could lower the need for reserve holdings (Central banks would simply borrow the required reserves in the market.) Total world liquidity could be increased or decreased, as the need arose, by varying members' quotas which would increase drawing rights at the Fund. However, unless the Central banks actually make use of these overdraft facilities, then no increase in reserves will take place, since all other transactions involve either the transfer of deposits between members or the exchange of one reserve asset (gold) for another (Bancor).

If we now compare Keynes Clearing Union with Triffin's plan for an X.I.M.F. (Expanded I.M.F.) we find a high degree of similarity. A new unit (Bancor) would be created to supplement current reserve assets and eventually replace the dollar and pound sterling. A unit of Bancor would be equal to a specific amount of gold, and each nation's currency would be fixed in value relative to Bancor. Members would acquire Bancor balances by paying into the X.I.M.F. either gold or foreign exchange, and Triffin would encourage the off-loading of dollar and sterling holdings on to the Fund, thereby converting the short-term obligations of the United States and Britain into long-term obligations which the Fund could liquidate gradually. Bancor would be an international reserve asset, bearing interest and gold guaranteed so that it would appear to be better than gold, but whether it is more acceptable than foreign exchange is unknown.

One of the main objectives of Triffin's plan is the deliberately controlled increase in international reserves. This is the outcome of fears which Triffin had that gold supplies would be inadequate and reserve currency country obligations could not be allowed to rise indefinitely without causing the system to collapse. What we should do therefore, is replace the reserve currencies by Bancor, the supply of which can be varied by the X.I.M.F. in accordance with current requirements. How is the steady 3–4% annual increase in reserves suggested by Triffin to be achieved? Firstly, as under Keynes plan, short-term overdraft facilities could be granted to deficit countries on condition that they followed the appropriate policies to correct their balances of payments. Secondly, new Bancor deposits could be created by allowing the X.I.M.F. to operate in the open market and buy securities. These purchases would be paid for in the form of Bancor deposits. In this way, the X.I.M.F. could adjust the growth of world liquidity in such a way that inflationary or deflationary biases were not imparted to this world economy, nor were strains imposed on the U.S. or British economies.

Criticisms of this plan have been made on the grounds that too much power would be put in the hands of the X.I.M.F. staff who, it is argued, are just as fallible as national governments and could therefore make mistakes concerning the required growth of reserves and so disturb the world economy. It is also argued that, since the X.I.M.F. would be buying or selling securities in the capital markets of Britain, the United States and Europe, then it either helps to finance the deficits of the two reserve currency countries or simply adds to the reserves of the surplus countries. Finally, it does nothing to improve the balance of payments adjustment mechanism and is therefore subject to the same dangers as the current system. Nevertheless, the degree of danger is considerably lessened since (a) the supply of reserves would not be dependent upon the haphazard influences of gold production and reserve country deficits, and (b) the reserve currency problem would be effectively solved. There is, indeed, much to commend Triffin's plan, but like all such plans, so much depends upon the political inclinations of member governments.[39]

It should by this time be clear that no single plan is capable of solving all the world's monetary problems, since each plan contributes to some solutions whilst it leaves other problems untouched. One way of eliminating the liquidity problem and making the adjustment mechanism more effective (i.e. flexible exchange rates) has at the moment little political support, so it would seem that we are stuck with a fixed exchange-rate system under which, nevertheless, adjustment to payments imbalances must take place. Concentration as a result has focused on plans to increase liquidity, and although agreement has been reached that increases are required, little agreement had been reached until recently as to how the increases should be achieved.[40] In 1967, however, at the annual meeting of the I.M.F., it was agreed in principle that the addition to reserves would take the form of additional drawing rights at the I.M.F. – the so-called *Special Drawing Rights*, or S.D.R.s for short. These drawing rights would be distributed to all I.M.F. members in annual amounts in proportion to their quotas; they would carry a rate of interest in order to discourage countries from trying to get rid of them too quickly, and could be saved by central banks as reserves. Countries in deficit would be able to draw on their S.D.R. account at the Fund and transfer them to the surplus countries, who would be obliged under the system to accept them as final payment. In this way, all that would happen would be that the I.M.F. would debit the S.D.R. accounts of the deficit countries and credit the accounts of the surplus countries. Thus, S.D.R.s would not be borrowings but would be unconditionally available to member countries which would use them, like gold, as the ultimate resource for purchasing other currencies. By increasing S.D.R. facilities as time goes on, international reserves could be increased independently of the growth of gold production or the continuance of U.S. deficits.[41] A prerequisite for the success of such a system is, of course, that member countries have confidence in these S.D.R.s, which in turn requires that deficit countries (at least initially) settle only part of their deficits by S.D.R. transfers, and that the United States and Britain remove their deficits. Whether or not this innovation can solve the problem of international liquidity remains to be seen. As Triffin says,[42] "Rio will only be a success if we all regard it as a starting point rather than a dead end, and as opening toward further evolution of the world monetary system a path long blocked until then by the age-old myths and taboos of conservative bureaucrats and nationalistic politicians."

[1] F. Machlup, "The Fuzzy Concepts of Liquidity, International and Domestic," being Ch. 12 of his *International Monetary Economics*, 1964.

[2] See R. Nurkse, *International Currency Experience: Lessons of the Inter-war Period*, 1944.

[3] The Bank for International Settlements (B.I.S.) was set up in 1930 to collect funds in connection with German war reparations. Nowadays, its main purpose is to achieve co-operation among central banks and promote international financial transactions.

[4] N. Kaldor, "The Problem of International Liquidity," *Bulletin of the Oxford University Institute of Statistics*, 1964.

[5] R. Triffin, *Gold and the Dollar Crisis*, 1961; also "The Evolution of the International Monetary System: Historical Reappraisal and Future Perspectives," *Studies in International Finance*, No. 12, Princeton University, 1964.

[6] W. Brown, "The External Liquidity of an Advanced Country," *Studies in International Finance*, No. 14, Princeton University, 1964.

[7] See also M. Fleming, "International Liquidity – Ends and Means," *I.M.F. Staff Papers*, 1961.

[8] See also Machlup, "The Need for Monetary Reserves," *Banca Nazionale del Lavoro Quarterly Review*, 1966.

[9] This is a member's quota minus the Fund's holdings of its currency.

[10] F. Machlup, *op. cit.*

[11] R. Triffin, "Gold and the Dollar Crisis," 1960.

[12] F. Machlup, "The Need for Monetary Reserves," Reprints in *International Finance* No. 5, Princeton University, 1966.

[13] W. Brown, "The External Liquidity of an Advanced Country," *Studies in International Finance*, No. 14, 1964.

[14] F. Machlup, *The Need for Monetary Reserves*.

[15] W. Salant, *et al.*, *The U.S. Balance of Payments in 1968*.

[16] R. R. Rhomberg, "Trends in Payments Imbalances," *I.M.F. Staff Papers*, 1966.

[17] This is Machlup's "wardrobe theory" of international reserves.

[18] P. B. Konen, "Reserve-Asset Preferences of Central Banks and Stability of the Gold-Exchange Standard," *Studies in International Finance*, No. 10, 1963.

[19] M. Fleming, *Essays in International Finance*, No. 58, 1967, Princeton University.

[20] R. Clower and R. Lipsey, "The Present State of International Liquidity Theory," *American Economic Review*, Papers and Proceedings, May 1968. See also the related papers by A. Kafka, P. M. Oppenheimer, G. Plescoff, F. M. Bator, R. N. Cooper and J. M. Letiche.

[21] H. R. Heller, "Optimal International Reserves," *Economic Journal*, 1966. See also P. B. Kenen and E. B. Yudin, "The Demand for International Reserves," *Review of Economics and Statistics*, 1965.

[22] R. Harrod, "A Plan for Increasing Liquidity: A Critique," *Economica*, 1961.

[23] R. Triffin, *op. cit.*

[24] See F. Machlup, *Involuntary Foreign Lending*, 1965.

[25] J. Rueff and F. Hirsch, "The Role and Rule of Gold: an Argument," *Essays in International Finance*, No. 47.

[26] See F. Hirsch, *Money International*, The Penguin Press, 1967, Ch. 30.

[27] F. Machlup, *International Monetary Economics*, Ch. 14.

[28] H. Piquet, "Some Consequences of Dollar Speculation in Gold," *Factors Affecting the United States Balance of Payments* (Joint Economic Committee, 1962); also A. Lerner, "Let's Get Rid of our Cross of Gold," *Challenge*, April 1964.

[29] X. Zolotas, *Bank of Greece*, Papers and Lectures, No. 7, Athens, 1961.

[30] F. Lutz, *Essays in International Finance*, No. 41, 1963, Princeton University.

[31] R. Roosa, "Assuring the Free World's Liquidity," in *Factors Affecting the United States Balance of Payments*, Joint Economic Committee, 1962.

[32] J. Williamson, "Liquidity and the Multiple Key Currency Proposal," *American Economic Review*, 1963.

[33] S. Posthuma, "The International Monetary System," *Banca Nazionale del Lavoro Quarterly Review*, 1963.

[34] E. Bernstein, *Further Evolution of the International Monetary System*, Moorgate and Wall Street, 1965.

[35] It has been suggested that the Fund retain part of C.R.U. deposits for its own use.

[36] Roosa bonds are medium-term obligations of the U.S. Government, denominated in the currency of the buyer.

[37] J. Keynes, *Proposals for an International Clearing Union*, H.M.S.O., Cmd. 6437, 1943.

[38] R. Triffin, *Gold and the Dollar Crisis*, Yale University Press, 1961.

[39] For a selection of variants on the Triffin Theme, see Machlup, *International Monetary Economics*, p. 336.

[40] See the Ossola Report – the Report of the Study Group on the Creation of Reserve Assets – a report by the Group of 10, issued in 1965.

[41] It is interesting to note that the smallest element in the stock of world reserves (I.M.F. drawings) has shown the fastest growth rate.

[42] R. Triffin, *Our International Monetary System: Yesterday, Today and Tomorrow*, Random House, 1968, p. 195.

Index